M000274098

SHIFTING GEARS

SHIFTING GEARS

One Family's Journey
Through the Automobile Age

AN AUTOMOTIVE HISTORY

William C. Shaffer III

First printing

Library of Congress Control Number: 2021906866
LC record available at https://lccn.loc.gov/2021906866

Publisher Cataloging-in-Publication Data
Shaffer, William C., 1950–
Shifting Gears: One Family's Journey Through the Automotive Age;
An Automotive History
p. cm.
Includes index
ISBN 978-1-7358078-0-5 (pbk.)
ISBN 978-1-7358078-1-2 (ebook)
Subjects: LCSH: Shaffer, William Caldwell, 1950—Family. | Automobiles—
History. | Automobiles—Social aspects—History. | Automobiles—
Technological innovations—History. LCGFT: History. | Biographies.
Classification: LCC TL15 | DDC 629.22209—dc23

Editing by Michelle Asakawa
Interior and cover design by Jane Raese

Printed in the United States of America

Contents

Introduction

THIS BOOK STARTED with a photograph—the one on the cover. It is a Ford Model T, the first car in my family, and the first car for millions of other families. But, to be more precise, the car is a brand new 1914 Model T. At first, I had no idea. I thought that all Model Ts were black and were virtually identical. I soon learned that was not the case, that an experienced eye could discern subtle differences across the nearly twenty model years of the "universal" car. In the photo, you will notice slight humps over each of the headlights. I learned that those are vents that dissipate the heat of the acetylene-powered headlights. And 1914 was the last year for those early headlights. Henry Ford finally replaced them the following year with electric lights, and the humps were gone. Personally, I had to learn the same lesson with my own first car, another "universal" automobile, the Volkswagen. They're not all exactly alike and like the Model T, it takes an automotive detective to arrive at the model year.

The person driving the Model T is William Caldwell Shaffer, my grandfather who was known as Will. He grew up on a farm near Williamsfield in central Illinois with one foot in the nineteenth century and the other in the twentieth. Will lived through the transition from human, horse, and steam power to automotive power. It was the mechanism under the hood of that car—the internal combustion engine—that fueled so many changes in his life. The impact was transcendent. The new power immediately provided freedom, independence, and eliminated much of the isolation and drudgery of farm life. Powered by the internal combustion engine, the automobile was soon followed by farm trucks, tractors, and combines, dramatically increasing productivity and ushering in a golden age of agriculture. Unfortunately, it didn't stop there. With the coming of the world wars, the new engine was harnessed to all manner of machines, including Sherman tanks and Hellcat fighter planes, to name a couple that became part of our family's journey.

Our story covers a century of automotive history, starting with the first uplifting transition from steam and horse power all the way to the present day, when the future of the combustion engine is very much in doubt. Along the way we'll see a kerosene byproduct called gasoline refined by Nikolaus Otto to create the first internal combustion engine and that engine added to a three-wheel cart by Karl Benz to produce the first automobile. Nobody paid it any attention until his wife, Bertha, took it on a 90-mile ride through the German countryside. Benz's automobile lit an explosion in Europe, and by 1900, there were some 130 automobile manufacturers in the city limits of Paris alone.

Bicycles had been invented in France and Britain in the 1880s and rapidly made their way to America, leading to the bike craze of the 1890s and creating a veritable army of bike mechanics who would soon turn their energies to making automobiles. That first automobile was built by the Duryea brothers, who grew up just a few miles from Will's farm. That 1893 Duryea Motor wagon was the first of over 2,000 car brands to debut in America. Very early, it was the steam and electric makes that topped the sales charts. But, it was Henry Ford that broke through that early maze. Though he soon dominated, he had to contend with the likes of Alexander Winton, David Buick, Ransom Olds, Walter Chrysler, the Studebaker brothers, and most menacing, Willy Durant and his General Motors juggernaut. Most of the other marques quickly disappeared but they provide engrossing backstories.

Many of those stories played out in the Williamsfield area. The first car in the area was a Winton, soon followed by a Duryea. There was a decided preference in the hinterlands for brands linked to farming. Studebaker made farm wagons before getting into automobiles. Moline built plows before developing the massive Moline Dreadnought car. Avery, the steam thresher manufacturer in nearby Peoria, saw brief success with the Glide. J. I. Case had even briefer success when it rolled out its automobile. It was Henry Ford, of course, that overshadowed all others. Having grown up on the farm, he was focused on easing the toil he experienced there. Ford produced the Model TT farm truck and followed that with the Fordson tractor.

Will bought that first car, a Ford Model T, but with a growing family there was no Ford option and he moved on to Buick. This was followed by Chryslers, Studebakers, even a Detroit Electric. On February 1, 1942, all automobile production ceased as the car companies turned to war production. The family's next generation would be driving Jeeps, Sherman tanks, and Hellcat fighter planes. After the war ended, pent-up demand meant anything on four wheels would sell. As this demand eventually settled down, the competition among the few remaining automobile companies was mostly fought with fins, chrome, and land yacht proportions. The family's third generation, the author's generation, missed this and ended up with much smaller automobiles—Volkswagens and Mustangs.

The end of our story takes us into the twenty-first century. The final chapter takes stock of where we have been and where we are going. The scrappy internal combustion engine is under assault. It is very unlikely to survive much longer. Your author has already capitulated, going electric in 2013. Coming full circle after three generations I may be going back to Ford. The new Ford electric Mach E is rolling out and I hear that you don't need a crank to start it.

1

The First Drive

WILL SHAFFER STEPPED OUT of the farmhouse into the bright sun. It was mid-July, not a cloud in the sky. The heat of summer had settled in. He started to cross the farmyard toward the barn. He had been working this farm for less than a year but still savored its location and the opportunity. To the north, past the barn, the property tumbled down a hill to French Creek. Across the creek and then across the old Peoria-Galesburg Trail stood French Grove, the original settlement in the area. It was initially called "The Barrens" but proved to be anything but that. The farm stretched east and south from the creek, totaling 160 acres. It was roughly five miles to each of the neighboring towns of Brimfield, Elmwood, and Williamsfield, and about 175 miles northeast to Chicago.

Will walked over to the north pasture to check on the horses. It was a day for rest for them. The oats were cut and threshed last week. Will turned and gazed back across the farmyard. All the farm buildings were painted white—the big barn erected with neighbors' help in the 1860s, the corn cribs, the many hog houses he had constructed, his equipment shed, and, of course, the old farmhouse with its picket fence. Everything was almost blindingly white in the midday sun. There was, however, one glaring exception. In front of the farmhouse stood Will's brand new, shiny black Ford. It was his first car.

Will was a man of twenty-nine, of medium height and build, wiry with dark hair and brown eyes. He had a strong jaw and, somewhat unusual for the age, was clean-shaven. He was a highly respected farmer with a large circle of friends. The residents of French Grove could rely on him much as he could rely on them. In just a few short years, he had built up a considerable farm operation.

Will walked around the Ford car. It was the touring model, with a can-
vas top, those acetylene headlights, kerosene taillights, and wood spoke
wheels. His wife Verne's uncle, Alex Reed, had also just bought a Ford at
the local agency in Brimfield, so they were able to compare notes with each
other on the new machine. The Ford was pretty basic, nowhere near as
flashy as this father-in-law's new Moline Dreadnought automobile.

As he was with all of this equipment, Will was meticulous in its care.
He had read the Ford owner's manual from cover to cover. Today, he would
be going on errands to Brimfield, and he had already checked the radiator coolant, dipped the wood ruler in the gas tank under the front seat to
check the level, and got under the engine to open the two oil petcocks and
checked the oil level.

It had been a good first year at the farm. The oats were in by mid-April,
the corn in May. He had increased his stable of hogs even while selling
quite a few to generate some current income. This enabled him to cover
living expenses, buy seed, engage a hired hand named Hank, and yes, purchase the Ford.

Most importantly, Verne and Will had recently welcomed their first
son. But wife and baby would not be joining him today. He would be going
solo into Brimfield to stop by the Ford dealer, gas up, and buy a few additional tire tubes, some heavier oil for winter, and a few things that Verne
wanted him to pick up at Winne's Market.

He mused about prior trips to town, before the Ford. Much earlier in
the day, he would be hitching up the horses to their buggy, then heading
out for a slow-paced journey that took close to an hour each way. That
would not be the case with the new car.

Will went over to the Ford. Leaning into the driver's side, he checked
that the hand lever was fully back, putting the engine in neutral and engaging the rear brakes. On the steering column he adjusted the spark lever on
the left several notches down, retarding the spark. On the right side he adjusted the throttle lever about two to three notches down to provide ample
fuel flow to start the engine.

He walked around to the front of the Ford and pulled out the priming
rod. Unhooking the engine crank, he pulled it up slowly several times to
prime the engine. Now ready to start, Will walked back around the car
and turned the key on the coil box to the "On" position. Back at the front,
he moved the crank down one last time and pushed it in to engage the
flywheel, taking care to hold the crank with an open palm. There had been

several recent stories of local farmers who had fully grasped the crank while yanking and then had the engine backfire. The backfire would explosively fling the crank backward, breaking a hand or a forearm. Will yanked the crank up vigorously and the Ford came to life.

With the midsummer heat, the oil was loose and viscous, quite unlike the sludge that formed in cold weather. Then, you sometimes had to deploy one strategy or another to turn the car over. Keeping the car in the barn overnight was one answer. Pushing the car down the big hill toward Elmore Road and engaging the clutch while rolling was another tried-and-true trick. And, there was another worry in winter with the oil stone cold. The clutch disk plates would stick together just enough to engage the transmission and the car would creep forward on its own. Standing in front of the Ford at the crank, you just had to be light on your feet.

Back in the car with the engine rumbling, Will moved the spark lever about halfway down to advance the spark and smooth out the engine. He pushed the clutch pedal halfway down and moved the hand lever to the vertical position. He then gently pushed the clutch pedal down until he felt low gear begin to engage.[1] The Ford emitted a shrill whining sound and started moving down the hill. Will let the clutch pedal out to move into high gear.

The dirt roads were in pretty good shape, maybe just a little dusty. There had been a Peoria County bond issue two years earlier that proposed paving Elmore Road, but nothing had come of it. Will turned onto Elmore Road, heading south. He moved the throttle lever down and he was quickly moving briskly, about 20 mph. On the left, he passed his broad field of corn, now about six feet tall and looking very good. He passed an 80-acre plot on the right that someday might make a good addition to the farm. It being July, the threshing season for oats and wheat was in full swing. The threshermen with their massive steam traction engines were very busy. About a mile south, he checked out the neighboring farm run by brothers Homer and Walter Tucker. At the southeast corner of their property, in the middle of an apple orchard, was Reed School, the one-room schoolhouse for the immediate area.

At the school, Will turned left and headed east on Forney Road. If he had continued south, he would have run straight into Elmwood. He kept motoring on Forney for about four miles, estimating that he was going about 20 mph on the dirt road. If he had a speedometer he might have known more precisely. If he could ever find a paved road, he understood that the Ford would top out at 45 mph. But, even at his present "dirt road" speed, he again pondered the dramatic difference between the errand with a horse and buggy, and now with the Ford. With the new car, it took all of fifteen minutes to reach Brimfield. Growing up in the town of Williamsfield, Will had been within a short walking distance to town. However, at French Grove, it was quite a journey to any of the three local farm towns without the automobile.

Will prepared to stop at the Knoxville Road intersection, pulling the throttle lever up, depressing brake pedal, and holding the clutch pedal halfway to engage neutral before coming to a full stop. He turned south on Knoxville for the final two-mile run into Brimfield. He noticed the fresh gravel improvement added to the roadway. A farm on the right had just reaped its wheat field. The wheat was standing in shocks, waiting for the threshermen to arrive. He crossed the Chicago, Burlington, and Quincy railroad tracks just west of town.

The road into town was in good shape. It had been oiled recently to keep the dust down. He had read in the Brimfield newspaper that the oil was too heavy to apply and the workers had to use Charlie Wocoff's traction engine to heat it up first. He remembered that it had only been last year that the town of Brimfield had voted against paving, feeling that dirt roads were just fine.

Brimfield was a pretty typical central Illinois farm town. It was originally settled in the 1830s and called Charleston. The name was changed shortly after as it turned out there already was a Charleston in Illinois. In 1838 the Frink and Walker stage line arrived, carrying mail and passengers from Peoria. During its heyday, the stage coaches were of the finest construction, drawn by four stout draft horses. In 1856 the Peoria and Oakhill railroad came west from Peoria through Brimfield, Knoxville, and Galesburg. A spur line of the Chicago, Burlington, and Quincy railroad was added in 1869. The current population of the town and surrounding township in 1915 was about 1,200.

Will rolled into town, passing Memler Brothers dry goods store. He spotted Henry Memler's brand new Studebaker parked outside. He continued on to Kelly Supply, the Ford agency in town, where he had bought the Ford earlier in the year. Again he had to deftly reduce the throttle and apply the clutch and brake pedals until the Ford came to a full stop. C. E. Kelly had been in town since 1910, when he bought the old McCabe Brick building, tore it down, and built an automobile sales and service shop. The

McCabe building was a former livery; now it was called an "automobile livery." Will ran into the service technicians Bill and Harry at Kelly, who mentioned they were working on G. A. Harper's new Ford before he headed out on a cross-country trip to New York. Kelly had recently run the agency's gas line out to the curb. The gas price was the same as on Will's previous visit: nine cents per gallon.

After filling the car's tank (it held ten gallons), Will went on to C. W. Winne, the grocers, to get the supplies on Verne's list. Because it was the middle of summer, quite a lot was happening in town. There would be a band concert on Saturday night. The Opera House was screening two silent pictures, *From Headquarters*, a police drama, and *Stars Their Courses Change*, a romance featuring Francis X. Bushman. Of course, the big news for the summer was the arrival of the traveling Redpath Chautauqua. They would be in Brimfield the following week with their mixture of lectures, music, and variety acts. The Brimfield organizing committee had bought 600 all-week passes to sell for the event.

With errands in Brimfield completed, Will headed back to the farm, retracing his route. At the foot of the hill leading up to the farm, he powered right up without any problem, in part because he had a full tank of gas. In the Ford, the gasoline was gravity fed to the engine. If your tank was low, the engine would sputter and die on a steep hill. The solution was to turn around, put the car in reverse and back up the hill, which Will had done on occasion.

He parked at the farmhouse gate and, before getting out, once again mused at the change in circumstances that the automobile provided. Along with a new farm and a new family, the future was certainly golden. Much had transpired since his early days in Williamsfield.

2

Coming to America

WILL, OR MORE FORMALLY William Caldwell Shaffer, was born in Douglas, Illinois, on February 1, 1886. Douglas was a small village four miles west of the slightly larger town of Yates City, which was six miles west of the even larger town of Elmwood. All three towns were on the Chicago, Burlington, and Quincy (CBQ) railroad. When the railroads were being constructed the railroad companies typically encouraged setting up towns every five miles. This was never an issue as local settlements fought to have the line run through their townships.

Will's arrival was just two days after a German named Karl Benz had completed his patent in Germany for what is considered the world's first automobile. Much would still have to happen before an Illinois farmer could buy his first automobile. This would involve a number of different transits across the Atlantic from Europe to America. Oil refining from Bucharest, the internal combustion gasoline engine from Germany, the concept of personal transportation with the bicycle from London, and the Benz horseless carriage would all be making the trek. In addition, Will's ancestors would have to make the crossing and eventually settle on prime farmland in the Midwest. In the meantime, it was still the age of horse and steam power.

It was Will's great-great-great grandfather, Heinrich Schafer, who would make the first move.[2] Heinrich was born in 1754 in the village of Biedershausen in an area of Bavaria west of the Rhine in southwestern Germany.

The village is within an area called the Palatinate, a part of the Holy Roman Empire that had been administered by a count since the tenth century.

The Palatinate rose to prominence and prosperity during the Middle Ages, but its later embrace of Protestantism led to a series of religious wars. The Thirty Years War (1618–1648) took a toll on the populace. The period of peace that ensued between Protestants and Catholics and the ruling elites was broken when the French king Louis XIV invaded the Palatinate and famously ordered every house and field set afire. This War of the Grand Alliance ended in 1697 with the area once again devastated. Peace lasted but a few years before the War of Spanish Succession erupted in the first years of the eighteenth century.

Farmers like Heinrich's father suffered the brunt in all these conflicts. And, the final peace did not necessarily bring a return to prosperity. The ruling elites among Catholics and Protestants taxed and spent lavishly. Inheritance laws mandated that property was to pass equally among all heirs, which meant that families that had amassed enough land to be profitable were forced to subdivide. This often resulted in a backslide into poverty and tenant farming. Opportunity in both war and peace proved limited.

At the close of the seventeenth century there was increasing awareness of the opportunity available in the American colonies. Britain was interested in increasing settlement and encouraged emigration, just as long as the emigrants swore allegiance to the British crown. William Penn had become the proprietor of vast lands in present-day Pennsylvania and Delaware, a result of money owed by British king Charles II to his father. Penn, a Quaker, and his agents sowed the seed of opportunity in the Americas, particularly in Protestant areas of Europe such as the Palatinate. Penn traveled several times to Europe in this effort. The first wave of German emigrants began in 1683, shortly after the end of the Thirty Years War. Penn's friend Francis Daniel Pastorius had purchased 15,000 acres west of Philadelphia from the Pennsylvania colony and founded Germantown that same year. The second wave began in the early 1700s as the War of Succession engulfed the area. The lead taken by the Palatinate emigrants in coming to America resulted in all German emigrants being called Palatines.

For Heinrich, who in 1771 was seventeen years old, there appeared to be decidedly limited prospects to remaining in Biedershausen. The path to sufficient land for farming was steep, and even if land was secured, the risk remained that all would be lost in another Palatine conflict. He made the decision to seek a better life in America, where land ownership and opportunity was in reach for anyone. He became part of the third Palatine wave.

Heinrich set out that summer on his own, traveling by foot east to Bingen and then catching a boat down the Rhine for the roughly 400 miles to Rotterdam. He was young and unencumbered by possessions, but equally unencumbered by money. In Rotterdam he signed a contract with a ship captain—Thomas Arnott of the *Minerva*—in order to pay for his Atlantic passage. The contract would require some level of indentured service once in the Colonies. Roughly half to two-thirds of young emigrants paid for their passage in this manner. He sailed on the *Minerva* in July 1771, along with 203 other passengers. The *Minerva* stopped at Cowes on the Isle of Wight to clear British customs and to swear allegiance to Britain. At this point, he was still Heinrich Schafer.

Out of Cowes, the *Minerva* set sail for the voyage across the Atlantic to Philadelphia. This normally took 6–8 weeks but depended heavily on the prevailing winds. In the eighteenth century, this was a dangerous journey. The time at sea, the small, ill-equipped ships, and the pressure to load as many passengers as possible was a deadly mix. Those on board endured poor food and hygiene, stench, misery, seasickness, fever, disease, and storms. Older passengers and young children were the most likely to not survive the sailing. Mortality was on the order of 5 percent for adults and 10 percent for young children (meaning that if records were kept, an estimated 10–20 passengers on the *Minerva* would have died and were buried at sea). It must also be noted that *when* you died was important. The contract stipulated that if you died on the first half of the journey, the captain was responsible for the crossing fare. But, if you died on the second half, you or your surviving relatives were responsible for the fare. A healthy seventeen-year-old like Heinrich stood the highest chance of making it.

And, Heinrich did indeed make it. The *Minerva* anchored on the Delaware River at Philadelphia on September 9, 1771. German residents from nearby Germantown rowed out to welcome the passengers. But, indentures had to remain on the ship until contracts for indenture had been negotiated and signed. This could mean up to two additional weeks confined to the ship, with a view of the American soil just a few hundred yards away.

Henry was contracted to serve his indenture with a tanning company.[3] Once this agreement was served, he established himself on a good financial footing. It is likely that he fought in the Revolutionary War, as a Heinrich Schaffer is listed as serving in a regiment in New York in 1779. In 1782 he married Mary Miller, a woman of German descent but born in America. He became a naturalized US citizen in Philadelphia in 1798.

The great German immigration had turned Philadelphia into the second-largest city in the British Empire; only London was more populous. But opportunity for farming lay to the west. Henry (he was no longer Heinrich) and Mary moved to Lycoming County, Pennsylvania, in 1800, renting land to farm. Renting was merely a transitory phase, as Henry moved quickly from renting to owning. The family grew with the birth of nine children.

It was soon apparent that more opportunity and better farmland lay farther west. Driven by cheap land, federal land programs, and publicity that flooded the East, Henry traveled to Ohio around 1810, where he bought a tract of land in Waldo Township, Delaware County (now Marion County), just north of present-day Columbus. He paid $1,080 for the acreage, a significant sum at the time. The property was still on the frontier, and it would turn out to be very close to the front lines of the coming war with Britain.

Because the new property possessed a stream, Henry erected a saw-mill and a gristmill on it, enabling timber and grinding work in addition to farming. He returned to Lycoming County while his sons William and James stayed on and worked on improving the farm. James had married Margaret Brooks, of Bucks County, Pennsylvania, in 1809. Her father, Benjamin Brooks, was an Englishman and an early settler of Bucks County. William had married Sarah DeWitt in 1810.

Two years later, war with Britain broke out. The War of 1812 was a minor theater of the Napoleonic Wars. Britain had blockaded the US ports to deny shipments to France. They also impressed—meaning kidnapped—Americans into service on their ships. Britain had allied itself with the tribes of the Northwest Territory (Ohio, Indiana, Illinois, Michigan, and Wisconsin) in order to create a buffer between British lands in Canada and the American colonies. The Indian confederation, led by Tecumseh, wanted to rid their lands of encroaching American settlers.

After the American Army of the Northwest under William Hull captured and then subsequently surrendered Detroit, William Henry Harrison took over command. He tried to recapture Fort Detroit but eventually fell back and constructed a fort in what is now Perrysburg, Ohio, on the Maumee River. This was Fort Meigs, located about seventy-five miles north of Henry's Ohio farm. James and his brother William joined the Army of the Northwest, serving under General Harrison.

In May 1813, British General Henry Procter and Tecumseh laid siege to
Fort Meigs. They failed to capture the fort and retreated after a week. James
and William both were involved in numerous engagements surrounding
the battle for Fort Meigs. James was with a party of eight that went down
the river to carry dispatches to General Harrison. The British and Indi-
ans attempted a second siege of the fort, which was also repulsed. The war
ended in late 1814 with the Treaty of Ghent. It confirmed a stalemate between the United States and Britain in the Midwest. The only loser was
the Indian confederacy, which would soon see the floodgates of western
immigration unleashed on their lands.

Henry, then age sixty, remained in Pennsylvania until the end of the
war. The following year he moved to the Ohio farm. He accumulated a
large holding, lived to be ninety-four, and died there in 1849. He left significant acreage, a huge barn, and a large stone residence. He named his son
James as his executor.[4]

Following his military service in the War of 1812, William remained in
Ohio with wife Sarah DeWitt and their children. After managing the reso-
lution of Henry's estate, James returned to Pennsylvania. He and Margaret
had a total of fifteen children. One of those was Benjamin Brooks ("BB")
Shaffer, Will's grandfather. BB was born in Pennsylvania in 1814 while his
father James was serving in the military in Ohio. He grew up in Grove
Township, Clinton County, Pennsylvania, farming during the summers
and lumbering the rest of the year. BB was destined to live a long and fruitful life, eventually moving the Shaffer (the spelling had finally settled to
"Shaffer") family farther west, to Illinois.

In 1838 BB married Elizabeth Caldwell, whose family had emigrated
from Londonderry, Ireland. She was born in Youngwomanstown (now
North Bend, Pennsylvania) about thirty miles downstream on the Susque-
hanna River. BB and Elizabeth had four children, William Caldwell (1839),
James Alexander (1841), Sara Jane (1844), and Benjamin Franklin (1848).
Then in 1849, at the young age of thirty-two, Elizabeth died. BB was left
with a family of four, with the youngest just over a year old. He married
again, to Phoebe Hess, in 1853.

Opportunities dramatically opened in the Midwest in the 1840s and
1850s. These were vast, virtually empty lands that were just waiting to
become prime farmland. Empty, that is, except for the numerous Indian
tribes that roamed there. The War of 1812 had dashed any British hope
of an Indian buffer nation. In 1812 Congress had established the Military

Tract, an area in Illinois of some five million acres, located between the Illinois and Mississippi Rivers in central Illinois. This tract comprised 207 entire townships and 61 fractional townships. The Military Tract included the present-day counties of Adams, Brown, Calhoun, Fulton, Hancock, Henderson, Knox, McDonough, Mercer, Peoria, Pike, Schuyler, Stark, and Warren. Furthermore, Congress had decreed that any veteran of the then coming conflict (the War of 1812) could claim 160 acres in these lands. Most veterans chose not to make a claim, and many parcels ended up in the hands of speculators. James and William Shaffer, though they had fought in the War, chose to remain in Pennsylvania and Ohio.

The year 1832 marked the end of the Blackhawk War, which had removed Native Americans from Illinois and thus from the Military Tract lands. Speculators and, in particular, railroad companies, moved in and flooded the East with circulars extoling the benefits of moving into the tract. In 1837 the steel plow was invented, then perfected and marketed by John Deere. This plow was particularly suited to the sticky prairie soils found in Midwestern prairie lands.

Of most importance, in the 1840s and 1850s land was cheap. Good farmland was generally available for as low as $1.25 per acre. Alternatively, with the 1841 Preemption Act, you could stake out 160 acres, live on it for fourteen months, and then buy the land from the government at $1.25 per acre. Railroad fever hit Illinois in the 1850s. Rail rights-of-ways typically included land along the route, and the railroads actively marketed their holdings. The rapid spread of railroads opened up the interior of the Military Tract, providing transportation to market for farmers. In 1862 Congress passed the Homestead Act, opening up a total of 270 million acres. Interested men would make a claim on 160 acres, pay a $12 registration fee, live on the land and improve it for five years, pay a $6 title fee, and then become the owner.

BB and new wife Phoebe decided to make the move, and they set out with the children in 1855. Early settlers faced a long journey, typically traveling by train, river, and canal to Pittsburgh, by flatboat down the Ohio River to the Mississippi at Cairo, and then up the Mississippi and Illinois Rivers to Peoria. From there, many settlers rode the Frink and Walker stage line to various points in the tract.[5] However, the stage lines were rapidly replaced by the railroads, and BB could travel most of the way from Clinton County by train. The last segment, from Peoria to Truro Township along what would become Knoxville Road, would still have been the stage in 1855 (the first rail line near Truro was just being completed that year).

Truro Township, about 40 miles northwest of Peoria, had first been settled in the 1830s. It was a township exactly like every other township in the
Midwest: surveyed into precise geometric squares irrespective of geography. Each township was six miles square, consisting of thirty-six one-mile-
square sections, each section containing 640 acres. Sections weaved back
and forth through the grid, with section 1 in the NE corner and section
36 in the SE corner. With horse-powered farming, 160 acres—one-fourth
of a section—was the typical farm size. One section in each township was
reserved and granted for schools, though it was frequently sold to finance
the schools. One-room schools were the rule except in larger towns. They
were sited so that no child had to walk more than two miles to school.
Towns were situated 5–10 miles apart, this being based on the travel time
of horse-drawn wagons. Travel at greater distances depended on stage or
steam. Steam, meaning railroad lines, was highly sought after. The towns
on the rail line prospered. Those small outposts not on the line soon faded.

Truro Township contained prime central Illinois farmland. The Spoon
River ran through the township, making so many twists and turns that it
logged over sixteen miles before exiting. The land north of the river was
hilly. The land south was more level. BB bought a 160-acre parcel south
of the Spoon about a mile southwest of what would become the town of
Williamsfield. As he had done in Pennsylvania, he worked the farm during
the summer and cut lumber the rest of the year. In time, his holdings grew
to 640 acres. With no desire to rest on Sunday, he was also a local minister.
By 1860, Truro Township's population had grown to over 700.

Farming 640 acres required a lot of power. It was before steam came
to the farm, so horses provided nearly all of that power. Farms of BB's size
would typically have six to eight horses. Of the many farm tasks, plowing
required the most power and necessitated keeping an additional one or
two horses over and above what the other tasks (harrowing, disking, cultivating, pulling wagons, etc.) would require. Farm technology innovation
then involved successively larger plows and harvesters like the McCormick
reaper. These all required draft or pull power, which horses provided.

There were other farm tasks, such as threshing, grinding feed, baling
hay, shelling corn, pumping water, and sawing wood, that required rotational or belt-driven power. Horses were adapted to this work but not very
efficiently or effectively. A large team of horses, up to fourteen, would be
hitched to a circular sweep and trod around in circles for hours at a time
while the gearing in the center of the sweep mechanism would translate

this motion into high-speed rotation to drive a belt. J. I. Case was a leading manufacturer of horse sweeps. Farmers like BB could not justify the high cost of such rigs and would contract out the harvest to a local thresher man who had the equipment.

BB retired from farming in 1870, moving to nearby Yates City and leaving the farm to his sons William, James, and BF. In addition to raising grain, they had a focus on thoroughbred stock such as Poland China hogs. Will's father, Benjamin Franklin ("BF") Shaffer, had arrived in Truro Township at age seven, along with BB, Phoebe, William, James, and Sarah. He attended the local Tucker one-room schoolhouse and then went to Yates City high school, graduating in 1866. While many farm boys skipped high school, the additional education would turn out to be a big plus for BF.

During this period the farm power equation dramatically changed. Larger farms and new implements required more power. The sulky plow became widespread at this time. With the sulky, the farmer could ride on top of the plow instead of walking behind it. This added a little more weight for the horses to pull. For the horses, size mattered. BF was the first farmer in the area to import Percherons, large draft horses that at 2,000 to 2,600 pounds were significantly bigger and heavier than American horses. The Percheron (also called a Norman) came from the old Le Perch province, just north of Paris. In the 1880s, roughly 5,000 stallions and 2,500 mares were imported. Percheron stallions were quite often crossbred with American mares. The goal was a strong, fast walker that was heavier and stronger than the existing 800–1,000 pound American horse. They were used in the Midwest primarily for plowing and hauling, and they significantly upgraded the power equation on the farm. By the 1930s, 70 percent of the draft horses on US farms were Percherons, and they were most prevalent in the Corn Belt states—Ohio, Indiana, Illinois, Iowa, Nebraska, and Kansas. Illinois was the epicenter.

In 1874, BF married Sara Lydia Foster at the Union Hotel in Galesburg. She had been a teacher. They settled on the farm in Truro and started a family. BF's brother William died in 1878 at age thirty-nine, cause unknown, leaving just brothers James and BF.

In 1881, BF was kicked by one of his horses. He was unable to walk without crutches for several years and remained partially crippled. An excellent farmer and very successful horseman, BF did not let the injury slow him down. Finishing his education helped prepare him more fully for a new life. Starting in 1882, just after sustaining the injury, he became a force in the community and lifelong seeker of challenges. BF decided to move the family to Douglas, the small outpost on the Chicago, Burlington, and Quincy (CBQ) rail line just west of Yates City. There, he opened a general store.

However, rather quickly BF sensed that Douglas was a dead-end town because the CBQ trains would likely not stop there. He became aware of a new rail line in the planning stages by the Atchison, Topeka, and Santa Fe Railroad. It would likely go through Peoria County in transit from Galesburg to Chicago. BF helped lead the effort to have the line come through the Truro crossroads. That effort was successful and became the singular event in the area's history, as a major rail line stop pretty much guaranteed a town's future.

With the township population over 700 and the railroad slated to arrive in 1888, a new town was immediately platted. It was named Williamsfield—"Williams" after the general attorney of the Santa Fe Railroad and "field," well, that was obvious. The line ended up a mile north of the Shaffer farm. The first train arrived in November 1887, pulling a boxcar to serve as a temporary depot. BF and family arrived in 1888. Good to be back home, he thrived. He was appointed the first postmaster of the town. He moved his Douglas general store merchandise into a two-story building erected by C. H. Tucker. He carried dry goods, groceries, queensware (crockery), hats, farm machinery, and the "largest line of boots and shoes between Galesburg and Chillicothe."

Just two years later, in 1890, with Williamsfield in the midst of accelerating growth, continuing health problems led BF to close the store. He passed the baton to his cousin, Frank Shaffer, who ran the town's main general store for years. That same year, BF's brother James succumbed to "consumption," which we now call tuberculosis. He was only forty-nine. James had been farming for many years, including raising Poland China hogs and Shorthorn cattle, and breeding Clydesdale draft horses.

With the railroad in place in 1888, town growth exploded. Williamsfield was a railroad stop between Chillicothe and Galesburg. A water tank was constructed for steam engine replenishment and a depot was built, replacing the temporary boxcar structure. In 1895 the Atchison, Topeka, and Santa Fe Railroad introduced service from Chicago to Los Angeles.

In just the two years since the railroad arrived, there were two general stores, two hardware and farm implement stores, two meat markets, a grocer, two barbershops, two lumber yards, a blacksmith, a livery, a veterinarian, a dry goods store, two restaurants, two grain elevators, a bank, a post office, a newspaper (the *Times*), two doctors (A. J. Morton and John Cole), a hotel (the Burt), and two churches—Methodist-Episcopal (ME) and Catholic.

And the town continued to grow. By 1895 Williamsfield had two more general stores, two farm implement dealers, a second hotel, a second elevator, a furniture store, drugstore, pool hall, undertaker, bike shop, millinery, three blacksmiths, and three fraternal orders. Frank Shaffer expanded his general store to include farm equipment such as McCormick reapers and sulky plows. The town was officially incorporated in 1896.

In 1890 a new grade school was erected, replacing the one-room Tucker school that BF had attended. It was a large, two-story structure built at a cost of $5,000. It had three sections—primary, intermediate, and advanced. By 1897 the Williamsfield Public School as it was called had 115 students across all grades. Also that year, the town installed gas street lights, replacing oil lamps. However, the civic shine was somewhat diminished as tiny Yates City had installed electric lights three years earlier. And, while Galesburg had twenty miles of paved streets, all was dust or mud in Williamsfield.

The town voice was the *Williamsfield Times*, founded in 1889. C. D. Benfield was the original publisher, but the *Times* building was destroyed by fire in 1890 and C. D. had no insurance coverage. The paper passed into the hands of Hugh Irish and was quickly restarted. A weekly publication, it covered everything about life in town. While some of content was very light, such as local comings and goings, the more serious events—sickness, accidents, deaths—were reported in great, even prurient detail.

This was a time when there was a much thinner line between life and death. Tuberculosis, smallpox, and diphtheria were constant threats. There was no shortage of things that could hurt you, make you sick, or even kill you. A farmer could cut himself on barbed wire, have it get infected, and be gone within days. Cancer was less of a concern, in part because most people did not live long enough for it to overtake them.

One recurring theme reported in the *Times* was runaway horses. Just about weekly, there would be a report of horses being spooked and taking the buggy or wagon on a terrifying ride that never ended up well. BF was not left out of this scourge. He had a runaway accident in 1893 when riding with son Thomas and another in 1896 with daughter Bertha. It was not the way you wanted to get your name in the paper.

Because most of the town buildings were constructed of wood, fire was another on-going story. In 1897 fire engulfed two entire blocks of town, destroying twenty businesses. Ironically, one of the buildings destroyed was the livery stable that housed the town's brand new horse-drawn fire engine.

With BF's brother James succumbing to tuberculosis in 1890 and BB dying a year later, the Shaffer acreage passed to BF and to James's widow Louisa (nee Oberholtzer), as defined in BB's will. Louisa's farm would be handled by her three sons—Joe, James Jr., and BB Jr. BF had a different situation, with his eldest, Tom, not interested in farming, the two daughters Bertha and Ada too young, and young Will only five. BF elected to retain the farm but rely on renting agreements to keep it going.

While his health prevented active farming, he had plenty of energy for other pursuits. He took on a new role as agent for the Santa Fe Town and Land Company, working out of the Woods Brothers drugstore building. His job was to market parcels that the railroad owned along its route right-of-way. He frequently traveled by train to Chicago on Santa Fe business. Additionally, in 1892 BF leased an elevator in town and started a grain silage business, advertising each week in the *Williamsfield Times*. He was competing with C. C. Davis, who had elevators in Monica and Laura in addition to Williamsfield. BF was a local school director and commissioner of roads for Truro Township. He was also active in politics, serving as chair for the Democratic Party in the town.

More than that, he was also a single father. He and his wife Sara had three children who died before the age of two, including one that was accidentally scalded to death. Sara was unable to cope with these tragedies. BF finally placed her in a facility in nearby Maquon, while arranging periodic visits. BF had to manage his kids and the treatment of his wife in addition to his long list of pursuits.

Since BB had arrived in 1856, the Shaffer clan had an outsized impact on Truro Township and the town of Williamsfield. Most was good, but not quite all. This was amply illustrated in BF's brother James's family. James had died of consumption just as the decade started and was not alive to see the good (daughter Vesper) or the bad (son Joseph). These were Will's cousins.

Joseph, or "Big Joe" as he came to be known, did not come into maturity quietly. He was twenty-two when his father James died of tuberculosis. BB died the next year and in his will counseled his executors (Joe's mother Louisa and Joe's sister Vesper) that any bequeaths to Joe and his brother Benjamin Brooks Jr. should be made only when they showed themselves to be "by their good and well-established temperaments, habits, and sound and business-like character . . . to be worthy, fitted, and capable to receive" their inheritances. The comment was prescient on BB's part.

Big Joe, according to the *Times*, was "for years the terror of Williamsfield" and called that "notorious Spoon River tough." He would steal and hide horses from a friend (O. E. Root, who quickly became an ex-friend) as a practical joke. While very successful with horses, he would neglect to pay livery charges. He rubbed many residents the wrong way with his antics while apparently building up his own grudges against certain individuals and businesses in town.

None of this was very alarming until the night of February 1, 1897. Joe, then twenty-nine years old, attempted to burn down the entire town. With a seventeen-year-old accomplice, he set fire to hay bales and carried them aflame to numerous buildings. The town's Davis and Seward grain elevator burned to the ground, destroying 3,000 bushels of corn, oats, and rye (including grain that Joe's brother Benjamin Brooks had stored there). The elevator was a total loss of $3,000.[6]

Joe was on the lam for four days. Sheriff Aldrich of Galesburg formed a posse armed with shotguns and revolvers. Joe was tracked to his home and gave up peacefully. The town had neither a sheriff nor a jail, so he ended up in a cell in Galesburg. The town newspaper that had routinely included such breaking news as "Mrs. JM Caldwell is indisposed" now had a real story on its hands. Joe's troubles were on the front page week after week, and not only in the *Times*. At trial, Joe considered pleading insanity but ended up pleading guilty to arson. He was sentenced to 1–20 years in prison. He was escorted by train from Galesburg to the state prison in Joliet.

Joe had requested that the train schedule of his departure not be published as he did not want the people of Williamsfield to see him off in handcuffs. Yet, he certainly misread the town. Joe was released on parole after twenty-three months to a town very willing to support his rehabilitation. Unfortunately for Joe, he quickly got in a fight with another farmer over a business transaction. That farmer complained, resulting in Joe breaking his probation and being sent back to prison.

Joe's sister Vesper represented the sharpest possible contrast to his incivility and behavior. She was born in the township in 1864, the eldest of James and Louisa's seven children. She went to the Tucker one-room school south of the crossroads through eighth grade, then attended St.

Mary's Girls School in Knoxville, a three-year religious prep school. This was quite unusual for the times, but then, Vesper was poised to take a different career path. Upon graduation, she traveled just five miles west to Galesburg to attend Knox College. She graduated from Knox in 1886 with an education degree and returned to Williamsfield to teach at the same one-room schoolhouse she had attended years before.

In 1889 she went to work for Dr. A. J. "Archibald" Morton,[7] one of the town doctors, as he set out to build up his "Gold Cure" program for alcoholism, opium, morphine, and cocaine addiction.[8] She helped Dr. Morton establish the National Institute in Williamsfield, where doctors from around the country were trained and licensed on the cure. This was a time when there were few established treatments for dependencies and limited scientific basis for the "cures" that were put in place. The practice operated out of an impressive three-story building at one end of town. The third floor of the building served as the Opera House and featured such traveling entertainers as "Martine the Wonderful," a magician.[9] Vesper was secretary for the institute.

In 1891 her father James died and named Vesper, then age twenty-seven, one of his executors. Given that her brother, Big Joe, was prominent in the will, this was not an easy task but one that she certainly had adequate preparation to do. She was long gone from Williamsfield by the time Big Joe went on his fiery rampage.

By 1893 Vesper decided, with the support of Dr. Morton, to become a doctor. She moved to Chicago and enrolled at the Northwestern University Woman's Medical School. At the time, women were not encouraged to become doctors and most medical schools were male-only. Northwestern had set up a separate medical school for women. During her medical training and for a brief time after graduating in1896, she returned to Williamsfield to assist Dr. Morton, handling female patients and delivering babies out of the National Institute building. As the Gold Cure business dwindled, Dr. Morton moved to Elmwood and Vesper moved to Chicago to set up a general practice.

3

Beginnings in Europe

WILL GREW UP in Williamsfield in the 1890s. Then known as "Willie," he saw his mother only when she was brought home from the facility at Maquon. Beginning in 1891, he followed in the footsteps of his older brother Thomas and sisters Ada and Bertha in going to the grade school in town. Will had Mrs. Pulver at the primary level. She was using Cyr's primers and first readers in her class. In 1899 Will was promoted upstairs to the advanced section (sixth grade) with James Welch as his teacher.

Growing up in Williamsfield in the 1890s, Will had a front-row seat to significant changes in farming and in rural life. The first change was steam power, which was experienced daily as the trains rumbled past town. Steam engines were naturally suited to rotary motion, and rotary motion is exactly what many farm processing tasks like threshing required. Even as early as the 1880s, threshermen began replacing horse sweeps with steam-driven machines. One common option was a steam engine mounted on a wheeled platform and driven by horses to the field. It would power a belt attached to a thresher. Typical of these units was the Westinghouse Agricultural Engine. It was available in 6-, 10-, and 15-horsepower versions.

It was at this juncture between horse and steam that the new concept of "horsepower" surfaced. What exactly did it mean? And how did it come about? James Watt provided the answer. In 1776 he had improved the steam engine that had been developed years earlier by Thomas Newcomen. Watt's steam engine doubled the power yield. To market his engines for the farm, he came up with a definition of work done by horses that correlated to what could be done by his steam engine. He looked at horses that lifted coal up a shaft in a mine, capturing the weight in pounds and distance in feet the coal weight traveled. He estimated that one horse could lift and move 22,000 foot-pounds in a minute. He increased this by 50 percent and pegged the measurement of one horsepower at 33,000 foot-pounds of work in one minute. This was the rather arbitrary unit of measure that has made its way down through the years. Later, when the power unit "watt" was named in Watt's honor, the result was that one horsepower equaled 746 watts.

The Westinghouse steam engine required 500 pounds of coal and 350 gallons of water to run and was typically managed by a crew of four or five men. A competing option was the steam traction engine. This was essentially a steam locomotive on ribbed steel wheels. It could be used in the fields to plow, as it was on the vast farms in the Dakotas. But in the Midwest it was largely used by threshermen at harvest time.

Locally, Hugh Carroll, with a large farm north of Brimfield, was a well-known contract thresherman. He was engaged for corn shelling and threshing of oats and wheat. He had an early steam traction engine in 1883, and then replaced it in 1899 with a Buffalo Pitts steam engine, a unit built by the H. G. Rouse Co. in nearby Peoria.

Another local thresher was Alf Whetzel, who started steam threshing for hire in 1893. He and his son eventually moved to an Avery steam engine and thresher. Avery was another local company, started in Galesburg but relocated to Peoria for better rail access. Avery's threshing machine, called the Yellow Fellow, was an enormous wood-and-metal contraption driven by the flywheel of the steam engine. It was nearly forty feet long and twelve feet high, a mass of gears, belts, pulleys, sieves, and hoppers. The shocks of grain went in one end, and the separate grain kernels dropped down into a hopper on the other. Even today, the threshing rig is a wonder to behold. The clatter, dust, belching smoke, heat, and sheer cacophonous noise assault the senses. The contrast with a threshing sweep, with the horses sedately walking around in circles, could not have been starker.

Will was soaking up both farm knowledge and book knowledge during this time. But, it was not "all work and no play." No, he had arrived as a youngster in the midst of the 1890s bicycle craze. As early as the start of the decade, the first bicycles began to appear in town. Seba Arnold was one of the first to buy a new bicycle, a high wheeler, and he was written up in the local papers. The high wheeler had made the journey from Europe and would have an outsized impact on the development of the automobile in America. But first, the bicycle had to significantly improve in order to go mainstream.

A bike precursor called a velocipede was invented by Pierre Michaux in the 1860s. By 1870 the high-wheeled bike was perfected by Englishman James Starely. Called the "penny farthing," it sported an extremely large front wheel and almost comically small rear wheel. The pedals were directly attached to the front wheel, meaning the bigger the wheel, the farther and faster the bike would go on one pedal rotation. But it was very difficult to ride, let alone to just get on. It developed a narrow following of enthusiasts who would participate in bike races. Those early cyclists quickly learned how bad American roads were and formed an organization, the League of American Wheelmen, to lobby for better roads.

In 1877 Colonel Albert Pope, an Eastern manufacturer, first encountered the English high-wheeler and decided to develop his own. It had a 54-inch front wheel, weighed 113 pounds, and sold for $337 (more than $8,000 in 2020 dollars). Meanwhile, in England, James Starely's nephew John had invented the safety bicycle. Its wheels were of equal size, and it sported pneumatic tires, a chain drive, and multiple gearing. With the safety bicycle, the craze was on, beginning in the United States in 1891 and with over three hundred manufacturers cranking out bikes by 1895. At the forefront, Colonel Pope sought to control the market by buying many of the bike makers. By 1895 he was called the "King of Bicycles" and was the country's largest producer. He sold his Columbia safety bicycle for $100.

Bicycle racing quickly became big business. Racers like Barney Oldfield and Carl Fisher were household names. Even a small rural town like Williamsfield was not immune to the fervor. Local stores joined in. M. C. "Mack" Spangler, who sold pianos and organs and was the town undertaker, began to sell a line of bikes. So did the W. D. Caldwell general store. A. C. Eliot opened a bike repair shop. In 1894 the Williamsfield Bicycle Club was formed, participating in races and rides to other towns. W. L. Wiley made the local newspaper by riding from Brimfield to Peoria and back, a distance of fifty miles. Will's older brother Thomas, who was attending Knox College in Galesburg, rode the twenty miles from the college to Williamsfield. There were bike races in town, even bike versus horse races. The Santa Fe railroad offered reduced prices to travel to a big bike race in Peoria. The *Williamsfield Times* covered it all, right down to local-interest blurbs such as, "David Cation is learning to ride a bike" or "Ona Shaffer has a new bike." (Ona was Will's cousin whose father, Frank, was now carrying Patee bicycles—locally made in Peoria—in his store.)

As quickly as the bicycle craze exploded, it was over. The recession of 1896 was too much for the oversupply of bike manufacturers, and the mania died down. But there was no turning back on what the bicycle represented. The genie was out of the bottle. The taste of personal freedom and personal transportation was too heady.[10] For small, rural farm towns like Williamsfield this was something new and wonderful—the freedom to hop on a bike and ride to the next town. More important for the next step to the automobile, the fading of the bike craze still left a new pressure for good roads and a large supply of experienced bike mechanics.

While steam power made a noisy entrance into farm life, another power source, likely little noticed, was a machine that local elevator operator J. M. Dungan installed in 1890. It made some noise but not nearly at the level of a steam thresher. It was an internal combustion engine powered by gasoline. He had previously used horses to drive a conveyor belt that raised the grain to the top of his elevator. He retired the horses in favor of this new stationary engine.

Several years later, C. C. Davis installed a similar unit at his elevators in Laura, Williamsfield, Monica, and Princeville. Like Dungan, he retired the horses that had previously been used to lift the grain. The local use of the gasoline engine accelerated. Local farmer Mark Tucker installed one to grind feed for stock. Joe Emery added a gas engine to pump water, grind feed, and do other farm tasks that required rotary power. The blacksmith in Brimfield used one to polish Deere steel plows. Miller and Sons bought an engine to run its sausage-making machinery. The *Brimfield News* ran its printing press with one. A pumping station was installed near Laura driven by a gas engine. Typical of comments about the new power source was, "It is as good about a farm as an extra man and a team of horses."

These first local gas engines were called "Otto cycle" engines. They were large and heavy. The 6-horsepower Otto engine was mounted on a stationary platform and weighed over a ton. It provided a dramatic improvement over steam power for certain jobs. Most important, power was immediately available on starting and the engine was instantly shut down upon completion. Initially, these engines were expensive, with a 4-horsepower Otto going for $680 in 1887. Yet, that rapidly changed. By 1903, the Sears Kenwood 6 horsepower engine, listed of course in the Sears catalog, sold for $199 and was substantially smaller and lighter. Several years later, a farmer could buy an Otto engine for just $42.

These engines were collectively called "Otto cycle" engines after the US patent holder, Nicolaus Otto, and like bicycles, they had made the journey across the Atlantic from Europe. The gasoline engine story had its roots in Romania, where in 1856 the first petroleum refinery in the world was built. The refinery distilled kerosene, a heavy component, which was then used to light the city of Bucharest. The refining process also separated out benzene and gasoline, lighter components that were initially just burned off. These were compounds that rapidly, explosively combusted. Combustion generates energy by burning a source material with oxygen. Slow combustion is the rotting of wood or rusting of iron. Fast combustion is the burning of coal or wood, or the kerosene that lighted Bucharest. Steam engines used fast combustion with an external firebox that heated water to steam, which would in turn drive a piston. This required very heavy components plus a large and heavy supply of fuel and water.

Explosive materials like gasoline or gunpowder could provide instantaneous combustion, as long as the process could be controlled. As the refineries ramped up the production of kerosene, there were more and more light components like gasoline to burn off. The fledging oil companies decided to price gasoline below kerosene and see if they could find a market. These newly affordable fuels led to efforts to use and control them. It soon became clear that if you mixed kerosene, benzene, or gasoline with air, vaporized and compressed it, then introduced a spark, you would have an explosion that could be harnessed.

And, this was exactly what the Belgian engineer Jean-Joseph Etienne Lenoir did in 1860. He designed an enclosed device that controlled the explosion without compression or carburation (to vaporize the fuel). The result certainly proved the potential efficacy of the approach, but it yielded an engine of very low power.

In 1862 the French engineer Alphonse Beau de Rochas added compression to the approach and, more importantly, designed the four-stroke principle upon which most modern automobile engines work. Under his design, the first stroke or cycle moves a piston down in a cylinder, drawing in a gas-and-air mixture. The second stroke compresses the mixture under piston pressure. The third stroke introduces a spark, which ignites the mixture, exploding the piston violently back down the cylinder. The fourth stroke opens a valve to expel the exhaust. The piston is connected to a rod that converts the up-and-down motion of the piston to the rotary motion of a crankshaft. De Rochas patented this concept but, critically, did not actually build the engine.

In 1870 an Austrian engineer working in Vienna, Siegfried Marcus, decided to build on the Rochas design. Austria also had a petroleum industry early on, and as in Romania, kerosene was the prized product. Marcus also quickly realized that gasoline was a better fit for internal combustion, as long as it was atomized in a cylinder. He developed the carburetion technique to do that and added an electric magneto to generate the spark for ignition. Since the design had four strokes but only one that actually generated power, he added a heavy flywheel to store the rotational energy and smooth out the power. He went on to mount this one-cylinder engine on a wagon. Since the flywheel was mated to the rear wheels, you had to lift the back of the wagon in order to start the engine. At the time, he was widely recognized as the inventor of the horseless carriage, fifteen years before Karl Benz, who would receive most of the glory.[11]

Although Marcus made significant strides in developing a workable internal combustion engine, it was Nikolaus Otto and some famous associates that further advanced the design, actively marketed it, and made it a worldwide phenomenon. Otto and his brother had built a replica of the Lenoir engine in 1860. Four years later, he teamed with Eugen Langen (who also provided the funding) and developed what they called an "atmospheric" gas engine. This was an engine without the compression phase. Otto exhibited it at the Paris World's Fair of 1867, and it won the Napoleonic Prize. Otto proceeded to sell 5,000 units of this stationary engine. In 1872 Gottlieb Daimler joined Otto's company as technical director. He brought in Wilhelm Maybach as an engineer. Daimler and Maybach upgraded Otto's design, adding compression. This was a true four-stroke engine, and it came to be called the "Otto cycle" or "Otto Silent Cycle" engine. Otto applied for a German patent but was rejected because of the patent granted to de Rochas nearly fifteen years before.[12]

Daimler and Maybach were both were convinced of the future of gas engines in automobiles. Otto was not interested, choosing instead to develop and market more stationary engines—engines that required 10–13 feet of headroom, weighed up to a ton per horsepower, ran slow (just 180 rpm), and compressed the gas mixture at a ratio of only 2.5 to 1. Such an engine was clearly not adaptable for horseless carriages. Daimler and Maybach left to form their own company and pursue an engine that would be adaptable.

There had been very limited work on gasoline engines in the United States before the Otto cycle arrived. The one that had some limited staying power was a constant-pressure engine developed by George Brayton in 1872. It did not have a compression stroke like the Otto four-cycle engine, resulting in a machine that produced significantly less horsepower by weight. The Brayton engine saw limited success, mainly with heavy, stationary implementations. Both the Brayton and Otto engines were on display at the 1876 Philadelphia Centennial Exposition.

The Brayton engine would eventually take an unusual place in automotive history due to George Selden, a part-time inventor and full-time patent attorney who saw it in Philadelphia. He succeeded in putting together a somewhat lighter version of the Brayton in 1878 but did not have the wherewithal to take it further. Instead, he took a page from the playbook of the French engineer Alphonse Beau de Rochas, who patented the four-cycle process without constructing it. However, Selden's patent was much more grandiose. In 1879 he patented the entire idea of the horseless carriage. He did nothing further except renew and extend the patent periodically.

Meanwhile, Nikolaus Otto applied for and was granted a US patent for his engine. In 1888 *Scientific American* magazine published a feature on the Otto gas engine, an article that had quite an effect on US tinkerers, particularly those who had been working on bicycles. His patent lasted until 1890, and the expiration led to a rapidly growing set of American companies producing four-cycle gasoline engines. By 1900 there were over a hundred companies. One of those was Olds Gas Power, a company started by Pliny Olds in Lansing, Michigan, to make steam engines. With his son Ransom, he moved on to stationary gas engines of Otto's design for use on the farm.

Back in Germany, Daimler and Maybach had left Otto and set about building an automobile. There was another German, however, who was already working on it: Karl Benz. Benz had a quality education as a mechanical engineer and had worked extensively on bicycles. He worked early on for the Karlsruhe Maschinenbaugesellschaft, an engineering company. He left the firm and started a steel fabrication company. He lost control of the company and proceeded to start a second company called Benz and Cie, which did achieve success and enabled him to spend time on his dream, a horseless carriage.

Working in Mannheim, Benz developed an engine based on the Otto design. He then set to work marrying the engine with a wheeled carriage. He bought many of the parts for his automobile from Heinrich's Kleyer's House of Bicycles in Frankfurt. Completed in 1886 and called the

Motorwagen, the machine was a tricycle with one-cylinder engine in back that generated 0.75 horsepower running at 250 rpm and weighed in at a svelte 220 pounds. His powered buggy featured many elements that would become standard in automobiles: spark plug, carburetor, water-cooled radiator, clutch, gear shift, rack and pinion steering, and differential. Out on the road, the top speed was 10 mph. Benz drove his invention in town, to great local amazement. But beyond that, he struggled to get any traction.

Luckily, he had a great assistant, his wife Bertha. Bertha Ringer Benz was the daughter of a wealthy family in Pforzheim, Germany. She had provided the funding for Karl's first two ventures. Now, she needed to expand her role. While Karl was a talented engineer, Bertha provided the rest of the needed "package"—planner, banker, accountant, and CEO. When Karl completed his Motorwagen, she helped get the patent approved in 1886.

But having built the first real automobile and having an approved patent for it were not enough. Things stagnated for a couple of years. In a theme repeated countless times in the ongoing history of the automobile, something else was needed. That something was marketing. And, for the first automobile, the required marketing was convincing the steam-and-horse public of the usefulness of this new contraption.

Bertha was aware that there was another German engineer (namely, Daimler) who was just a few miles away and was also working on a horseless carriage. She realized just what was needed. Unbeknownst to Karl, who was busy in his shop tinkering, on August 5, 1888, she loaded her two sons in the Motorwagen, pulled on the huge flywheel in back to start the engine, and set off to travel cross-country from Mannheim to Pforzheim. This was a distance of sixty-five miles without any real roads, just country lanes. Karl Benz's newest Motorwagen was an upgrade, with a single-cylinder, 2.5 horsepower engine that would now power the carriage at 25 mph. As there were no gas stations, Bertha would stop at chemist shops along the way and buy ligroin, a petroleum solvent. She also made repairs—fixing the ignition with her garter, clearing the fuel line with her hat pin, and having a cobbler put leather shoes on the brakes.

The threesome arrived in Pforzheim in twelve hours, whereupon she sent a telegram to Karl, explaining where she and the kids were. The telegram was really not necessary as Bertha had created a sensation all along her travels. Rural onlookers seeing this strange tricycle contraption without a horse, driven by a woman, was enough. After visiting with her family for a few days, she drove back, using a different route. The publicity created a backlog of orders, and Benz and Cie soon became the world's largest automobile company. Bertha's ride was the first of countless automotive "attention grabbers" that would soon include endurance runs, speed records, challenge races, hill climbs, and many more.

Meanwhile, working in competition with Benz were Daimler and Maybach. After the two had left Otto in 1882, they worked to perfect an engine design specifically for a motor vehicle. The closest Otto engine at the time was a stationary unit that weighed 750 pounds and ran at 180 rpm. The two engineers knew that if they could reduce the size and weight, they would have a viable motor vehicle. Maybach's key innovation was carburetion, using a float atop the fuel to control the atomization. They initially used benzene but soon determined that gasoline worked better. They also realized that greater rpm was a key to achieve more power. In 1883 they completed and patented an internal combustion engine with four cylinders that ran at 900 rpm and weighed just over 100 pounds. They also worked on compression, realizing that greater compression would also be a key to an engine that was both powerful and lightweight. In 1885 they tested the new engine on a bicycle. By the next year, they had assembled their first four-wheel motorcar. Like the Motorwagen, it was more like a horse buggy with an engine mounted underneath the back seat.

By 1891, though wary, Daimler needed funds and decided to go public. He formed DMG (Daimler Motoren Gesellschaft). Sure enough, like many of the auto pioneers that followed, he was forced out, along with Maybach in 1893. Two years later, his friend and DMG director Frederick Simms lobbied to bring them back and they returned with a substantial financial package. During this time, they were developing more powerful automobiles with four-speed transmissions, the engine in front, and a steering wheel instead of a tiller. They were also selling their automobiles. Their dealer in Italy, Emil Jellinik, pressed for faster and faster Daimlers. He offered to buy thirty-six high-performance Daimler Phoenix cars for a total of $130,000 if they named them after his daughter. The Phoenix was a 2,200 pound car with a 5.9-liter engine putting out 35 horsepower with a top speed of 55 mph. Daimler had no problem in changing the name. Jellinik's daughter was named Mercedes.

Early automobiles were not solely a German story. After all, it was the Frenchman de Rochas who had patented the concept back in 1862. In 1887, Rene Panhard and Emile Levassor saw a boat in Paris powered by the Daimler-Maybach engine. They licensed the engine and set about building an automobile around it. In 1891 the "Panhard and Levassor" car debuted, and it was not just a buggy with an engine in back. Their car was quite a modern configuration, with a front-mounted engine, a radiator in front, rear differential, and clutch-driven gearbox. They called the entire design the "Systeme Panhard."

At the same time, Armand Peugeot, a bicycle maker and developer of a steam tricycle, had also caught automotive fever. He met with Panhard and Levassor as they had the French license to the Daimler-Maybach engine. Daimler shipped one of his cars for Peugeot to examine. Peugeot also purchased a Benz car and had it broken down. In the end, he decided on using the Daimler engine and had his first car on the market in 1892.

Panhard and Levassor and Peugeot entered cars in the Paris-to-Rouen race in 1894. A steam tractor entered by Count Albert De Dion finished first but was disallowed. The Panhard and Levassor and Peugeot cars were declared co-winners. Though disappointed, the count decided to switch from steam to gasoline. He engaged engineer George Bouton to design an engine. Bouton created an improved design, fitted to a tricycle frame, that achieved an astonishing 3,500 rpm. The count started selling automobiles in 1899 under the De Dion–Bouton brand. By 1900 this was the largest auto manufacturer in the world, though with an annual production of only four hundred cars. The count also licensed his engine to over 140 emerging automobile companies.[13]

One of those licensees was Louis Renault. In 1898 he used a Bouton engine to power his first car. He added innovations that included a driveshaft, universal joint, and steel frame. By 1900, Paris alone had over 130 automakers within its city limits, making it for a short time the epicenter of the automobile industry in the world.

4

The First Cars

I N 1899, WILLIAMSFIELD was a bustling town. Aside from the occasional bicycle, local travel was by foot, horse, or horse-drawn buggy or wagon. The streets were dirt and lined with hitching posts. Yet, behind Gale Street were the Santa Fe tracks. And, Galesburg was only twenty miles west and thirty minutes away by train. Furthermore, Galesburg had one unique attraction—the "Big Store."

With the "Big Store," O. T. (Orson Thomas) Johnson had created the largest department store in the Midwest south of Chicago. Ahead of its time, it was a massive three-story brick building housing thirty-four departments across 125,000 square feet of floor space.[14] A local Galesburg doctor, E. V. Morris, had the distinction of owning the first automobile in town. It was a Winton Phaeton, and he was one of the initial twenty-one buyers of one of the first production cars in the United States. His automobile caused a sensation in town. This was 1899, and as the *Chicago Tribune* had stated that June, "automobiles are few." In fact, the article indicated that though there were perhaps a hundred or more automobiles in New York City and Chicago, Cleveland only had twelve, St. Louis possibly six, the District of Columbia one, and there were none in Minneapolis or St. Paul. Furthermore, the story indicated that the entire state of California might have just three. So, little Galesburg was certainly very competitive.

One of those who more than noticed the Winton in town was Bert Chappell, Johnson's store manager. For years, Johnson had enticed customers in the surrounding towns to make the trip to the "Big Store" as it was universally called. For Williamsfield folks, there was a special $1 fare to take the train to Galesburg. Chappell suggested that this amazing new machine would be perfect for advertising the store with a drive through the local towns, and Johnson agreed.

In 1899 Williamsfield, it must have been quite a shock to see a buggy making its way down Gale Street without a horse. The Winton automobile, driven by Albert Gale (yes, of the Gales as in Galesburg), became the first car in Williamsfield. It also became the first car in Brimfield, Elmwood, Laura, and French Grove before the day was out. At each stop, Gale distributed store fliers, gave a few rides, and patiently explained the workings of the "horseless carriage." And, horseless carriage it was, described by the *Williamsfield Times* as "a doctor's buggy, with one seat beautifully upholstered in leather, accommodating three people with gas motor, chain drive, steering tiller and gear levers." Will, at thirteen, would have been there or, failing that, would have been sorry he missed it. Chappell returned the Winton to Dr. Morris at the end of that fateful day.

Later that year, F. B. Snow of Wyoming, Illinois, purchased another pioneering automobile, a Duryea Motor Wagon. Hearing the hullaballoo surrounding the Winton, Snow challenged Dr. Morris to a race. With a winning streak of twelve victories, Snow's Duryea seemed unbeatable. The race was a hundred miles on a dirt track in Peoria with the winner taking $1,000 and, more importantly, bragging rights. The Duryea conked out after twelve laps, and Dr. Morris and his Winton cruised home for the win. His average speed over the course was 29 mph. Two years later, the doctor traded his Winton in for an electric car, something more suitable for a country physician.

The Winton car was the work of Alexander Winton, a feisty Scot from Cleveland, who had graduated from making bicycles to automobiles. In the United States the list of manufacturers, sellers, mechanics, and tinkerers of bikes that made the transition was indeed long: The Duryea brothers, fresh from the farm, were building bikes in Peoria. Elmer and Edgar Apperson had a bike repair shop in Kokomo, Indiana, that was frequented by Elwood Haynes. Colonel Pope, as we have seen, was making a quarter of a million "safety" Columbia bikes in Hartford, Connecticut. John Willys was selling bikes in Elmira, New York. Thomas and Charles Jeffery were bicycle makers in Kenosha, Wisconsin. The Dodge brothers, Horace and John, were building Evans and Dodge bicycles in Detroit. George Pierce was building bikes in Buffalo, New York. Louis Mooers was making Peerless bicycles in

Cleveland. William "Bill" Knudsen was a bike mechanic at his brother's shop in Copenhagen. Tom Cooper and Barney Oldfield were not making bikes but were becoming famous by racing them across the country. Then, there were a couple of bike mechanics in Dayton, Ohio—Wilbur and Orville Wright—who had other designs than building a horseless carriage. Finally, there was a young man named Henry Ford who was riding a bike to work as an engineer at Detroit's Edison Illuminating Company.

Missing from the early chase to build an automobile were the carriage makers. Roughly five thousand in number, they would become a factor later. But in the early automobile days, their business was still strong and they were slow to see that their industry was doomed.

For the prospective inventor, the missing ingredient was a lightweight power source. The Otto engine was the key. Though Nicholas Otto obtained his US patent in 1876, his focus remained on producing large, heavy stationary engines. For the would-be horseless carriage inventors, news of progress in Europe and articles such as the 1888 *Scientific American* feature on the Otto engine were especially instructive and galvanizing. Certainly Europe had a substantial head start in both gas engine propulsion and automobiles. But by 1891, the newly arrived *Horseless Age* magazine estimated that there were in excess of three hundred inventors working on automobiles in the United States. Heading up this burgeoning wave of automotive invention were two brothers from a small farm within twenty miles of Williamsfield.

Just who built the first automobile in Europe would later become a matter of great controversy. The same thing happened in the United States, though here it had the added drama of pitting brother against brother. The brothers were Charles and Frank Duryea. Charles was born in 1861 on a farm in Canton, just south of Williamsfield. His brother Frank was born eight years later after the family moved to a farm in Wyoming, Illinois, just north of Williamsfield. Though both brothers grew up and worked on farms, they quickly left farming behind. Again, bicycles entered their stories. In 1882 Charles moved to Washington, DC, and began to work for H. S. Owen, a bicycle importer and repair shop. Frank soon joined him there.

In 1890 Charles moved to Chicopee, Massachusetts, a suburb of Springfield, intending to start building his own bikes. He arranged for Frank to join him there. The bicycle start-up stalled, and Charles used the summer of 1891 to explore the concept of a motor-driven wagon. While in DC, he had visited the US Patent Office to read up on patents relating to gasoline engines and motor wagons. Then, on a trip back to the Midwest, he had examined a gas engine at the Ohio state fair. While living near Hartford, he visited a local manufacturer that was building a Daimler-type engine. He also spoke to an engineer at Colonel Pope's bike company, comparing notes on building an engine.

Once Charles felt he had a usable concept in place, he asked Frank to join him in building the design. With limited funds, they procured a used horse buggy, built a one-cylinder Otto cycle engine, and added a friction transmission that linked to a tricycle differential that they obtained from Pope. Steering was by tiller.

With substantial progress but the work incomplete, Charles moved back to Peoria. He had set up the Rouse-Duryea Cycle Company and was again focused on launching a new bicycle design. Meanwhile, back east, Frank completed the first motor wagon, but he was less than satisfied. Without even as much as a road test, he dismantled the engine and carriage and started work on an improved second machine. He made major changes, starting with constructing a brand new engine, one that was heavier and more powerful than the first. This change necessitated upgrading many of the other components, including a stronger carriage, pneumatic tires, and a drum and leather belt arrangement for the transmission.

On September 21, 1893, under the cover of darkness, Frank rolled out the new motor wagon for its first trial. The engine performed well, but the transmission was balky. The wagon traveled all of six hundred feet. Though less than successful, this first trial was reported in the Springfield paper the next day. This is generally regarded as the first US automobile.

Frank had a mental list of changes that needed to be made. But first, he took time to travel to Chicago in October for the World's Fair, called the 1893 Columbian Exposition. He met Charles there, and the two were able to see the Daimler quadricycle and numerous Otto engines on display. As reported by *Horseless Age*, there were many amateur engineers working on automobiles, but mostly in isolation. In Chicago, a number of these future automotive pioneers showed up, including Alexander Winton, Elwood Haynes, Charles King, and Henry Ford. Henry had traveled from Detroit specifically to see that Daimler engine.

Frank returned to Chicopee and had the wagon ready for a second run in November. It was more successful than the first run but ended with the same problem—a failure of the transmission linkage. Frank worked until mid-January 1894 to reengineer the entire clutch assembly. On January 18, with the new transmission in place, he proceeded to put six miles on the wagon, driving through the streets of Springfield. This second motor wagon was destined to be the ultimate low-mileage car. Shortly after the successful run, it was stored in a local Springfield barn. Later, it was moved to a barn in Peoria, where it remained until 1920, when it was acquired by the Smithsonian. Today, it is sitting in the Smithsonian Museum of History and Technology with perhaps twenty miles on the odometer (that is, if it had an odometer).

Charles and Frank had built their first automobile but needed a push to really get into business. An opportunity surfaced in 1895 when the *Chicago Times-Herald* staged the first automobile race in the country. It was a fifty-four-mile loop from Chicago to Evanston and back, finishing at the center of the 1893 Columbian Exposition grounds. The purse was $5,000, with $2,000 going to the winner. It was billed as the "Race of the Century."

Automobiles were so new that the paper couldn't agree on what to call the vehicles. It settled on "Moto Cycle." There were nearly eighty entrants, including Frank in his second car. Elwood Haynes also planned to have his car in the contest and was a pre-race favorite. However, he was stopped by police while traveling on Michigan Avenue into town and ordered to have his car towed by horses as it was apparently unlawful to have such a machine on city streets. His car was subsequently damaged in what may have been the first US auto accident, and he was unable to repair it in time for the race.

The race was to be held in early November, but only two cars were ready. It was rescheduled for Thanksgiving Day, which, unfortunately, was a day of heavy snow. Only six cars made it to the starting line—the Duryea, three Benz automobiles, and two electrics (a Morris and Salom Electrobat and a Sturges Electric). Hiram P. Maxim, who worked for Colonel Pope and hoped to have a Columbia automobile in the race, instead rode as the umpire in the Sturges car. The electrics were out of the race early as the cold severely limited their battery range. Only two cars finished. Frank Duryea crossed the finish line first with a time just over ten hours, earning the $2,000 prize. One of the Benz cars was the other finisher. It was driven most of the way by Oscar Mueller, but on the return leg he fell unconscious from the cold. Riding as umpire with him was Charles King of Detroit. He had planned to enter his own car in the contest but it was not ready in time. With Mueller slumped by his side, King took over the tiller and finished the race. Though the race was certainly less than the *Times-Herald* had planned, the national coverage raised awareness of horseless carriages.

The following year, Charles and Frank organized the Duryea Motor Wagon Company in Springfield and produced thirteen vehicles. That same year, Frank took one of the new motor wagons to England and scored a dramatic victory in the London-to-Brighton race. He was offered $250,000 for the European rights to the Duryea automobile, but Charles was late in responding and the opportunity slipped away.

Charles and Frank spent a couple of years trying to make a go of manufacturing cars, but selling fewer than twenty cars per year was not enough to be profitable. They quarreled often and finally split in 1898. Frank formed the Stevens-Duryea Company, focusing on more expensive cars. The company was very successful, producing quality engineered cars until 1927. Charles went through several automotive companies, mostly with very limited success. He then spent his later years asserting that he, with some engineering help from his brother, was responsible for the first American automobile.

As mentioned, Elwood Haynes of Kokomo, Indiana, was in Chicago for the *Times-Herald* race. Haynes had been very successful in the gas field, and like many of his would-be inventor peers he sought to build a horseless carriage. He considered and rejected both steam and electric approaches. When he saw the Otto engine at the 1893 Chicago Exposition, he knew he had found his power source. He purchased a two-cycle, single-cylinder Sintz marine gasoline engine and then contacted the Apperson brothers, who ran a local bicycle and machine shop. He asked them to mate the engine with a buggy on bike wheels. The completed car weighed in at 820 pounds and had a top speed of 8 mph. The first run was on July 4, 1894. Haynes and the Appersons formed a company and built cars in their spare time until 1898, at which time they got serious, if only for a time. They parted company in 1901, not on good terms, and went forward as two companies—Haynes and Apperson. Both companies built excellent cars and lasted into the 1920s. And, both companies continued to make the assertion that they had created the first US automobile, albeit with the caveat that they had invented the first production-oriented machine.[15]

One inventor who was not in the Chicago race was Alexander Winton. He was building a car for the contest, but it was not ready in time. Winton was born in Scotland in 1860 to a father who was a marine engineer. He immigrated to New York City at age nineteen and initially worked for a steam engine manufacturer. He followed in his father's footsteps, becoming a marine engineer on ocean-going steam vessels for five years. Back on dry land, he moved to Cleveland and was an early entrant into bicycle manufacturing in 1891, specializing in high-end bikes. He rode the bicycle-craze wave until it crested and the industry became bloated with manufacturers. At that point, Winton turned his energies to building a horseless carriage.

Winton knew that steam was too heavy and impractical to power a horseless carriage. By 1896 he had built an experimental one-cylinder car. Well-versed on marketing from running his bicycle business, he managed to get an article in *Horseless Age* magazine in November 1896, and then a second one two months later. By the following year, he had built a two-cylinder, 10 horsepower machine. He drove it from Cleveland to New York City, a total of five hundred miles, and had a writer for *Horseless Age* along to document the journey. (He failed to report to the magazine that he loaded the car on a train for the return trip.) In March 1898 he sold his first car. He ended up selling twenty-two cars that first year, including one to James Packard, who would quickly figure prominently in automobiles. Another car went to O. T. Johnson in Galesburg. The 1898 Winton was a buggy design with a 6 horsepower, one-cylinder engine running at 200–1,000 rpm. It featured bicycle tires, tiller steering, and a two-speed transmission of gears and chains. Speed was controlled by a button on the floor.

One of the early giants of US automobiles had no connection with bicycles except perhaps riding them. His forte was engines. His name was Ransom E. Olds. He would pioneer many of the approaches to making and selling automobiles that would became standard in the industry. Born in 1864, Olds worked for his father Pliny in Lansing, Michigan, selling gasoline-heated steam engines. In 1887 he built a rudimentary steam wagon. He continued tinkering, building prototype electric and gas-powered vehicles. The company had switched to producing Otto gas engines, and Olds was clear that this was the way to go. In 1893 he was at the Chicago Columbian Exposition to get a look at the Daimler car. In 1895 he wanted to enter the Chicago race but, like Winton, did not have a car ready in time.

Working with a small team back in Lansing, Olds completed his first car in August 1896 and drove it through the streets of Lansing. He commented that his motor carriage "doesn't require care in the stable and only eats on the road." The first car had worked well, in part because of his vast experience with engines. The next year he organized the company as Olds Motor Vehicle Company. After selling just four cars, he realized that his capital was insufficient for accelerated production and secured nearly $200,000 from Samuel Smith, a Michigan copper and lumber baron.

Together, they set up Olds Motor Works and began car operations in earnest in 1900. With this huge injection of cash, Ransom Olds proceeded to develop eleven prototypes. None of these pilot cars were getting much traction in the market as they were predominantly big, heavy, and expensive machines. He decided to build a small runabout. The frame was a buggy with a curved front end, typical for small horse-drawn buggies at the time. Olds and his engineer Horace Loomis developed a planetary transmission with two forward speeds and one reverse. It was powered by a one-cylinder, 7 horsepower engine running at 500 rpm with a simple chain-drive transmission. It was a mere 98 inches long (by comparison, a Volkswagen Beetle is 160 inches long) and weighed in at seven hundred pounds.

In March 1901, a fire raced through the factory. All of the prototype cars were destroyed except the little runabout. Ransom decided to go with it, pricing it at $650. To stir up a little publicity he engaged twenty-one-year-old Roy Chapin to drive the car, now christened the Curved Dash Oldsmobile (though officially the Oldsmobile Model R), eight hundred miles from Lansing to New York City for the 1901 New York auto show at Madison Square Garden. Chapin had quite the adventure driving up through Canada and back down into New York State. Fearing that he would arrive late to the show, he took a shortcut by driving on the Erie Canal towpath before motoring into Manhattan. He had used thirty gallons of gasoline and averaged 14 mph on the trip.

This was not the only publicity stunt that Ransom Olds tried. He took a one-cylinder but more powerful Olds car that he called the Pirate down to Daytona, Florida, in 1902 for a race with Alexander Winton. Winton brought his own racer, called the Bullet. They raced on the sand at Ormond Beach in time trials. Though neither would claim victory, they both reported top speeds of 57 mph, a speed unheard of at the time.

Once on display at the New York show, orders poured in for the little Olds car. Initially, Olds could only build one or two cars per day. So, he decided to use suppliers and headed to Detroit. He first went to see Henry Leland (of Leland and Faulconer, a leading machine shop) and secured an agreement to supply two thousand engines. He then proceeded to the Dodge Brothers (Horace and John) machine shop, and came away with a contract to provide two thousand transmissions. He sourced ball bearings from Hyatt Ball Bearing, a company run by the Alfred P. Sloans, father and son.[16] With these suppliers in place, Olds was able to ramp up production to ten cars a day. By 1902 he had four thousand orders and was able to produce 3,299 Olds cars. Total US car production that year was nine thousand, and Olds was the number-one producer. However, to put this number in perspective, nearly a million horse-drawn buggies were sold that same year.

Still, Olds's little Curved Dash Oldsmobile was a phenomenon. It even spawned its own popular song, "In My Merry Oldsmobile," in which you didn't just go driving but went "automobubbling." Ransom Olds had constructed an efficient roadmap for automobile success—build one model and build it efficiently—and utilized marketing and dealer networks to drive volume. For Olds, the future looked bright.

However, unfortunately his future would not be with the Olds Company. In 1904 Samuel Smith installed his son Frederic, who was all of twenty-five, as head of the company. The Smiths wanted to build expensive cars. Olds did not. Olds was forced out, and adding insult to injury, the Smiths retained the name "Olds" and threatened Ransom about using it for another car company.

Ransom Olds had the last laugh though, or perhaps even a couple of laughs. He walked out the door with $500,000 and within a year had his own automobile company up and running; quite cunningly called REO (Ransom Eli Olds was his full name). REO hit the ground running with nearly a thousand cars sold in 1905 and was outstripping Olds the following year. The Smiths stopped production of the Curved Dash in 1907 and tried to sell $4,500 luxury automobiles. Sales cratered. By 1908 it was a distressed manufacturer that Willy Durant bought and added to his General Motors (GM) grab bag of companies.

Several others were early on the automotive scene. The aforementioned Colonel Pope moved from bicycles to automobiles and produced an electric car in 1896. He hired Hiram Percy Maxim, a recent MIT graduate, to head up his Columbia motor division. Two years later, he merged his company with the Electric Vehicle Company, which was making electric taxis in New York City. From 1899 to 1901, Columbia was the largest automobile manufacturer in the United States, albeit with annual sales under a thousand. Along the way, Pope and the Electric Vehicle division parted ways. Pope made several subsequent forays into the automobile business, but none were successful. He declared bankruptcy in 1907.

Electric automobile sales were no better back at the Electric Vehicle Company. However, the company had an asset that held some promise. In

1899 George Selden had sold his automobile patent to William Whitney, one of the financiers of the company. They just needed to figure out a way to monetize it, and once they did, it was to cause untold damage to the automotive industry in its early years.

Very early on, steam was still a factor in automobiles. Francis and Free-lan Stanley, brothers in Watertown, Massachusetts, sold their photographic business to Eastman Kodak and built their first car, a steamer, in 1897. They sold the rights to that first car to John Walker (publisher of *Cosmopolitan* magazine), who developed the steamer into a brand called Locomobile. The Stanleys proceeded to develop a more advance steam automobile and formed their second company, Stanley Motor Carriage. They secured a factory in Bridgeport, Connecticut, in 1900 and began production, selling four thousand steamers by 1902. In 1906 a Stanley Steamer set the world speed record at the same Ormond Beach oceanfront course, clocking at 127 mph.

Early on, gas-powered automobiles were noisy, hard to start, and expensive. For a brief period, steamers held sufficient advantages to be successful and overcome some of the inherent issues with steam power. They needed up to thirty minutes to develop pressure. They needed to stop for water every 30–100 miles, and they needed gasoline fuel to heat the water. Yet despite those limitations, by 1905 there were over one hundred steamer brands on the market.

As for electrics, they comprised up to 40 percent of the market even as late as 1910. Thomas Edison was an early buyer of an electric automobile (a Baker) and would later work with Henry Ford in an attempt to revive the concept. But the negatives of electrics quickly caught up with the makers. They were heavy, had very limited range and limited charging options, and were much more expensive to buy and run.

A watershed event for the budding US automotive industry was the first dedicated auto show, held in New York City in November 1900. At the time, the United States was a nation of seventy-six million people, with eighteen million farmers, ten million bicycles, and roughly four thousand cars. A year earlier, an automobile parade had been held on Madison Avenue, providing the seed of the idea for a show and a brief glimpse of the future. The show was held at Madison Square Garden (this was the second incarnation of Madison Square Garden, located at Madison Avenue and 26th Street). The streets outside the Garden certainly did not reflect what was being shown inside the Garden. Horse cars had been replaced by cable-driven trolleys, but the streets were dominated by horse-drawn Hansom cabs, buggies, and wagons.

However, walking to that first show in 1900, one could spot an occasional exception to normal nineteenth-century urban transportation: Hansom electric cabs. The Morris and Salom Electrobat electric car had debuted in 1894, and a group of financiers in the city had sought to replace horse-drawn Hansom cabs with Electrobat-based machines, which looked just like a Hansom cab but, of course, lacked the horse. They even developed a system to swap out batteries in order to avoid long charging downtimes. This became the Electric Vehicle Company. It enjoyed brief success in New York before its business model succumbed to overexpansion.

There were thirty-four different makes at the New York show. Gas models included cars built by Duryea, Knox,[17] Winton, Daimler, De Dion–Bouton, Peerless, and Haynes-Apperson. There were seven steamers including Stanley, Locomobile, Foster, and McKay. Electrics included National, a former bike maker, Riker, Baker, and the Electric Vehicle Company. At the time of the 1900 show, the rough breakdown of the industry had steamers at 40 percent, electrics at 38 percent, and gasoline models at 22 percent.

Fast-forward four short years, to the 1904 New York auto show, and there were now 152 exhibitors, including Franklin, Pierce, Knox, Peerless, Jeffrey, Olds,[18] Electric Vehicle, Apperson, Winton, Pope, Studebaker, Packard, Cadillac, Duryea, Mercedes, Panhard and Levassor, and oh, one other—Ford. By this time, the term "automobile" had come to be accepted, replacing horseless carriage, motor wagon, motocycle, polycycle, mocle, and even scoot wagon.

With all this progress in automobiles in both Europe and the United States, what was happening out in the hinterlands, in farm country? It turns out that quite a few automobiles were being built there. For one, Frank and Charles Duryea had set up shop in Peoria. And they weren't the only shop in town.

Farmers knew that Peoria was where the big Avery threshing machines and steam traction engines were built. John Bartholomew, who had grown up on a farm a mile north of Elmwood, had gone to work at Avery in 1879. He had been stationed at an Avery plant in Des Moines, Iowa, for several years. There, he had started a side business making peanut roasters. When Robert Avery died in 1892, Bartholomew returned to Peoria and rose to be president of Avery. Once back in Peoria, he again started another side business—this time building an automobile. A prototype was called the

Bartholomew, but when he formally started production in 1902, the car was renamed the Glide, as in the company's ads: "Ride the Glide, then decide."

While O. T. Johnson's one-day campaign with the Winton marked the first car to rumble through the local towns, the first car owner in the farming countryside belonged to Williamsfield. In 1903 Charles Elliott bought a Glide, one of only twenty-five built by Bartholomew in his first year. It was a red, one-seat runabout, one-cylinder with tiller steering, looking not all that different from the best-selling Curved Dash Oldsmobile. The next year saw another Glide buyer in Williamsfield, Noah Tucker. He purchased a two-cylinder model—and then decided to go all in and become a Glide dealer.

This sudden veritable explosion of automobiles in town prompted the town board to decree a speed limit of 4 mph within the village (this was the average speed of a horse and buggy). There subsequently sprouted up many Glide dealers in the small towns around Peoria. Charles Bartholomew, John's younger brother, opened a Glide dealership in Elmwood. Brimfield eventually had two Glide dealers. The Glide enjoyed success in part because it was a local company and, more importantly, because it was produced by a company with a farm equipment background, so it was trusted.

Williamsfield having bragging rights for the first car was a cause for some consternation on the part of the other "non-automobile" towns. The Elmwood newspaper wrote, "Ho, all ye little crossroads towns like Brimfield, Elmwood, Farmington, and Princeville. Take off your hat and go way back and double up while Williamsfield's brand new automobile goes sailing by." The *Brimfield News* lauded "Billtown" as a step ahead of the other towns. The *Williamsfield Times* took the longer view, stating that "these machines will probably soon become so common that their passage will not excite newspaper comment." Yet, for the time being, automobiles did excite newspaper comment. Virtually every automobile purchased was duly reported in the paper. This continued until the 1930s, when new car purchases did indeed become all too common.

In 1902 it was reported that the first car in Canton had run into a horse and buggy, killing the horse. If there was a touch of symbolism in that, it was not noted at the time. That same year, there was a short-lived attempt to create a local taxi company between Buda and Sheffield, about five miles north of Williamsfield. Zephaniah "Z. E." Williamson was behind the effort. He was one of the very small numbers of buyers for the Milwaukee steamer. The company lasted just two years before it folded. One of the Milwaukee Steamer drivers laid off in the bankruptcy was W. H. McIntyre, who would go on to start the McIntyre High Wheeler buggy automobile, which would experience similar results.

Chicago staged its first auto show in 1901. Exhibitors included Winton, Knox, Studebaker, Electric Vehicle, Locomobile, Pierce, Jeffrey, Stearns, Peerless, Packard, Apperson, Ford, Bartholomew, and Pope. In 1904 Charles Elliott became the first local to trade in a car, replacing his Glide with a bright red Duryea built in Peoria. He then turned around and became a dealer for them. The first car in Elmwood was jointly purchased by Marshall Lott and Harry Schenk, two partners in the Bank of Elmwood. It was also another Glide. The local paper reported it as a "scoot wagon," the early name that had generally been retired several years before.

5

A Pretty Good Engineer

I N 1898 ALEXANDER WINTON was just getting started. Like many early
carmakers, he focused on low volume, expensive cars for those that
could afford them. One of his very early buyers was James Packard, a
successful manufacturer of incandescent lamps. He professed to have many
problems with his new car that he repeatedly voiced to Winton. He even
taunted Winton that even he could build a better motorcar. Winton finally
said "go ahead and build one." Packard took up the challenge. He also took
two of Winton's key engineers—William Hatcher and George Weiss—and
was able to roll out the first of many luxury Packards in 1899.

Winton had lost a customer and two key engineers. His factory chief
(Leo Melanowski, who had previously worked at Panhard and Levassor)
recommended a young up-and-coming engineer he had recently met. This
engineer had been to the 1893 Columbian Exposition and was also present
for the 1895 *Times-Herald* race. He had already designed and developed
several automobile prototypes. Winton agreed to an interview with the engineer but was not impressed and did not hire him. The engineer was, of
course, Henry Ford. Not only was this a missed opportunity for Winton,
but the snub would come back to haunt him several years later.

Henry Ford did not invent the automobile. He was still working for
Thomas Edison in Detroit as the European and American pioneers rolled
out their designs. Yet, he did more than anyone else to jump-start the

automotive revolution. How did this Michigan farm boy, just two generations removed from the Irish famine, climb to such heights? There is no simple answer to that question. The best approach is to start at the beginning and work forward from there.

In 1819 Henry's grandfather John Ford took over the family land lease in Cork, Ireland. John Ford's younger brothers Samuel and George, without even options to rent farmland, immigrated to America and settled west of Detroit in Dearborn. The Irish potato famine struck in 1845, and after two years of misery John Ford, his wife Thomasina, and a family that included young son William traveled to Cork City on the coast. There, they boarded a ship bound for Quebec. The Atlantic crossing had not improved much since the Palatine emigrations a century earlier. Thomasina died en route and was buried at sea. The ship traveled up the St. Lawrence to Grosse Ile, an island just short of Quebec City, where an immigration facility like Ellis Island was set up primarily to quarantine disease. Many thousands who had survived the arduous Atlantic crossing ended up dying on this island as the close quarters was a natural breeding ground for disease. John and his children survived and continued their way up the river to Kingston, across Lake Ontario to Buffalo, and across Lake Erie to Detroit.

John Ford was reunited with his brothers and purchased a farm in Dearborn. William was twenty-one. He worked his father's farm for a period, then purchased half of the eighty acres and began raising wheat, hay, sheep, cows, and hogs. In 1861 he married Mary Litogot, a woman of Belgian ancestry, at the home of Thomas Maybury.[19] Henry Ford was born two years later in Springfield Township, in what is now present-day Dearborn, and eight to ten miles west of Detroit. As a lad, Henry walked several miles each weekday to the Scotch Settlement School, a typical one-room schoolhouse. He was taught using McGuffey readers, which combined reading and instruction with a heavy focus on character and duty to parents, God, and country. His teacher there was John Chapman, and when Chapman moved to another school (Miller) in 1873, Henry followed him.[20]

The seminal event in young Henry's life was the sudden death of his mother from complications in childbirth. He had developed no love of farm life and was to say years later that "it was the mother on the farm that I loved." To be sure, at age thirteen his interests were already elsewhere. Fascinated by machinery, he took apart watches and reassembled them. He marveled at the McCormick reaper that his father bought and the productivity it delivered. He was especially intrigued by the Nichols and Shepard steam traction engine that a neighbor farmer had purchased. Seeing lo-comotion on the farm roads without horses planted the seed that would eventually take over his life.

Given the proximity to Detroit, Henry Ford had options. And so, with his father's blessing, he left school at sixteen and walked the eight miles to the city. He started a job at the Michigan Car Company, a maker of railroad freight cars. He lasted just six days, as other workers in the shop were not happy that he worked at a much faster pace than they did. Ford used his father's connection with James Flowers to secure a position at the Flowers Brothers machine shop, an operation that manufactured brass and iron fittings. There were more machines than workers in the shop, a veritable toy store for Henry. He learned engineering and machining on the job. He may have heard mention of another apprentice who had previously worked in the shop before he arrived, David Dunbar Buick.

A year later, Ford took a position with Detroit Dry Dock Company, a builder of steam ships. He was now working on steam boilers. The owner, Frank Kirby, was one of the great naval architects of his time, specializing in large steam vessels that plied the Great Lakes. Frank took Henry under his wing as an apprentice. Ford returned to the farm at harvest time in 1880 and 1881 to help his father.

After two years, he left Detroit Dry Dock and returned to Dearborn. His father provided him with a forty-acre forested parcel, hoping it might entice him to give farming a try. Instead, he bought a circular saw, rented a 12 horsepower gas engine, and used the rig to cut timber. He processed over 200,000 board feet of oak and sold it, but did no farming. His neigh-bor James Gleason had recently purchased the Westinghouse Agricultural Engine, a portable steam engine used to power a threshing belt at har-vest. Already very familiar with steam power from his stint at Detroit Dry Dock, Ford learned everything he could about the 6,900-pound machine and landed a part-time job with Westinghouse to demo the unit to farmers and support installed units in southern Michigan. In his spare time, he proceeded to develop his own small steam engine.

In 1884 Henry Ford attended the Goodsmith, Bryant, and Stratton Busi-ness School in Detroit to learn the essentials of business and accounting. When he returned to Dearborn, he had the opportunity to work on Otto cycle gas engines that were being used on neighboring farms. By 1888 he secured steady work by traveling back and forth to Detroit to work on both steam and gas engines. With so much exposure to various power plants, the idea of building a motor wagon started to form in his mind.

During this period living in Dearborn, he met, wooed, and married Clara Bryant. His father provided the couple with a small cottage, once again hoping that farm life would somehow seep in. Clara and Henry designed a bigger house and Henry used part of his harvested lumber to construct it. Yet, he continued to commute into Detroit to work on engines.

In 1891 he was offered a position at Edison Illuminating as a night engineer. He confided to Clara that the job not only provided a good salary but would afford him the time and environment to pursue his vision—building a horseless carriage. They moved to Detroit and ended up renting half of a duplex house at 58 Bagley Avenue. It conveniently had a shed in back where Ford could tinker. That same year, he taught an engineering class at the YMCA. One of his pupils was Oliver Barthel, someone who would soon provide him with a valuable connection.

After two years at Edison, Ford was promoted to chief engineer, a job that placed him on call at all hours but critically gave him even more free time to work on his machine. His first challenge was building a lightweight Otto cycle engine. Working from an article in *American Machinist* magazine, Ford constructed a very primitive one-cylinder engine in his shop and ran it successfully, with Clara's help, at the kitchen sink. As the engine had no muffler, it no doubt woke up their son Edsel, who was just a few months old. Ford moved on to a more complex engine, again pulling the design from engineering articles.

Around this time, he ran into Oliver Barthel, who was now working for a wealthy and nationally known engineer and inventor with sixty-four patents to his name. The engineer, Charles King, was also working on a horseless carriage. King had seen the Daimler engine at the Chicago Exposition and was using John Lauer's machine shop to fabricate his own design. In March 1896, King and Barthel drove King's wooden-wheeled automobile through the streets of Detroit at 7 mph, marking the first automobile in the city.[21] Henry Ford rode his bicycle to watch the test.

Inspired by King, Ford threw himself into his automobile project. With his natural ability to get others to see and work his vision, he had four colleagues from Edison (David Bell, James Bishop, George Cato, and Spider Huff) assisting him, all on their own time. He secured cylinders, pistons, and rings from Detroit Dry Dock. His friends there also forged a crankshaft. Charles King supplied a key and difficult component—the cylinder valve. Ford dispensed with a carburetor and simply positioned the gas tank at an elevation above the engine. He exposed the two cylinders so no water cooling was required. He added two little bulbs to the top of each cylinder to drip down oil for lubrication.

Ford secured iron for the frame from Barr and Dates and a buggy seat from C. R. Wilson. For the transmission, he had a leather belt running from the flywheel to a gearing countershaft that drove a bicycle chain to one of the rear wheels. A lever was used to tension the belt and engage or release the drive wheel. He also added a differential at the rear, remembering this requirement from the steam traction engine he had seen as a boy. He performed much of the metalwork himself in his shed. Struggling with ignition after several failed approaches, Ford decided to simply drill a hole in the cylinder and inserted a spark circuit connected to a dry cell battery. Amazingly, it all came together. To start the engine, Ford had to connect the battery, open two fuel petcocks, and then hand-turned the large flywheel.

The finished vehicle was a compact, five-hundred-pound unit with a metal frame, four bicycle wheels, a two-cylinder, 4 horsepower engine running at 500 rpm, two driving speeds controlled by the tension lever, and a tiller for steering. There was no reverse and no brakes. In June 1896 it was complete enough for a test drive. However, there was one small problem— the machine was too wide to get out of the shed door. This was no time for a slick engineering solution. Ford took a sledge hammer to the door jamb, and the machine was rolled out onto the street. It was four in the morning on June 4, 1896. Given that it was still dark and the motor carriage had no brakes, Ford added a single headlight to the front along with a little electric bell to announce the vehicle was bearing down. In addition, he had one of his colleagues (James Bishop) ride ahead on a bicycle to warn anyone venturing onto the street. Ford took the second car in the city of Detroit out on Bagley Street and up Grand River Avenue, reaching 10 mph in low gear and 20 mph in high gear. Despite needing a couple of adjustments, the trial was a success.

Ford called the machine the Quadricycle. Throughout its development, he continued to work at Detroit Edison. His manager there (Alexander Dow) invited Ford to the annual Edison convention in Manhattan Beach, New York. While there, he was able to talk about his automobile with Thomas Edison. Ford expected a lively discussion about electric cars, but Edison urged him to keep on improving his gasoline car. Upon his return,

Ford sold the Quadricycle to Charles Ainsley for $200 and started work on his second car.[22]

With the moral support from the master inventor, Ford redoubled his efforts. His second car was completed in 1898, another runabout. It was dramatically more complex than the Quadricycle, improved in every way. It featured a two-cylinder engine, battery ignition, and a larger flywheel connected to real transmission gearing. Ford added a carburetor of his own design, and yes, the second car had brakes. The following year, he completed a third car, another runabout. Besides enhanced engineering, there was another focus for these two cars. He needed to transition from machines that proved the concept to ones that could lead to commercialization. To that end, the new runabouts were upgraded with running boards, brass fixtures, a padded seat, high wheels, and a full suspension.

Though Ford had successfully built three automobiles, he was still in full tinker mode, wanting to constantly improve on his designs. But in 1899, he decided that it was time to get serious about building cars for a living. He informed Alexander Dow at Edison of his intention to resign. Dow offered Ford the position of general superintendent at an annual salary of $1,900 (equivalent to $59,000 in 2020). But Ford's mind was made up and he resigned from Edison.

His first step was lining up financial backers. William Maybury, a family friend and now Detroit mayor, introduced Ford to William Murphy, a local lumber businessman. In July 1899, Ford took Murphy on a sixty-mile, three-and-a-half-hour ride to Pontiac, Michigan, and back. Murphy was suitably impressed, and by the next month he had lined up a group of Detroit movers and shakers to come up with $150,000 in funding to incorporate the Detroit Automobile Company. It went live on August 5, 1899 with a small factory on Cass Avenue for production.

Ford hired his former associates Spider Huff and Harold Wills. The transition from inventor to producer was not easy. Ford had no experience in production and did not realize the steps he must take to move from engineer to manufacturer. The investors expected cars to roll out of the plant, sales to be made, and their investments to earn a return. Working on his own, Ford had all the time in the world. He was a perfectionist who would not freeze designs but continue to fine-tune them. Now as the principal of the Detroit Automobile Company, he continued in his old ways, often spending considerable time away from the plant floor just "thinking." In two years, the company produced fewer than twenty cars.

In the midst of this low output and after running through $86,000 of investor money, Ford expressed his desire to pause production and build a race car. This was not a crazy idea. In the early days of the automobile, winning races was a standard approach to increase interest and raise your profile. In addition, the larger engines and higher speeds of racers required excellence in all components, resulting in a better car. However, investor patience at Detroit Automobile Company had already worn thin, and the company folded in January 1901.

Ford did not seem to lose any sleep over the failure of his company. Instead, he immediately pleaded his racing case directly with William Murphy, who agreed to provide $5,000 to underwrite the development of a race car. It was the summer of 1901, and Ford decided to gear up for a race scheduled in October at nearby Gross Pointe. He again enlisted his colleagues from Edison—Huff, Wills, and Barthel—and the team went to work. Henry designed a fuel-injection vaporizer and Huff engineered the spark plugs. Fitted with two huge cylinders—each was seven inches in diameter and displaced 538 cubic inches (by comparison, the Quadricycle displacement was 64 cubic inches)—the engine generated 26 horsepower. Ford and his team used up the $5,000 provided by Murphy in materials alone. The completed 2,200-pound racer was called Sweepstakes and clocked out at 72 mph in pre-race tests. The car was a monster. Henry was apprehensive about driving it and enlisted Tom Cooper, the nationally famous bicycle racer who lived in Detroit, to coach him.

The Grosse Pointe track was a one-mile oval track. The race was set up to host several car classes, including steamers, electrics, and an unlimited class for vehicles weighing over two thousand pounds. There were twenty-five entries for this heavyweight class, but come race time, only one other entrant joins Ford and his Sweepstakes car for the race. That other entrant happened to be that carmaker that was not impressed with Henry Ford only a few short years back: Alexander Winton. His entry was a 70-horsepower behemoth called the "Bullet". The winner would take home $1,000 plus an elaborate cut-glass punch bowl with a classic strawberry, diamond and fan pattern. Winton especially coveted the punch bowl. The racer cars were each manned by a driver and a mechanic. Winton jumped out to a large lead as Ford was more cautious in the turns, in part because he was driving the Sweepstakes racer with Huff crouched on the running board. Ford gradually cut into the lead and when Winton ran into engine trouble around lap seven, Ford and Huff cruised home for the victory and the prizes. The Sweepstakes racer averaged 45 mph over the race course. Of the over eight thousand spectators in attendance, several would figure prominently in Ford's future plans—Alexander Malcolmson, James Couzens, Tom Cooper, and Barney Oldfield.

Ford was certainly right about the value of racing. Within a month, he had another set of wealthy backers lined up to form a second enterprise—the Henry Ford Company. These new investors were led by none other than William Murphy, willing to give Ford another chance.

At the same time, Ford had also reached a side agreement with Tom Cooper to fund the design and build of a new, more powerful racer. Cooper, who had earned in excess of $100,000 racing bicycles, agreed to put up $5,000 for the effort, with the stipulation that Ford build not one but two racers—one for Ford and one for Cooper. Cooper provided a machine shop at 81 Park Place for the work. While Ford and his team were busy working on the racers, Roy Chapin of Olds Motor happened to be driving a Curved Dash Oldsmobile in town and had a spring break. He stopped at a nearby machine shop looking for a quick repair. This, of course, turned out to be Henry Ford's racing shop.

With the new company, Ford and his team worked on a production car during the day and the enhanced racer at night. Murphy, aware of the experience of investors with Ford's previous venture, enlisted Henry Leland, the principal of a well-respected machine shop in town, to work with the Ford team and ensure that progress was made toward a production car.[23] Not surprisingly, Ford and Leland, both headstrong individuals, clashed repeatedly. Murphy and the investors finally stepped in and reached an agreement for Ford to leave the Henry Ford Company. Ford parted with $900, the new racer design, and a promise from Murphy to not use the Ford name.

With Henry Ford gone, Murphy and his investors considered folding the nascent company. Studebaker had been pressing Leland for the new engine he had developed that Olds had turned down. However, Leland suggested to Murphy and his investors that they back him in developing a new car. They agreed, and per the Ford stipulation, the company name was changed. It would now be called Cadillac, after the French explorer who founded Detroit. Leland proceeded to use Ford's production design, added his new 10-horsepower engine, and produced the first Cadillac, the Model A. In January 1903, three Cadillacs were taken to the New York auto show. The outstanding quality, fit, and finish of the car (standard for Leland work) and the $750 price generated an amazing 2,286 orders before Leland's sales manager declared "sold out." Production of these orders immediately put Cadillac at number two in sales, just behind the Olds Curved Dash.

Meanwhile, Henry Ford seemed unfazed about the turn of events and rededicated himself to the second generation of racing cars. Harold Wills designed the new cars, which sported four huge cylinders with a total displacement of 1,156 cubic inches, generating 70–100 horsepower. The cars were essentially enormous engines mounted on a rugged frame. Dubbed the Arrow and 999 after two very fast express trains, they were truly dangerous machines. The crankshaft and valves of the engines were fully exposed, producing a deafening noise and a spray of oil into the driver's face. Cooper was afraid to drive either car and suggested fellow bicycle champion Barney Oldfield.

In October 1902 the second Grosse Pointe race was held, and Ford's competition was once again Alexander Winton. Oldfield had never driven an automobile before and had just a week to master the new racer. Five cars were entered in the five mile unlimited race, including Winton with his monster Bullet racer. It was no contest. Oldfield drove with abandon and lapped all of the other racers, finishing a mile ahead of the second place car. He won in record time, averaging 55 miles per hour for the entire course. Winton's Bullet broke down and did not finish. Cooper and Oldfield envisioned a new career to replace bicycle racing. They purchased the 999 racer from Ford, agreeing to use the Ford name in races around the country, further advertising the Ford brand.[24] In 1904 Spider Huff and Frank Day raced two of Ford's cars in a Wisconsin race. Day crashed his Arrow and was killed. Ford bought the Arrow racer, repaired it, and renamed it the Red Devil. He finally summoned the courage to drive the car himself—on a straightaway carved out on frozen Lake St. Clair. He set a new land speed record of 91 mph.

Despite racing success, Henry Ford now had two failed ventures in his wake. But in 1902, with the 999 victory at Gross Pointe, Ford's profile rose ever higher and he was again looking for backers. Furthermore, he seemed ready to give up racing in favor of building regular cars.

Ford knew Detroit coal supplier Alexander Malcolmson from his Edison days and sought him out. With a long-time interest in automobiles and having followed Ford's career to date, Malcolmson agreed to pull together a group of investors for a new company. Most were relatives and friends. The enterprise was initially called the Ford and Malcolmson Limited but was subsequently changed to the Ford Motor Company. The new company stock was structured so that Ford and Malcolmson split a 51 percent ownership stake.[25] It began operating on June 16, 1903.

Malcolmson knew enough about Ford's personality to give him free rein, but he also knew he would have to assist Ford in moving expeditiously to real production. He aranged for a Strelow factory on Mack Avenue in Detroit to be used. He also secured an agreement with the Dodge brothers to build engines, frames, and transmissions for 650 cars.[26] In agreeing to the arrangement, the Dodges would have a commitment for $162,500 in components as long as they dropped their supplier contract with Olds. Early cash flow problems led Malcolmson to offer one hundred shares of the new company to the brothers in lieu of outright cash payments. Accepting the stock turned out to be the best decision they ever made.

Malcolmson also wanted to keep close tabs on his investment, so he assigned his coal office manager, James Couzens, to be Ford's office manager. Couzens, a short "bulldog" Canadian, did much more than just oversee: he demanded advance payment from dealers, just-in-time delivery from suppliers, did the hiring and firing, and was savvy in marketing. Most importantly, working with his sales manager Norval Hawkins, he built a huge dealer network, signing 450 agencies by 1905 and growing it to seven thousand dealers by 1913. He was clearly the missing piece from Ford's first two failed ventures.

With the Dodge brothers providing engines, transmissions, and frames and additional suppliers providing bodies, wheels, and tires, the initial bulk of the work for Ford's workers was assembling each car. The first car out the door was the Ford Model A. It was similar in overall design to the buggy-style automobile that Ford had patterned after the best-selling Olds Curved Dash. Henry Leland's Cadillac Model A had taken full advantage of Henry's drawings after he left, though the engine was a new design. However, Henry's Model A was a significant and rugged upgrade over Leland's car. It sported a steering wheel versus a tiller, sturdy artillery wheels versus bicycle wheels, and was powered by a two cylinder 8 horsepower, high torque engine versus one cylinder. Debuting in June 1903, the Ford Model A was initially slated to sell at $750, but Couzens raised the price to $850 based on heavy demand. The very first Model A was sold to Ernest Pfennig, a dentist in Chicago. Five more went out within the week. The Model A cleared about $150 per car, just as Couzens had predicted.

Within three months, the company had generated enough profit to pay back most of the initial investments to the shareholders. Over the next nine months, a total of 658 cars were sold, generating $98,000 in profit. Ford became the number-three automaker in the United States, just behind Olds and Cadillac. By the end of 1904, Ford had outgrown the plant on Mack Avenue and the assembly operation was moved to a new three-story building on Piquette Avenue. This was in an area called Milwaukee Junction and was home to a number of other automobile manufacturers, including Hupp, Cadillac, Oakland, and Packard.

6

The Golden Age

IN THE EARLY YEARS of the new century, Williamsfield continued to prosper. It might have been said to have entered its "golden age." Though smaller than neighboring Elmwood and Brimfield, it was nearly always in the forefront of advancements. Through passenger train service from Chicago to Los Angeles included an optional stop at the Williamsfield depot. Most of the daily train traffic, however, was freight related, with many trains stopping in town to replenish their water stores. In 1912 Williamsfield was wired for electricity and a steam plant was installed to provide the power. Of course, little nearby Yates City had electricity in 1894 so Williamsfield could not crow too much.

The one-room Tucker school was replaced by a large, full grade school in 1900. This was followed in 1901 with a new multi-story high school. As in most farming towns, the high school had a three-week vacation period in the fall during threshing time. The new high school saw its first commencement in May 1904, with Ona Shaffer, daughter of general store owner Frank Shaffer, among the graduates.

The *Williamsfield Times* was a big civic booster. It had long lobbied for a county fair–style show in town, and in the fall of 1903, the Williamsfield Horse Show debuted. It featured an opening parade down Gale Street and a host of agricultural competitions. Awards were given not only for the various horse categories (draft and roadsters, for example) but also for the best poultry, grain, and vegetables, and best domestic skills, like quilting and cooking. BF was especially proud of his giant Poland China hogs. They had been sired by the 1,000-pound hog "Junction Chief." The horse show drew large crowds from the surrounding towns and became an annual event.

Traveling shows came to town, including acts like the Great Ferrante, the Prince of Magic. These shows were held at the National Institute building until it burned to the ground in 1903. Thereafter, the traveling acts played at the ME (Methodist Episcopal) Church. More elaborate shows, such as the Redpath Chautauqua, would set up to run for a full week and featured a wide variety of music and speakers.

There was a much thinner line between life and death in these years. The *Williamsfield Times* used much of its ink covering accidents, sickness, and death, sometimes in the grimmest way possible. Years before the discovery of sulfa drugs, many illnesses and infections would lead inexorably to death.

Williamsfield had been a pioneer town with the automobile. In the early years of the twentieth century, it was witness to a transition era between the horse and buggy and the automobile. An emblematic episode of the shift occurred in 1906 with local farmer S. R. Boley. An automobile had broken down outside town. The motorist hired Mr. Boley to haul the car to Peoria. Boley hitched a team of horses to the car and then added his buggy to the back of the car so that he had a comfortable way to get back home. Well past the turn of the century, Frank Shaffer was still selling buggies at his general store. Even so, it was the last gasp for buggies. As late as 1911, the Reverend Ward bought an elegant new buggy, one of the last reported purchases before automobiles completely took over.

Yet, it was a crossover era, with buggies and wagons gradually giving way to automobiles. The *Times* even used different terms when covering one versus the other. If it used the term "drove," it meant the writer was talking about a buggy or wagon pulled by a horse. The term "motored" was applied if he was talking about an automobile. Buggy and wagon "runaways," where the horses were frightened by a loud noise and took off, remained a weekly occurrence and common staple in the newspaper. With the introduction of the automobile and its explosively loud gasoline engines, there were many more buggy and wagon "runaways" whenever the two met. As an example, Mrs. Shuglue's buggy horse was frightened by Noah Tucker's new Glide automobile and took off, resulting in a buggy crash. Mrs. Shuglue was shaken but not hurt.

By 1910 the horse-versus-automobile friction was front and center. The local papers covered any related incident. And they added rules (sometimes facetiously) for automobiles to follow to avoid any such conflict. One rule suggested that "on discovering an approaching team, the automobilist must stop off to the side and cover his machine with a tarpaulin painted to correspond with the scenery." Another instructed, "in case an automobile approaches a farmer's house when the roads are dusty, it must slow down to one mile an hour, and the chauffeur lay the dust with a hand sprinkler worked over the dashboard."[27]

The automobile population continued to grow, at first with the early adopters. Theo Bass purchased the first car in Farmington, a $750 Cadillac Model C Runabout.[28] He strategically waited for a mid-year price reduction. Edwin Preston bought the first automobile in Canton—a car made in Galesburg and naturally called the Gale. Thresherman Hugh Carroll, a very early automobile adopter, was already buying his second car, a Moline. The Moline was a monster automobile nicknamed the "Dreadnought" after the massive battleships. This was fitting for a man who ran steam tractors weighing over thirty tons. Another local thresherman, Alf Whetzel, ordered an REO in 1908.

Yet, the early adopters—the wealthy, country doctors, mailmen, and those few others who just wanted to be at the front of a new technology—were giving way to a much wider penetration of cars in the Illinois farm country. In 1907 the Illinois Motor Vehicle Act mandated automobile registration and license plates for the first time. The state reported car registrations that year for Ford, Cadillac, Winton, Olds, Buick, Cameron, Jeffrey, Star, Autocar, REO, Buckeye, Briscoe-Maxwell, Bartholomew, Haynes, Studebaker, Franklin, White, Pope, Electric Vehicle Co., and a host of others. Williamsfield kept leading the pack, with not one but two Ford agencies. But the other towns—in particular, Brimfield—were not far behind.

As of 1914 the streets in Williamsfield were still dirt, still dusty. The *Times* had shamed the town into oiling the main street during the summer months and frequently mentioned the fact that Galesburg already had twenty miles of paved streets, but to no avail.

In 1903 Will Shaffer began the three-year program at Williamsfield High School. Older siblings Bertha and Tom had already graduated, and his sister Ada and cousin Ona were two years ahead of him.[29] The high school had a new principal, R. C. Woolsey, who was young, energetic, and willing to shake things up.[30] He would develop a very special attachment to his first graduating class, Will's class of 1906. One of his innovations was developing sports teams. Despite its small enrollment, the school began to field teams in football, baseball, and track. The first football game was played in 1904, with Williamsfield beating Oneida. Of course, all the boys played, there being only ten boys in the senior class. Will played right end. He also ran the long distances in track. The star athlete was Floyd Wesner. Williamsfield High sports were an immediate hit with the town and especially with the *Williamsfield Times*, which began front-page coverage of the games. Williamsfield did very well against Brimfield and Elmwood, and even beat the B team from large powerhouse Galesburg High. One sport that did not get added until several years later was basketball. Given Will's size and speed, that would have been a good fit. The most important impact of sports was keeping the farm boys in school until graduation. There still remained that three-week vacation at threshing time.

Will's graduating class of 1906 with ten boys and seven girls was the largest graduating class in town history.[31] Spurred in part by R. C. Woolsey, the class had a reunion each year for several years then every five years thereafter, lasting well into the 1950s. Of course, over time the reunion participant numbers dwindled. Most shockingly, Floyd Wesner was the first to go, succumbing to tuberculosis in 1910 at just twenty-one.

By the time that Will graduated Williamsfield High, his older brother Tom was the druggist in nearby Oneida. Tom had graduated from high school in 1895 and attended Knox College. Upon college graduation in 1899, he went on to pharmacy school in Des Moines. He passed the pharmacy exam in 1901, got started as a pharmacist, and very soon thereafter had his own drugstore.

For Will, it was pretty clear that the Williamsfield farm was his to take over, assuming that is what he wanted. His grandfather BB had retired. Uncles William and James had died prematurely. Cousins Big Joe, James Jr., and Benjamin Jr. were all farmers but had separate landholdings. With father BF sixty years old and partially crippled, the bulk of the work would fall to Will.

But first, Will took time out to attend Browns Business School in Galesburg. This was actually one of a chain of business colleges located across the Midwest and started by George Brown. It had grown to twenty-nine locations by 1908. The schools offered accounting and business management, with a special focus on farm administration. Typical of Brown's advertising was the line "a business education is the trotting mate to up-to-date farming."

BF and Will formed a farm operation called "Shaffer and Son" that raised oats and grains, with a livestock focus on Poland China hogs. The hog operation was going well. BF would market their mature, "hippo" size hogs as far away as Mississippi and Kentucky. Unbeknownst to Will, he was about to catch a very favorable "wave," which would later be called the golden age of agriculture. Perhaps the wave metaphor doesn't apply here, as farm work in 1908 was still back-breaking labor, even with new horse-drawn sulky plows and tillers.

The year 1906 ended on a sad note. Will's mother and BF's wife, Sara Foster Shaffer, died that November, at age fifty-five. She had been at the Macomb facility for mental patients for nearly twenty-five years, ever since her complete breakdown due to the tragic loss of multiple children.

In 1905, BF was an officer of the new Williamsfield and Dahinda Mutual Telephone Company. Their work included the first phone line to the BF home. The following year the multiple telephone companies in the area had to meet to rationalize coverage and to set up a common switchboard. BF also made annual trips to Fairhope, Alabama, for treatments on his crippled leg.

Big Joe Shaffer had gradually come to the realization that the longer he remained in Williamsfield, the higher the likelihood that another altercation would send him back to prison. Therefore, in 1908 Joe traveled to Saskatchewan to look at farmland. Canada had set up a similar land policy to the US Homestead Acts, offering 160 acres to anyone who paid $10 and settled on the property. The area around Regina was wide-open prairie and ideal for large grain farms. Moreover, additional acreage could be had for prices far lower than the going rate of roughly $100 an acre for Illinois farmland. Joe secured a large holding in Milestone, Saskatchewan, a town not unlike Williamsfield. It was built on the New Soo railroad line and was named after the manager of the line (C. W. Milestone). And like Williamsfield, it prospered with the arrival of the trains.

Come first harvest in the fall of 1911, he shipped two steam units—traction engine and threshing machine combinations—from Williamsfield by rail using the CBQ line to St. Paul, the Great Northern Railroad to Winnipeg, the main Canadian line to Regina, and the New Soo branch line to Milestone. He was joined in the harvest at the Milestone farm by brothers Benjamin Brooks Jr. and James Jr.[32] James had recently purchased an Inter-State automobile and had taken his uncle BF along for the 1,200-mile drive to Milestone. They wrote of plenty of mud along the route. BF stayed for a couple of months and then returned by train. Eventually, Big Joe decided to relocate permanently to Milestone. His reputation in Williamsfield and the threat of breaking parole certainly factored into the move. He became a naturalized Canadian citizen and lived out his days there.

Vesper Shaffer opened a general practice in 1897 in Chicago at the Reliance Building at 32 North State Street, partnering with another woman doctor—Dr. Gertrude Thompson. She was also on the staff at the Frances Willard and Mary Thompson Hospitals (the latter founded for women due to the continuing discrimination toward women doctors). Vesper was one of the first doctors to use the "twilight sleep" procedure to relieve the pain of childbirth.[33] She conducted 824 deliveries in the years 1915–1922, mainly in private homes.

Vesper lived northwest of downtown Chicago, near Logan Park, sharing a turreted brick Victorian house on Logan Boulevard with Dr. Thompson. She commuted to the office and on rounds with a horse and buggy, or sometimes took the Blue Line trolley, which initially ran down the streets but was elevated in the late 1890s.

Will had settled into farm life on the Williamsfield farm, working with BF. Yet, little did he know that this would not be his chosen patch of earth to farm. In early 1911 he met a vivacious, adventurous young woman from Elmwood who was accomplished, highly respected, and quite striking looking. She was Verne Ivy Reed, a fourth-generation member of the omnipresent Reed clan from nearby French Grove. Verne had been born in Wahoo, Nebraska, where her father, John Henderson Reed, had briefly farmed before returning to French Grove. She had attended the one-room school at French Grove. An accomplished horsewoman, she showed off her equestrian skills with a spirited seven-mile ride to Brimfield for ice cream at Carson's Drug Store, then another fast ride back to French Grove. Verne attended Galesburg High School, graduating with the class of 1907, followed by Bradley University in Peoria, graduating with a two-year associate's degree. The family moved to the Glendale area of California for two years before returning to Elmwood. Some say she left a boyfriend out on the West Coast.

In 1911 Verne met Will. There followed a series of dinners here and there, which were duly recorded in the local papers. Dates over the course of two years led to a marriage proposal and an acceptance. They were married in September 1913 and settled in at the Williamsfield farm.[34]

Verne's father, John Henderson Reed, was a very successful man, born on the Reed farm in French Grove, and schooled at Reed School, the one-room schoolhouse in the Tucker apple orchard. He graduated from Elmwood High School and from business college in Peoria, then married Margaretta "Detta" McCoy in 1884. John and Detta moved to Wahoo,

Nebraska, for several years; as was noted earlier, Verne was born in Wahoo, in 1888. Extremely unusual for farm families, Verne was an only child. The family moved back to French Grove in 1890 and purchased the farm next to the land of John's father, Joseph Spriggs Reed. Like his father, John was a stout man. He sported a handlebar mustache and walked with a wooden leg, a reminder of the rigors of farm life. He was a very successful farmer, raising grain and hogs. He helped organize telephone service in French Grove, with a line to his house installed in 1901. He was elected road commissioner of the township and traveled the area in one of the finest carriages. In 1912 he purchased a Moline automobile.

The Reeds were among the earliest settlers in French Grove. They came early and came in numbers. In later years the Reed family picnics were legendary. The Reeds had emigrated from Northern Ireland in the late eighteenth century, settling first in Wheeling, West Virginia. Verne's grandfather, Joseph Reed, left Wheeling in 1850, traveling for twenty-one days with his sister Rachel to Illinois, where he rented land at French Grove. Joseph had left his sweetheart, Elizabeth Henderson, in West Virginia. She subsequently moved west that same year, traveling with her parents by steamboat on the Ohio River to St. Louis, up the Mississippi to Keokuk, Iowa, and overland to West Point, Iowa. Once settled in French Grove, Joseph loaded up a horse and carriage and drove the 100 miles to West Point, intent on marrying Elizabeth. He showed up, secured her hand, and they rode back in the carriage together. Within a few years, they purchased land just south of French Creek, 160 acres in sections five and six of Brimfield Township.

In 1899, in a familiar reminder of the dangers of farming, Joseph was kicked in the lungs by one of his horses. The injured area became infected. He traveled to Indianapolis for treatment, but the doctors were unable to stem the infection and he died. A year prior to Verne's marriage to Will, her father John was injured in the same manner as his father. The injury developed into an abscess, and, much like his father Joseph, the abscess became infected. Without modern sulfa drugs, he had no chance. Verne's mother Margaretta was left with the farm.

Will and Verne had settled in at the BF farm in Williamsfield. By 1914, Margaretta concluded that the French Grove farm would be better served in the hands of Will and Verne. She made the offer, and they decided to make their new life in French Grove. Will discussed the move with BF and the two agreed to have an estate sale at the Williamsfield farm. It was conducted in February 1915 and included eighteen horses, twenty head of cattle, eighty hogs, and an array of farm implements.

Will and Verne moved to the 160-acre Reed property on Elmore Road in the spring of 1915.[35] The farm was in the northwest corner of Brimfield Township in Peoria County, Illinois. It was a half-mile south of the pioneer community of French Grove that had been first settled in 1837. The county was well watered, bisected by five rivers in addition to the Illinois River. Brimfield Township was one of the richest agricultural sections. French Creek ran through the north end of the farm, then meandered southwest eleven miles to join the Spoon River at Macomb, which in turn joined the Illinois River at Havana, forty miles downstream of Peoria.

Will and Verne made a good team to tackle farming. Will was an experienced, smart young farmer. He had grown up on the farm and had been well-schooled by BF along with his uncles. To that substantial base, he added the education he received through high school and Brown's Business College, certainly above and beyond most farmers at the time. Verne had also grown up on the farm and had completed junior college. Both were ready for the new challenge.

Their timing was very good. The golden age of farming that had begun at the turn of the century peaked in 1914, with a combination of rising prices and increased farm productivity due to new technologies. In addition, the expanding US population and new international markets would ensure that prices remained high. Farmland values were still affordable but had already risen fourfold since 1850, when land could first be homesteaded. Average farmland in Illinois was valued at $108 an acre in 1910 and would rise to $188 an acre by 1920. And Brimfield Township acreage was certainly not average farmland. Considering that by 1919 the average Illinois farm was valued at $23,500, it was not a financial stretch for a farmer to invest in new technologies like automobiles, trucks, and tractors.

The USDA published a prescription for a successful 160-acre farm in 1915. At a minimum, you would need two strong draft horses plus their harnesses to start. The horses would pull a broad range of implements including heavy and light wagons, plows, cultivators, mowers, grain drills, corn planters, reapers, binders, disks, harrows, rakes, manure spreaders, and, of course, a buggy. To this list, you needed to add all the seed and livestock that you would be raising. It was a significant investment just to get started. Will had a head start with the estate sale and the implements and livestock moved over from the Williamsfield farm.

7
The Alphas

THE RAPID SUCCESS of the Model A was a result of the new brand awareness Ford achieved through racing, the masterful execution by James Couzens, and, most of all, by Henry Ford. Despite his two initial company failures, Ford exhibited a number of attributes that separated him from so many others trying to make automobiles. He was an experienced engineer, hired the right people, fostered teamwork, and most importantly, had a single, unwavering vision.

Ford understood from experience what an automobile would do for those toiling in farm country. He wanted to build an affordable "motorcar for the great multitude", a "universal" car.[36] At the time, the majority of automobiles were targeted in the $2,000 and up price range. He was particularly attuned to sell his automobile to farmers. He is quoted as saying, "To lift from drudgery off flesh and blood and lay it on steel and motors has been my most constant ambition." Asked years later why he did not seek more input for his vision, he supposedly remarked: "If I had asked people what they wanted, they would have said faster horses."

More than the vision, he believed he understood how to achieve it, stating that "the way to make automobiles is to make one automobile like another, to make them all alike." Yet, even with the success of the Model A, he was being tugged in a different direction by Alexander Malcolmson and the other investors. Adamant about building a luxury car with high profit margins, they essentially dictated that Ford build an upscale automobile. It was designed by Wills and Ford, and featured a four-cylinder, 24 horsepower engine, with a shaft drive and fancy appointments. It sold for

$2,000. In keeping with the alphabetical scheme it was called the Model B and was announced in October 1904.

Meanwhile, Ford and his team continued work on the Model C, an improved version of the Model A with a two-cylinder engine that was located under the front seat with the fuel tank under the hood. A touring version of this model, somewhat more luxurious, was dubbed the Model F. Since the Dodge Brothers continued to provide the chassis, engine, and drive train, they were given latitude by Ford to contribute to the design process. While the Models B, C, and F posted good numbers, none survived past 1905.

Malcolmson again exerted his view and forced the development of another high-end car. This became the Model K,[37] a $2,800 premium car guaranteed to go 60 mph. Couzens was busy managing nearly all of the company operations except design and engineering. But he was not blind to the deteriorating relationship between Ford and Malcolmson. He clearly saw the handwriting on the wall and knew that one of them would have to go.

Ford continued to be focused on his universal car. The breakthrough result was the Model N, not just another iteration but a big jump in design. It incorporated some of the features of the Model K, including the spark and throttle levers on the steering wheel, the planetary transmission, and the magneto-based electrical system. But perhaps even more important, it used a new steel alloy called vanadium. Henry had seen European racing cars using this alloy. It was significantly stronger than regular steel but weighed far less. Ford asked Wills to take the lead in finding a source and converting as many components as possible to this new material. The results were dramatic. The Model C weighed 1,250 pounds while the Model N slimmed down to 800 pounds. The completed Model N designs were blueprinted and carried to the Dodge Brothers shop, which continued to be Ford's principal supplier, building the engines, transmissions, and frames.

Ford concluded that the emergence of the Model N was the right time to move forward on the fractured relationship with Malcolmson. He devised a strategy that would force Malcolmson and several other investors out of the company while at the same time addressing two other critical issues he was facing. He engineered a cut in dividends from $100,000 in 1905 to just $10,000 in 1906. He would use the savings to set up a new company called Ford Manufacturing. It would manufacture and sell components to Ford Motor Company at such prices that there would be no profit for Ford Motor Company, thus effectively reducing the value of Ford Motor shares.

At the same time, the Ford Manufacturing operation would enable him to reduce his dependence on the Dodge Brothers, reducing the cost of components and allowing the flexibility to reduce the price of his cars.

Malcolmson and several other investors that had pushed for expensive cars were not invited to invest in Ford Manufacturing. In addition, Malcolmson had formed another company called Aerocar to produce luxury automobiles. Since Aerocars competed directly with the Model K, he has asked to resign from the Ford Motor board. He conceded that he had lost control and sold his shares to Henry Ford for $175,000. His Aerocar venture went bust by 1908. He sold the factory to Hudson Motors and returned to the coal business, where he was very successful. Several other Ford Motor investors also sold their shares, certainly to their later great chagrin. This maneuver raised Henry Ford's holdings to 58 percent and gave him much greater control.

Meanwhile, Ford moved aggressively on his manufacturing plan. He leased a factory on Bellevue Avenue and began to outfit it with a wide range of machine tools. He bought the tools from Walter Flanders, a burly Vermonter, who impressed Ford with his cutting-edge ideas on manufacturing. Flanders recommended Max Wollering to manage the shop, aided by Pete Martin. Flanders joined a year later. The plant was organized in logical tool sequence and part progression. The movement of work from station to station was done by hand trucks. The process was aptly demonstrated by engine manufacturing. Cast iron engine blocks were hauled by horse and wagon from a Detroit foundry. Flanders supplied a special machine tool that would drill eight holes in the block, an early harbinger of the thousands of specialized tools that would be set up at the Highland Park and Rouge plants. The engine block would then be mounted on a rotating jig that would ease the installation of the crankshaft, pistons, rods, cams, flywheel, and oil pan. By the end of 1906, the Bellevue operation staffed with 125 men was producing 50–75 engines per day as well as other components.

An important additional benefit of the new component manufacturing was the improvement in part quality. Ford felt the path forward to high volume automobile production was built on interchangeable parts. This meant that each part was built to such a tolerance that it was interchangeable on any car being assembled. Henry Ford and his team had long complained about the parts coming from the Dodge Brothers; that they fell short of the blueprints or patterns and required additional adjustment or rework to be installed. The wisdom of Ford's view on interchangeable parts was further endorsed in 1908 when the Royal Automobile Club of England awarded Henry Leland and Cadillac the Dewar Trophy for the work on interchangeable parts.[38]

The Model N was announced at the 1906 New York auto show (the show car was actually missing the engine) with a price of $500. At that price, with the Ford name and the quality of the car, Henry Ford left the show with close to twenty thousand orders. Buyers could have any color they wanted as long as it was maroon (not the black that would later become the standard). Wollering noted the price was too low and Couzens boosted it up to $600. Back from the show, Ford promised the very unrealistic production of ten thousand cars for 1906. He moved the manufacturing operations at Bellevue Avenue to Piquette, installing the heavy machines and engine assembly on the first floor, component assembly on the second floor, and final assembly on the third floor. Where the original factory on Mack Avenue (fittingly a converted wagon factory) was capable of building seven cars per day, production at Piquette ramped up to an average of 80 cars per day, with a one-day record of 101 cars set in 1908. Actual production for the year was eight thousand, short of Ford's prediction but still astounding. The sales of the Model N vaulted Ford to the number-one position in US car sales for the first time.

In early 1907, Ford quietly merged Ford Manufacturing back into the Ford Motor Company. Flanders left in early 1908 to form the E-M-F automobile company, taking Max Wollering with him. Ford asked Sorensen and Martin to take over factory operations.

Following the success of the Model N, Ford released the models R and S. They represented upscale modifications to the base Model N. At this point, with all of these "alphas" behind him and annual sales of fourteen thousand and growing, he felt it was time to stop working on incremental changes. He decided to start with a clean sheet and begin working on what would be his opus. By this juncture, he had been working on gas engines, steam machinery, machine tools, and automobiles since 1880, nearly thirty years. Now, he had the profits coming in to truly create something special. And unlike Ransom Olds, he had drive, guile, vision, and single-mindedness to outmaneuver those who might get in his way.

In 1907 he had a secret room built in the northeast corner of the third floor of the Piquette factory and assembled an impressive engineering team. The core team included Joseph Galamb and Charles Balough.

Both men had been trained at the Royal Technical Institute in Budapest. A third Hungarian added to the team was Eugene Farkas. He had Spider Huff working on ignition and Harold Wills on metals and machine tools. Charles Sorensen, a big, tall Dane originally from Copenhagen, had joined Ford in 1905 as a pattern maker. Ford and Tom Cooper had met Sorensen at a pattern shop that did work for Charles King when looking for patterns for the 999 and Arrow racers. Ford could read blueprinted engineering drawings, but he relied on Sorensen to translate each design into a wood model so that he could properly visualize it. The secret room featured a blackboard along with a camera to capture the ideas that were drawn up. And finally, there was a rocking chair for Henry.

Ford laid out the overall design vision to the assembled team. He aimed to create an automobile that had more power than the Olds Curved Dash; was light, sturdy, and high enough for the muddy roads of the day; big enough for a family; simple to operate; inexpensive to own; and would sell for a low price (he had $500 in mind). At the 1906 New York auto show, he stated that the future of the automobile "was dependent upon the production of a car for the ordinary man. I considered that I was an ordinary man and I wanted what ordinary people wanted, and I put my efforts towards developing a car that would meet what I conceived to be the ordinary man's car." Ford went on to describe that this did not mean creating an ordinary car. No, it had to be built of the best materials, using the best automatic machines, with processes to continually drive down the cost. The end product needed to be sturdy, light, and easy to maintain.

It all started with the engine. It was a 177 cubic inch, four-cylinder in-line L-head (all cylinders lined up on one side) design that put out 22 horsepower at 1,600 rpm. It was quite large for what was a very light car, thanks to the vanadium steel. It provided an outstanding weight-to-power ratio of sixty to one, resulting in the speed and acceleration of much more expensive cars. Ford decided to do a single casting for the block and relied on Sorensen's pattern skills to make it work. The original engine had an open tappet chamber, allowing you to see the valve stems and tappets move. A separate cylinder head was added later, a first and a design that made it easy to repair the engine. The first roughly one thousand units produced at Piquette had a water pump. Because the water pump had some issues, Ford changed to thermosiphon cooling, where cooled water flowed by gravity. This was also a simpler and cheaper arrangement, both Ford design criteria. Likewise, there was no fuel pump. Instead, the gas tank was situated under the front seat but elevated above the engine. The same held true for lubrication—there was no oil pump. A sheet metal pan was designed that held oil for both the engine and transmission. The crankshaft running through the pan splashed oil to lubricate the components.

The pan was supplied by the Keim Company, a former bicycle manufacturer that had turned to sheet metal fabrication when the bicycle market cooled. Ford and Sorensen had visited the Keim plant in Buffalo. They met a young stamping operator there named William Knudsen, who was completely covered in grease from keeping the stamping machine running. He was an outsized individual, at 6' 3" and 230 pounds, who would go on to fill an outsized role at Ford and beyond. Knudsen, known as "Big Bill," was a recent arrival from Denmark, where he had worked as a bicycle mechanic in his brother's shop in Copenhagen prior to immigrating to the United States in 1900. Though he was just a machine operator when Ford and Sorensen visited, it was not long before he rose to be Keim's plant superintendent. Ford subsequently bought the company in 1911. When a strike interrupted production in Buffalo, he had all the machine tools loaded on rail cars and moved the entire operation to Detroit. That included Big Bill.

Spider Huff was responsible for ignition, and he designed a unique magneto for the job. The magneto concept was largely invented by Robert Bosch in 1897 while working for the Otto Company. The magneto replaced the dry cell batteries that were used in most other cars at the time. Huff's design had sixteen magnets affixed to the outer edge of the flywheel. These magnets passed through iron cores with copper wires, inducing a current. The generated current was routed to four ignition coils housed in a wooden box mounted on the dash, one coil for each cylinder. The coils raised the voltage, enabling a spark to jump across the spark plug in each cylinder. To ensure engine timing, a lever mounted on the steering column altered the point at which the coil fired for each cylinder, either advancing or retarding the spark.

Initially, generating a spark was the sole job of the magneto. As all Model Ts produced until 1919 had no battery or generator, the magneto was the entire electrical system. In the testing of the magneto, a problem surfaced. The Model T engine would conk out, indicating that the current experienced a momentary drop. Henry Ford suggested insulating the magnets with a varnish mix. Thus modified, the engine ran continuously for weeks. It showed that the design process in the secret room on the third floor also had a strenuous debugging process out on the factory floor.

Side and rear lights on the Model T were powered by kerosene. Initially, Ford used an acetylene process to power the headlights. A brass tank on the driver-side running board had water in top and calcium carbide crystals in a chamber below. The water was dropped into the crystals, forming acetylene gas that was piped to the headlights and taillights. Ford's major supplier of this lighting was Prest-O-Lite, a company started by former bicycle racer Carl Fisher and partner James Allison. Fisher had a bicycle shop in Indianapolis and later set up what was considered the first automobile dealership in the country. The Prest-O-Lite product made him rich and provided the resources to drive his many other innovations.

Later, headlights were fed by the magneto with less than satisfactory results. The headlights varied in brightness as you slowed down because they depended on how fast the flywheel was turning.

Focused on simplicity, Ford decided on a planetary transmission, which had long been used on European cars. In the United States, it had been first employed by Duryea and then adopted by Olds, Cadillac, and REO. Yet, the more advanced automobiles had already shifted to the eventual standard, a sliding gear transmission. Henry felt that sliding gear transmissions were more difficult to drive while being heavier, more complex, and more expensive. It did not help that a test car built with the sliding gear approach had problems, which further hardened Ford's conviction against its use.

The key advantage of the planetary transmission was that the actual gears were in constant mesh so there was no need for a real clutch to move the gear into position. There were three "planetary" meshed gears rotating around a master "sun" gear. You did need a lever or pedal to select which of the three meshed gears would engage with the rotating flywheel and transmission shaft. However, you were limited to just three gear selections: two forward and one reverse. The Models N, R, and S all used planetary gearing, but Ford tasked Joe Galamb to come up with an improved design. That new design necessitated three pedals and a lever. Yet, the planetary transmission was indeed improved and remained constant until 1927; that is, through fifteen million automobiles.

A final area of focus for the design team was the frame. The roads in towns and cities were not great, but the roads in farm country were downright miserable. The frame design had to accommodate that. Again, Ford's prime directive was simpler, lighter, and less costly. The key innovation was a three-point triangular design where the frame would flex under the stress of uneven roads. It used the principle of the three-legged stool that is always

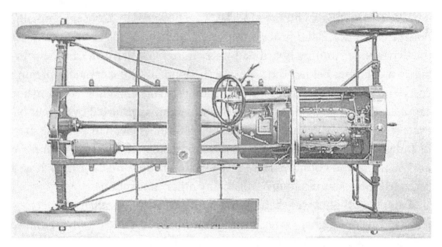

1908 Model T chassis showing the thin but strong vanadium steel frame with triangular spars that helped navigate the poor roads of the time. (Ford Motor publication, "Watch the Fords Go By.")

on the ground with each leg carrying load, as opposed to a four-legged stool. The frame was also of minimalist design but made stronger and lighter by use of the vanadium alloy. Henry designed the universal joint and differential at the rear axle to adjust the driven wheels to the road. Oh, and one other change was made: Ford moved the steering wheel to the left side.

Early on, the car was assembled at the Piquette facility from supplier parts. This was certainly out of necessity, but the resulting lack of control would eat at Henry Ford. He would move toward more in-house parts and subassembly production at the first opportunity. The principal supplier of engines and transmissions continued to be the Dodge Brothers. Frames came from Parish and Bingham. Brass thermo-siphon radiators were supplied by several companies, including McCord Manufacturing. First Model T bodies were all wood, with a wood-framed steel body introduced in late 1912. Shells produced by C. R. Wilson (whose superintendent was Fred Fisher, later of Fisher Body). Axles came from A. O. Smith, a former bicycle maker in Milwaukee. The metal stampings such as the oil pan were made by Keim, still in Buffalo at the time. Henry Ford had been approached early on by carriage salesman Harry Firestone, who sold him four tires for one of his initial alphabet cars. Firestone became one of four tire suppliers for the Model T.[39] Many items were left off the automobile, even such basics as gas, oil, and coolant gauges. This gave rise to a huge aftermarket for Ford parts and conversion kits. Sears alone had over five thousand items for the car in its weighty catalog.

Though it was truly a revolutionary automobile, it was just assigned the next letter and so became the Ford Model T. It was designed as an inexpensive "universal" car but featured many innovations not found in other cars at the time. Those included the use of vanadium steel, a single-cast engine block with a removable cylinder head, the splash lubrication system, the flexible three-point frame, and the unique magneto ignition.

The car was the product of an outstanding team. Henry Ford provided the vision, leadership, and drive. James Couzens kept Ford grounded and the operation running smoothly. Ford pulled together an exceptional team of engineers and provided a collaborative environment. Charles Sorensen converted engineering diagrams to prototype patterns that Henry could visualize and from which parts could be made. The manufacturing team, including Flanders, Martin, and Sorensen moved the company away from total reliance on the Dodge Brothers and started Ford down the road of the assembly line, mass production, and what would soon be called "Fordism." This team came together and worked through the Models A through S before arriving at the Model T, then focusing heavily on production of that universal car for what would turn out to be the next twenty years.

The car was not perfect. There were certainly issues, but one could have assumed that those would be worked out over time. The one person who did not believe that was Henry Ford. He did not see the need for major changes. His decision to retain the hand crank helped keep electric cars in business until 1920 as easy starting was a major advantage of the electrics. Continued dependency on the magneto delayed both electric starting and electric lights for years. The planetary transmission was awkward and limited but remained in place until 1927 through the sheer force of numbers. Changing tires was a major headache as the rim needed to be detached from the wheel and the inner tube replaced and inflated like a bicycle tire. Industry trends such as high-compression engines, color choices, interior appointments, and annual model changes were generally ignored. Then, there was the long simmering issue: what would a Model T owner do when ready for a second car?

By the summer of 1908, Ford Motor had been the leading US automobile company for two years, thanks in large part to the Model N. The new prototype was completed by mid-summer and rolled out of the secret room, down the elevator, and out onto the street. Henry took the first drive and reportedly remarked on returning, "I think we've got something here." In September, he drove the prototype nearly 1,400 miles from Detroit to Iron Mountain (on Michigan's Upper Peninsula), by way of Chicago and Milwaukee, and back. Ford entered two cars in the four-thousand-mile race from New York City to Seattle in October. After twenty-two days of negotiating all manner of roads, the Fords finished first and third.

Production was ready to go by September, and the announcement was made on October 1. The price of the touring model was set at $850 (which was $250 more than the Model N). Though that bought you a great car, the windshield, top, speedometer, and acetylene tanks were options. The Model T debuted at the New York automobile show in January 1909. Unlike the 1906 appearance of the Model N, the Model T did, in fact, have an engine under the hood. The quality of the car, the price, and Ford's reputation all factored in a flood of orders. Norval Hawkins, the accountant turned sales manager hired by Couzens, had already started building company-owned branches in major cities (Boston, Chicago, Buffalo, Kansas City, New York City, Philadelphia, and Detroit), followed by franchised agencies in smaller towns. The number would reach seven thousand agencies by 1913.[40] Very quickly, however, the volume of orders for the Model T outpaced production, and Couzens and Hawkins were forced to notify dealers to stop taking orders.

The first 2,500 Model T automobiles were unique as Ford attempted to work out the kinks and hone in on a standard configuration. The early transmissions were redesigned into the familiar three foot pedals and one lever. The water pump was dropped in favor of the thermo-siphon radiator. The maroon-painted carriage was offered early on but was dropped in June 1909 in favor of green or black.

With the Model T, Ford accelerated its lead over the other automobile companies, growing 90 percent each year over the car's first three years. Sales were 18,000 in 1909 and grew to 32,000 the following year as production moved from Piquette Avenue to a new plant at Highland Park. The Models N, R, S, and K were discontinued after ten thousand Model Ts had been sold. Sales continued to skyrocket, growing to 70,000 in 1912 and 168,000 in 1913. By this time, Ford had driven the price down to $525, with every intention to keep going lower.

Through stubbornness and a laser focus on near-perfection, Henry Ford had shepherded his vision of the "universal" car to fruition. The drive to making this car available to virtually anyone, especially farmers, was now his challenge. The near downfall of Henry Ford early on was his constant tinkering and total inability to freeze a design. Now, with his "this is the car" mentality, he switched gears completely and totally. The stubbornness remained, but the drive for perfection in engineering was replaced with a drive for perfection in manufacturing. It seems odd, given his lifelong experience of working with machines. In the new Ford organization, the manufacturing plants managed by Bill Knudsen were ascendant while the engineering department languished. Again, his mantra continued to be to "make automobiles is to make one automobile like another, to make them all alike, to make them come through the factory just alike." Though incremental enhancements were made each year, none dramatically changed the look of the car nor did the changes keep up with competition. Of course, one area of substantial innovation was the price, which continued to trend downward through the years.

Pushed by demand and prodded by the Dodge Brothers for more capacity, Ford purchased sixty-three acres at Highland Park and engaged Albert Kahn to design a purpose-built factory. Kahn, who had built the Packard automobile plant in 1903, used reinforced concrete to enable much more open interior factory spaces. Ford wanted the building to be four stories so that assembly could start on the top floor and use gravity to flow car production down to street level. To create adequate light, Kahn had 75 percent of the outside of the building done in glass. Bill Knudsen, the engineer who had come along with the Keim acquisition, was tasked to work with Kahn to turn Henry's concept into reality. Highland Park was the first of upwards of a thousand architectural commissions that Kahn did for Ford.

The first roughly ten thousand Model Ts were built at Piquette, which ceased production at the end of 1909. The plant was then sold to Studebaker. The Highland Park complex opened in 1910. Initially, Model T production was similar to the Piquette plant, with the cars assembled in individual work spaces on saw horses and the component parts carried to each chassis. The change to a flowing assembly line came gradually but in large part due to Clarence Avery, Sorensen's assistant. Avery had been Edsel Ford's teacher at Detroit University School and was familiar with the ideas of Frederick Taylor, who espoused a scientific manufacturing process where time and motion analysis expunged every last wasted motion. Of course, if you asked Henry Ford he would say that their methods were simply expedient adaptations to dramatically increasing volumes.

Once in the much larger space at Highland Park, Sorensen and his team expanded the experimentation in more efficient manufacturing. The sheer volume of orders for the Model T dictated a move away from the current static process. The new approach, a moving assembly line, was started in one department—flywheel/magneto production. Instead of each worker assembling the complete magneto, a line of workers, each assigned a specific task, would perform that repetitive operation as the work-in-process magneto moved by. In the first pass, magneto build time was reduced from twenty minutes per worker to thirteen minutes. Changing to an upright workspace and adjusting the speed of the line reduced the build time to five minutes.

The assembly line was then applied to engine assembly. The baseline was the time it took one man to assemble the Model T engine, start to finish. With the line approach, the time per man was essentially cut in half. With the line approach, the time per man was reduced to 226 minutes. But, Sorensen and his team saved the best for last. That would be final assembly, which occurred on the first floor. For four months starting in August 1913, the team tried different variations. An initial setup with a rope tow was quickly replaced with a moving chain. The base Model T frame started moving down the line, while forty-five different operations were applied, adding the engine, gas tank, dashboard, wheels, and radiator. The line was further modified by creating two parallel work platforms, one high, staffed by tall men, and one low, staffed by shorter men. The results were astounding: an 88 percent reduction in man-hours for chassis assembly, from twelve man-hours per chassis down to 1.5 man-hours.

The assembly line approach very quickly spread throughout the entire plant. Now, Model T production would begin on the fourth floor and descend gradually as it moved across four floors and through eighty-four stations. At the end of the line, a man would sit on the gas tank, start the car, and drive it outside to the side of the building, where a chute was set up from the second floor that allowed the appropriate body to be lowered onto the newly minted chassis. The completed car was then driven directly to a rail car for shipment to the dealer. Daily production at Highland Park climbed to 5,400 cars, with peaks to 10,000 cars in a day. For the 1911 model year, Ford built 78,000 automobiles with nearly 7,000 workers. By the 1914–1915 model years, production was over 300,000 cars with just twice the number of workers. This miracle of production soon had a name, one that bestowed the credit on Henry: "Fordism."

Henry Ford was single-mindedly focused on making the Model T more affordable. The new manufacturing processes created the space to make this happen. It certainly helped that the Model T was the only automobile ever built at Highland Park, and that it was virtually unchanging year after year. There was very little engineering change, and the tools and dies were only changed when they wore out. Ford sold over 170,000 Model Ts in 1913, generating $89 million in revenue and $27 million in profits. He paid $11 million in dividends and used some of the rest to lower the price of the car from $525 to $440.

One measure of "affordable" was the amount of time a Ford employee needed to work in order to buy a Ford car. From 1912 to 1915, Ford worker wages needed for the purchase of a Model T dropped from sixty-four weeks to sixteen weeks. A key part of this drop was Ford's announcement in 1914 of the $5 day pay rate for Ford workers, doubling in one pen stroke worker salaries. This move predictably infuriated other industry titans. But, Ford's view of the role of the industrialist was quite different. His goal was to "make the best quality of goods possible at the lowest cost possible, paying the highest wages possible." Of course, an additional reason for the $5 day was the 378 percent turnover rate of Ford workers at Highland Park, mostly due to the monotony of the assembly line. Even so, Ford was inundated with thousands seeking Ford jobs.

The other part of the affordability equation was the dramatic drop in the Model T price year after year. At Piquette, the unit price was $825. By 1915 at Highland Park, it had dropped to $390. Of course, Henry Ford's peers in the automotive industry felt that much of the savings should have gone to shareholders, not customers. Ford disagreed. Those sixteen weeks of wages guideline for buying a new Ford car held for the next fifty-five years.

In 1909, in the midst of Ford's Model T ramp-up, there was one distracting piece of business for Henry Ford to address—the Selden patent. George Selden had kept his patent active ever since he first filed it in 1879. He had a vehicle crafted, but it never worked nor did it go into production. It used a Brayton cycle engine for propulsion, not the far more prevalent Otto four-cycle design.[41] He had sold rights to the patent to William Whitney of the Electrical Vehicle Company, while retaining partial rights for himself.

As Whitney's electric taxi business declined, he turned to Selden to see if they could construct a framework to use and enforce the patent. They put together an organization called the American Licensed Automobile Manufacturers (ALAM). With the threat of patent infringement, they charged a 1.25 percent royalty on each car sold, with one-fifth going to Selden, two-fifths to the Electric Vehicle Co., and the remainder to the ALAM. For automobile manufacturers, there was actually a benefit to joining ALAM and paying the royalty, aside from not getting sued for infringement. The ALAM arrangement would, in effect, create a cartel where only members were officially licensed to sell cars. Nonmembers would be subject to lawsuits. Once up and running, ALAM's initial target was Alexander Winton. He initially fought the issue in court but soon capitulated and signed up. He was joined by Studebaker, Knox, Packard, Pierce Arrow, Olds, and Cadillac as members.

Henry Ford was initially amenable to ALAM. He met with ALAM head Frederick Smith, the same Smith who had orchestrated Ransom Olds's exit from his own company. Smith told Henry that he couldn't join, that his company was a "mere assemblage place" and not a real manufacturer. Thus, Ford would be liable for the ALAM royalties. To say that Henry Ford was upset was an understatement. He may have believed that it was the work of Henry Leland of Cadillac working behind the scenes to bar Ford's admittance. More likely, it was probably just another shady move by Smith. In any case, it would prove to be a costly decision. Never one to shy away from a fight, Ford decided to contest the patent in court. Despite having a strong case and able representation, Ford lost his case in 1909, with the judge ruling for Selden and ALAM. This cast Ford Motor Company as a nonlicensed automobile maker. Ford would have to pay back royalties of 1.25 percent on each of the fifty thousand cars he had sold since 1903. ALAM took out advertisements stating that any customer who bought a Ford would be subject to a lawsuit. Norval Hawkins, Ford's marketing chief, struggled to expand the dealer network because of the swirling confusion and inherent risks. Billy Durant, anxious to expand his nascent General Motors conglomerate, thought he might be able to buy Ford at a distressed price because of the tenuous situation.

Of course, Henry Ford would have none of this. He took out his own ads, assuring that his customers would be protected. More importantly, he decided to appeal the court ruling. In 1911, before a different judge, the court ruled in Ford's favor. The verdict hinged on the fact that the Selden patent only covered automobiles with the Brayton engine, of which there was only one in the world and it did not run. The ALAM group fell apart. Ford, having opened Highland Park just the year before, could move forward at high volume unencumbered.

8

Yet Another Model T Purchase

HE RISING DEMAND for automobiles meant opportunity for agencies
in the local towns. Generally, local buyers looked to local agencies
to secure a car. Williamsfield and Brimfield led the way in establishing new agencies.

William Radcliffe was the first dealer in Williamsfield, selling Overland, then adding Metz, Ford, Studebaker, and even farm implements.
Noah Tucker was the Glide agent in town. Dimmick Brothers started as
the Ford agency, later replaced by Charles Boley, who had pooh-poohed
automobiles earlier but now was a full-fledged convert.

Brimfield had Auto Sales and Reinhart selling Studebakers and Maxwells. Yet, the big dealer in town was Kelly Supply, who had the Ford
agency. Cornelius Kelly had purchased the "McCabe Brick" building in
town for $500 for his new agency. In a sign of the times, the building had
been a livery for years, with blacksmiths shoeing horses and polishing steel
plows. For that matter, Kelly was himself a sign of the changing times. His
father, Michael Kelly, was a well-known local breeder of Percheron draft
horses. His prize stallion Tom was 2,070 pounds and sixteen hands high
(64 inches). The elder Kelly would make the rounds in the spring with
Tom. The stud terms were $10 for a live colt. His son decided to make a
clean break from horses and move on with automobiles, although he did

use a team of draft horses to pull his oil wagon around the area, delivering kerosene and gasoline.

The town newspaper was puzzled by Kelly's purchase, as the village and surrounding territory had very few cars and there was already an auto company in town (Brimfield Auto Sales, selling Buicks). This did not deter Kelly. He sold two Fords that year, nine the next year and well over a hundred by 1916. He grew his operation to seven Ford sub-agencies, five salesmen, and fourteen mechanics, blanketing the central Illinois farm country.

With nearly two thousand automobile brands surfacing in the early years of the twentieth century, only a handful had a sufficient profile and enough success to create a network of local agencies. For first-time prospective buyers like Will, you could catch the train to Chicago and stroll along Michigan Avenue, where well over a hundred makes were clustered in what was called Automobile Row. Though Detroit had the most automobile manufacturers, Chicago had very early embraced the horseless carriage, with exhibits at the 1893 Columbian Exposition and the first major automobile race back on Thanksgiving Day 1895.

The first dealer in Chicago was the Ralph Temple agency, set up in 1899 to sell the Curved Dash Oldsmobile. But, extensive brick-and-mortar car agencies did not take off until 1905, when Henry Ford selected Chicago for his first dealership outside of Detroit. He and James Couzens were involved in the planning of the Ford showroom at 1444 Michigan Avenue. This Ford agency put the stamp of approval not only on the location but also on what an automobile showroom in a major city should look like.

This being Chicago in 1905, a city at the forefront of modern metropolitan architecture, most brands followed Ford's lead in retaining architects and constructing impressive buildings. As a result, the standard auto agency was at least three stories with a high-ceiling first floor to show off new models. Expensive brands like Studebaker, Locomobile, Packard, Peerless, and Pierce-Arrow competed for the most lavish building. The Studebaker building was seven stories. The Locomobile building had highly polished hardwood mosaic floors and giant fluted ceilings to create an impressive setting for their cars. This one building sold a quarter of the total output of Locomobiles and featured a service department with fifty employees. With one in seven Chicago cars electric, brands such as Detroit Electric, Broc, Ohio Electric, and Standard Electric also set up shop along the Michigan Avenue thoroughfare. Foreign brands were also represented, including Fiat, De Dion–Bouton, Renault, Berliet, and Isotta.

The stretch along Michigan Avenue from 12th to 30th streets south of the river was transformed from a leafy residential boulevard to a string of automotive palaces. The avenue had been paved in the 1890s and provided a smooth roadway for prospective buyers to test-drive new automobiles. With steady automobile traffic, it became the least likely avenue in town to see a horse and buggy. It was called the "most imposing automobile row of any city" (by the *Chicago Tribune*, of course), even including New York and Detroit. People came to the Row from across the Midwest. It was the one place to see a Moline, Badger, Cutting, Knox, or any number of other cars that lacked local agencies. In the summer, an auto show was conducted on the street, featuring more than 120 models.[42] In 1911 just one person in 250 in Chicago owned an automobile, but interest was intense and the numbers were rapidly increasing.

The Row also represented in microcosm a view of the brutal nature of the automobile industry at the time. Automobile brands were constantly coming and going. Of the 120 brands represented on Michigan Avenue in 1911, seventy were gone by 1915. Another twelve exited the industry before 1920. Twenty more did not make it to 1930. Ten more survived to the Depression but were gone by 1940. The steam brands were all gone by 1920. Several of the electric brands hung on until 1930. Nearly 30 percent of the brands lasted less than five years.

As of 1940, that left roughly nine makes still standing from the 1911 Automobile Row—Ford, Buick, Cadillac, Hudson, Pontiac, Olds, Overland, Packard, and Studebaker. They were joined by a select few post-1911 brands—Chevrolet, Chrysler, Desoto, Dodge, Plymouth, Lincoln, and Mercury. Certainly at the time, it was not clear how savage the infant industry was and just how dramatic the fallout would be. Yes, there were many, many choices. Yet, many choices would be incredibly short-lived.

Into the second decade of the twentieth century, the penetration of automobiles in the area surrounding French Grove increased dramatically. And, the selection of automobiles in this farming country followed several common themes. First, there was a preference for cars that were built locally. This was simply a carryover from other major purchases that local farmers made at the time. They were more likely to buy the Yellow Fellow threshing machine from Avery because it was made twenty miles away in Peoria. Second, there was a wide variety of brands purchased simply because there were so many choices. If one wanted to stray from the top sellers like Ford, Buick, and Olds, one could easily do so. With such a young industry where it was very easy to put together a new car but very hard to get traction, it was hard for the buyer to pick winners or losers, to choose an automobile that would survive. The brands that had traction as national leaders quickly set up agencies in the rural areas. And finally, more expensive cars started to appear, just as upscale buggies replaced basic carriages twenty years before.

The first cars in Williamsfield were the Glides. And they were local makes built by a farm equipment manufacturer, namely by John Bartholomew of Elmwood and the Avery Company, and built in Peoria. Glides continued to be popular. Charles Bartholomew, John's brother, was the dealer in Elmwood. His sales included one to Marshall Lott in town, three in Williamsfield, and one to Hugh Sloan in Yates City.

Two early sales in Brimfield were Mitchells, which happened to have an agency in Galesburg. One Mitchell went to the town doctor, Alfred Knapp, and the other was purchased by Henry Memler, who ran the general store. John Cowell of Williamsfield also bought a Mitchell. The automobile was designed and produced by Henry Mitchell, a wagon and bicycle maker in Racine, Wisconsin. He experimented with a motorcycle before selling the bicycle business. The experience gained, though, led him into the automobile business in 1904. He decided to focus solely on cars and sold his wagon business to John Deere. Things were going quite well until a styling change made in 1920 gave the front of the car a "drunken" look. This was the beginning of the end. The company declared bankruptcy in 1923, and what was left was purchased by Charles Nash, a former associate of Billy Durant.

In 1910, local mailman Charles Fourney purchased a Halladay for his route. The Halladay was built by Streator Automobile in Peoria. Though it was a purely assembled car made from other company components, it was technically local. The Halladay brand was gone by the following year.

By then, Sears had grown to be a major factor in farm life. Its catalog offered greater selection and lower prices than the local general store, and ordering from home made it almost more "local" than the local store. Sears was anxious to get into automobiles. Its management initially discussed branding an automobile built by a local Chicago machine shop engineer named D. W. Cook. However, the offered price was too low and Cook turned it down. Sears found another supplier, and it found its way into the 1908 Sears catalog: a runabout selling for only $395.

In 1911, O. J. Tharp, the Elmwood music teacher, bought a Sears automobile. He was one of only 3,500 total customers. Though the Sears automobile was a pretty good car, management quickly determined that they were losing money on each one sold. Sears dropped out of the new car business within two years but remained very much a part of the automobile aftermarket business. Their catalog became a major supplier of parts for the Model T and other makes. Sears made another run at marketing a car in the 1950s with the Allstate automobile. The results were similar.

Meanwhile, Cook found a suitable facility to build his own car. It was the former Brown Corn Planter factory in Galesburg. His car debuted in 1905 and was named, of course, the Gale. The marketing slogan for the Gale—"climbs like a squirrel and eats up the road like an express train"— garnered some initial buzz, but the company lasted all of two years.

Studebaker was a very familiar name to farmers. The company had been selling sturdy farm wagons since the Civil War. While starting with electric cars at the turn of the century, by 1910 Studebaker was making well-appointed gasoline cars, including a six-cylinder model. Henry Memler of Memler's Department Store moved on from his Mitchell to the Studebaker Six. Joseph McCoy, a French Grove farmer, also purchased the Studebaker Six. Joseph was Dan McCoy's father and Dan was Verne's first cousin. He would soon become the automobile guru of the area.

With the J. I. Case Company, you couldn't get much closer to farming connections. The leading maker of steam traction engines and gasoline tractors had tried to enter a car in the 1895 *Chicago Times-Herald* race won by Frank Duryea. In 1910 Case bought the Pierce-Racine Automobile Company and soon rolled out their first automobile. Like Case's farm engines, it was a sturdy piece of machinery. Earl Gray of Williamsfield bought one in 1913. Though the Case automobile struggled to gain traction, the company had deep pockets and the car division persevered until 1926.

Verne's father, John H. Reed, purchased a Moline from Kelly Supply in 1912. Molines, made nearby in Moline, Iowa, were known for their ruggedness. Moline cars were winners of several endurance races, which led to the tagline "Car of Unfailing Service." Sometimes referred to as Dreadnought Molines, they featured a battleship as their hood ornament. This was a four-cylinder, 35 horsepower touring car with dual ignition (magneto or electric starter), thermo-siphon cooling, a three-speed sliding gear transmission, and luxury interior. The car weighed nearly three thousand pounds. It sold for $2,400, about five times the price of a Model T. The Moline was developed by W. H. Van Dervoort, an engineer and partner with the Root & Van Dervoort Company. The company had started out making

railroad parts and then developed a best-selling stand-alone gasoline engine that was marketed by John Deere. It moved on to the Moline automobile in 1904. The car had a good run, but the company did not survive Van
Dervoort's early death in 1921.

John Reed's cousin Franklin W. Reed, who was a real estate agent in
Peoria, also bought a Moline that year. His Moline replaced a Cutting Forty.
He may have become nervous about the future prospects of the company,
a common feeling in those early days. Cutting the company and Forty the
car certainly were symbolic of the times. The car cost an impressive $1,200
and had four cylinders, a sliding gear transmission, a foot accelerator, and
both magneto and electric starter. The issue was not the car but financing,
or rather the lack of it. Ironically, the ads for the Cutting Forty stated, "Our
directors are prominent men of affairs, several of them identified with successful automobile companies. The future of the Cutting 40 is not problem-
atical, it is assured." The company promptly folded in three years. Well over
two thousand auto companies were formed in the United States, nearly all
in the first decade of the twentieth century. Mismanagement and competition knocked out most. The 1920–1921 recession, the Big Three hegemony,
and the Great Depression finished the job.

By the 1910s, more expensive cars were starting to appear in farm towns.
Of course, the Cutting Forty and Moline were two. As part of Billy Durant's
General Motors, Cadillac underwent a repositioning from a low-priced
competitor of then market leader Olds to a top luxury make. F. P. Pulsi-
pher, an Elmwood real estate broker and financier, purchased a Cadillac in
1911, when the base price of a Cadillac was $1,700. William Oakes of French
Grove bought a Cadillac in 1915, by which time its price had escalated to
the $2,000–$3,000 range.

In 1914, C. H. Pulver of Williamsfield bought a Hudson. The company
was started by Roy Chapin, the same young man who had driven the Curved
Dash Oldsmobile eight hundred miles to New York City in 1901. He had recruited Howard Coffin, an engineer who also worked at Olds. They secured
financing from Joseph Hudson, the Detroit department store magnate.
Hudson established their niche as having the first low-price six-cylinder
cars. By 1914, all Hudsons were six cylinders and generated an eye-popping
76 horsepower at 3,000 rpm. Also attracted to this powerful car was Ora
Clark of Williamsfield. He traded a team of horses for his Hudson.

A couple of automobiles were especially successful in competing with
Henry Ford and his Model T, or should we say relatively successful given

the dominance of the Model T. In 1911, no less than six citizens of Elmwood bought Maxwells. One of those was Dr. David Morton. He was the town physician and the son of A. J. Morton of Williamsfield and Gold Cure fame. The Maxwell brand was started by Jonathan Maxwell, an engineer who had worked at Buick. It was funded by and included in the United States Motors conglomerate that Benjamin Briscoe was attempting to put together. Maxwell developed two- and four-cylinder cars similar to and competing with the Model T. In 1911 the entry-level Maxwell was selling for $600 (the Model T was $680 at that time). One addition was a special runabout model called the Doctor Maxwell. It was designed and marketed to physicians who made house calls, a persuasive selling point for Dr. Morton. In 1911 Maxwell had climbed to fourth in US sales, behind Ford, Overland, and Studebaker.

Charles Bartholomew, who had the Glide agency in Elmwood, added the Overland. The car proved popular not only in Elmwood but also in Yates City, Brimfield, and Williamsfield. Overland had a rocky start but became a major success thanks to one person, John North Willys. The company was founded in 1902 with a little one-cylinder car developed by the engineering graduate Claude Cox and funded by Indianapolis buggy manufacturer Charles Minshall. But it was John Willys who took the company to the pinnacle of success.

Willys grew up in the Finger Lakes area of New York. Like Henry Ford, he left schoolhouse learning at age fifteen to start his first enterprise, a laundry. As a master salesman in the Billy Durant vein, success came easy. He moved on to repairing bicycles, then selling them. By 1898 he had bought a sporting goods store in Elmira and significantly expanded his bike business. Yet, when he saw his first automobile in 1899, he instantly knew that bicycles were fading and cars would be the next wave. He bought a Pierce Motorette, the little motorized buggy with an imported De Dion–Bouton engine that started George Pierce on his road to fame. He then signed up as an agent to sell Pierce-Arrow and Rambler cars.

Willys could sell as many cars as he could obtain, but supply was always an issue. When Pierce-Arrow moved upscale and Ramblers were tough to secure, he knew he had to find an alternative. Looking around for a readily available and economical option, he discovered Overland, based in Indianapolis. He ordered the entire Overland production for the 1906 model year (only forty-seven cars) and followed that with an order for five hundred more for 1907. He sent a $10,000 check to lock down his supply.

When no cars arrived, he traveled to Indianapolis and discovered that the recession of 1907 had bankrupted Minshall and he had shuttered the plant. Willys jumped into action. He put up $350 of his own money to pay workers and get the plant restarted. Then he sweet-talked the local banks into providing essential financing, and proceeded to have the first cars for 1908 built in a circus tent.[43] Willys quickly raised production for 1909 to an incredible 4,907 cars, and with his usual marketing savvy, all of them were quickly sold. This was good enough for eighth place in US sales.

The company was rechristened Willys-Overland. Needing a much larger factory, he learned that Colonel Pope's huge plant in Toledo (producing the Pope-Toledo automobile) had also succumbed to the 1907 recession. Acquiring the plant at a discount, Willys dramatically ramped up production, rising rapidly to become the number-two automaker, just behind Ford, with annual production of 150,000 automobiles. He stayed up in the rarified air from 1912 to 1918.

Willys then decided to challenge Henry Ford and the Model T head-on with a car priced at less than $500 but with electric lights and starter. Unfortunately, when the Model T fighter rolled off the line in 1919, the target price had risen to $845. Meanwhile, Ford had added an electric starter and reduced the Model T price to $395. Willys's challenge fell flat.

Interestingly, the fortunes of Maxwell and Overland shared a common history. Both were rescued from near bankruptcy by a former railroad engineer named Walter Chrysler, who will factor later in this story. Like Billy Durant, John Willys was highly leveraged with bank financing and would finally lose control of the company during the Depression. Though he died in 1935, his company would make a comeback with another little car called the Jeep. And, the Overland name would make a small comeback of its own with the naming of the Grand Cherokee Overland in 2002.

With so many automobile makes, there was bound to be a shake-out. While assembling and pushing an automobile out the door was relatively easy, growing an infant operation to a profitable, sustainable company was not. To be successful required financial resources, marketing, and producing the right car at the right price, at a minimum. Many of the early local cars did not make it.

Williamsfield certainly led the pack in experimenting with off-brands. Fred Hurlbut bought a 1911 Rambler. The company was started by Thomas Jeffery in Kenosha, Wisconsin, making Rambler bikes, soon becoming the second-largest bike maker in the United States, after Colonel Pope. He sold his bike business to Pope and started making automobiles. Unfortunately, he died suddenly in 1910 and was succeeded by his son Charles. Though Thomas Jeffrey had spent most of his life building up the Rambler name, his son decided to rename the automobile the Jeffrey in his father's honor. The newly rechristened cars went nowhere. Charles then had a brush with death, surviving the sinking of the *Lusitania* in 1916. He promptly sold the family business to Charles Nash.[44] Nash, looking to rebound after being tossed out of General Motors by Billy Durant, renamed the company Nash Motors and almost immediately turned it into a success. Actually, it was quite a lot more than a success as Nash Motors lasted well into the 1950s, when it was folded into American Motors.

Harry Galpin bought a Metz roadster in 1915. Charles Metz had won the 1885 New York State High Wheeler bicycle championship. In 1893 he moved on to making Orient bicycles, then motorcycles, and finally put together an automobile in 1898. He left the company for a period to become, of all things, an automotive industry columnist. But, when the company was in financial distress in 1909, he returned and came up with a unique marketing plan. You could buy the Metz roadster on the installment plan. However, this was unlike any other automobile installment plan. Once you placed your order, you were shipped fourteen separate packages of components, each priced at $25. After you assembled all of the components, you had yourself a very nice automobile for the thrifty sum of $378. Metz did very well until he decided to go upmarket in 1919 with a fully assembled car at over twice the price. Metz was gone by 1921.

Lloyd Nelson bought a Crow-Elkhart in 1915. The company built a perfectly serviceable automobile. In fact, it offered to build automobiles for other companies. Crow-Elkhart was unable to properly focus on its own brand and ramp up production to a profitable level. The company did not make it through the mini-recession of 1920–1921.

Phil Maher of Elmwood and Mary Tucker of Williamsfield both opted for Franklins in 1911. Syracuse, New York, engineer John Wilkinson had designed an air-cooled car and was able to get funding from Herbert Franklin, a local manufacturer. The Franklin became the most successful air-cooled automobile in the United States, though it must be said it was one of the only ones. Quite ironically, Franklin dealers rebelled in 1923, wanting to add a fake radiator in front in order to have a more conventional-looking car.[45] Wilkinson resigned in protest, but Franklins soldiered on until the Depression. In an interesting local note, there were two and only two Franklins in Brimfield in 1921 and they somehow managed to crash head-on into each other. Thankfully, no one was hurt.

James Shaffer Jr., Will's first cousin and the younger brother of Big Joe, had purchased an Inter-State automobile in 1912. With the closest agency eighty miles east in Streator, James would have likely taken the train to Chicago, where he could have seen the car at Inter-State's 1354 Michigan Avenue showroom. The Inter-State was a four-cylinder, 40 horsepower touring car built in Muncie, Indiana, that sold for $2,400. Thomas Hart, the principal of the company, worked overtime to promote the Inter-State brand. He started by calling it "the best automobile made in America, even though everyone doesn't know it" and then ratcheted up the hyperbole with the line "the greatest achievement in the history of motor car development." It was without a doubt a well-engineered car. In fact, in 1912 it was one of only two automobiles in the country with an electric starter, the other being Cadillac. This addition was used to try to appeal to women drivers. Yet, none of these promotions significantly increased sales, and in 1914 the company fell into bankruptcy. It was purchased by Ball Corporation, the maker of Mason jars, which continued producing cars until World War I interrupted production. Ball never made it back to making Inter-States, closing shop in 1919.

Jones Gale of Williamsfield bought a McIntyre from the William Radcliffe agency in 1912. McIntyre had started out making a high-wheeler Motor Buggy, an automobile that looked really and truly like a buggy without a horse. Use of the term "buggy" for an automobile did not turn out to be a good move as buyers were looking for a real automobile, not a buggy. Though the name was quickly dropped, the company never escaped the association and was in receivership by 1915.

Russell Farquar and Willie Murphy of Williamsfield both bought an Empire automobile. This was a car with a storied birthing but a short-lived life. It was "sired" in 1909 by early automobile and bicycle royalty from Indianapolis—Carl Fisher and James Allison, the two principals who had made millions with Prest-O-Lite headlights. Fellow investor Arthur Newby had turned the National automobile from a limited-volume electric into a popular gas car. Unfortunately, all of these principals got sidetracked. They were focused on building the Indianapolis Speedway, and the Empire operation was left to wither.

In Chicago, Dr. Vesper Shaffer was still making rounds in a horse and buggy. Her partner, Dr. Thompson, had purchased an automobile in 1902 and was likely the first woman in Chicago to own a car. In a sign of the perilous times on Chicago streets, where many different conveyances were competing for the roadway, a man stepped in front of Dr. Thompson's car as she was traveling along at only 10 mph. She swerved to avoid him, but struck him and crashed into another automobile. Though she was a doctor and immediately on the spot, the man was fatally injured. Dr. Thompson was exonerated of any blame but certainly chastened about driving on Chicago streets.

Despite this, Vesper had already made the decision to move on from a horse and buggy. It was actually getting more dangerous to make her rounds by horse and buggy. She was traveling at 4 mph while competing with the growing number of automobiles traveling at 30 mph or faster. She had a six-mile ride from her northwest residence to the office in the Reliance Building. There were many options for this travel. The early omnibus lines had given way to horse cars, horse-drawn trolleys, and by 1890, the first electric trolley lines. And by 1900, many of the trolley lines had been elevated, freeing up the streets.

But, Dr. Shaffer needed to make house calls and travel between her office and the two hospitals where she had credentials. By 1910 there were 12,000 cars and 58,000 horse-drawn conveyances on Chicago streets, with the number of cars growing dramatically as buggies and wagons plummeted. Chicago had 90,000 cars by 1920 and 300,000 by 1925, when the number of horse-drawn vehicles had sunk to 15,000. Electrics were popular as in-town cars, with roughly one in seven automobiles electric. Their numbers totaled 12,000 by 1911.

Once Vesper decided it was time for a change, the change she made was not a surprise. While electric cars were falling farther and farther behind their gasoline competition, they still held their own in several customer segments—city women with money, city doctors, and delivery vehicles. As a female physician, Vesper met two of those targets. With an electric, there was no issue with range in town. But with most current gasoline automobiles, hand cranking the engine was an issue. It was both hard and dangerous. Furthermore, bending down and cranking the engine was considered unladylike. Conversely, driving an electric car was considered unmanly. Her male counterparts would opt for a gas model like the Doctor Maxwell model. Unbeknownst to Vesper, the starting crank on gasoline automobiles was soon to be a thing of the past. An electric starter would appear on the 1912 Cadillac, and within a few years, many cars (but not the Model T) had replaced the hand crank.

In Chicago, Vesper had the Automobile Row showrooms and up to twenty different brands of electric cars to choose from.[46] Electric cars generally had ranges of 60–100 miles and top speeds of 25 mph. The lead-acid batteries would take about twelve hours to recharge. It was the price of the batteries that dictated the list price and appointments of electric cars. The lead manufacturer was Detroit Electric. Clara Ford and Thomas Edison had Detroit Electrics, a fact that quickly made it into their advertisements. These automobiles were produced by Anderson Electric, formerly Anderson Carriages, which had been a maker of all manner of carriages up to and including very ornate opera coaches.

Detroit Electric models started at $2,000 and could escalate to $5,000 or more. At those prices, customers expected more than the buckboard styling of the Curved Dash Oldsmobile. Given their carriage background, many electrics were styled after Hansom cabs or even opera coaches. The high-end Detroit Electric models were over seven feet tall, with fully enclosed bodies. The interiors were designed to look like a Victorian sitting room, replete with expensive upholstery, deep Turkish cushions, mirrors, and flower vases. The passengers sat in comfortable chairs in front facing backward while the driver controlled the car from the rear seat. Not surprisingly, given the much faster speed of an automobile, having the driver in back quickly came under review and was banned in many cities as unsafe. Detroit Electric's response made an odd situation even odder. Its leadership elected to equip both the left front and left rear seats with full controls—steering tiller, accelerator, and brakes. One could drive from either the front or rear seat, depending on the local ordinances.

This kind of fancy, ostentatious automobile would have had no attraction for Vesper Shaffer, both in terms of style and price. Yet, as electrics continued to lose ground against gas automobiles, Detroit Electric and other electric manufacturers (Baker, Rauch and Lang) made a number of significant adjustments. They added Victoria, roadster, and runabout models that dispensed with all the expensive luxury trappings and drove the entry prices below $2,000. The Victoria models were especially attractive. Patterned after Victoria carriages, they were adapted to look like a conventional gasoline automobile, including a large, extended front end that one might think even housed a gas engine. Instead, it was of course filled with batteries. In fact, the Detroit Electric Victoria looked surprisingly like the Doctor Maxwell, without the crank, that is. It was a simple, utilitarian two-passenger touring automobile with a folding top.

Vesper made the change from horse and buggy to an automobile around 1910, the peak of electric sales. The Victoria model sold for $1,900. It was not a huge premium over the Doctor Maxwell, which then listed for $1,375. In Chicago, Detroit Electrics were shown in an impressive enameled terra cotta showroom at 2416 Michigan Avenue. With a range of up to eighty miles, Vesper's new electric car was not made for the trip to Williamsfield but would be just fine in Chicago, joining roughly four thousand other electrics on city streets.

As for Will and Verne, they were certainly not going to buy another buggy in 1915. They were just starting out at French Grove but were in good shape financially. The French Grove farm was a long buggy or wagon trek to the any of the local towns. In Williamsfield, the farm had been just a mile from town. While there was still a small general store, post office, and church at French Grove crossing, residents were still isolated.

Once Will and Verne agreed to purchase an automobile, the decision of which model to buy was not too surprising. Ford was a juggernaut. The Highland Park factory was producing a thousand Fords daily. One in three cars sold were Ford Model Ts. The percentage was significantly higher in Central Illinois farm country. In the local counties, a survey in 1917 found 73 of 158 cars listed were Fords, or 46 percent. The next frequent makes were Overland, Buick, and Studebaker. A long list of brands brought up the rear including Maxwell, Chalmers, Haynes, Cadillac, Chevy, Olds, REO, Jeffery, Mitchell, Dodge, Glide, Oakland, Paige, Hudson, Inter-State, and Moline.[47]

Henry Ford was proud of his connection with farming and farm lo-cales. He was clear that part of the impetus for the universal car was to get farmers "out of the mud." He was even known to demonstrate a Model T on the farm, having one of the rear drive wheels raised to attach a belt and proceed to shell corn. The Model T that had originally listed for $850 in 1908 was now selling for $440 (roughly $12,000 in 2020 dollars).

The first Model T in the area was sold to Al Hurd, a farmer in Wil-liamsfield. By 1914, Ford Model Ts were the dominant car on local roads. Will and Verne's relatives were buying Fords. Alex T. Reed, brother of John H. Reed and Verne's uncle, bought a Ford in June from Kelly Supply. William Caldwell Reed, another uncle of Verne's who worked the Reed farm in French Grove, also bought a Ford that month from Kelly. Henry Reed, another French Grove Reed but unrelated to Verne, bought a Model T that July.

Part of this rush on Model Ts in 1914 and 1915 was due to Henry Ford. He had sold 168,000 Model Ts in 1913 and wanted to ramp up production at Highland Park to 300,000 in the 1914 model year (which ran to August 1915). He announced a challenge. Any Ford purchaser between August 1, 1914, and August 1, 1915, would receive a $50 rebate if the 300,000 target was achieved. With the cash rebate, the net cost of a Model T was only $390. This was quite a bit less than a team of horses while being considerably faster. Kelly Supply was on board with the offer, posting an ad weekly. Charles Boley with the Ford agency in Williamsfield also worked the offer to great effect. He sold new Fords to ten local residents including town doctors Dr. Harlan Hubbell and Dr. Loyal Davis.

In the end, it was a pretty easy decision. Will and Verne ordered a 1914 Model T from Kelly Supply. Will's Model T was delivered to Brimfield on a railcar, disassembled and standing upright. In this configuration seven Fords could fit on one railcar in the space where only two assembled cars would fit. It took the Kelly Supply mechanics about half a day to put each Model T together. All Model Ts on the arriving railcar were black, whereas in prior years there had been dark blue, green, and maroon options. This was actually the first year that all Model Ts were black. As mentioned, it was also the last year for gas headlights and taillights. There was also less brass than prior years, and Ford had started to move from leather to leatherette for the seats. The wooden ignition coil boxes were now metal. Finally, due to supplier shortages, there was no speedometer (the blow softened by a $50 reduction in the price). For farmers on rural unpaved roads this was not a serious shortcoming. It was said that you could gauge your speed by the level of vibration of the Model T. If the car was really shaking, you were going 40 mph.

Illinois had started licensing motorcars in 1907. When Will and Verne registered the car, it was assigned license plate R7112. This five-digit plate numbering was to expand to six digits in 1916 and seven digits in 1925, a sign of the explosion in car registrations. Another early Illinois motor vehicle law set speed limits, though initially they were set in minutes per mile rather than miles per hour. The law also levied a $200 fine if you did not shut off your car off to avoid frightening an approaching team of horses.

On July 22, 1915, Henry Ford announced that 308,213 Model Ts had been sold in the 1914–1915 production year, surpassing the challenge target. Ford paid out $15 million in $50 rebates, including a check to Will and Verne. Of course, Ford led auto sales again for the year. A distant second was Willys-Overland, at 48,000 sales, followed by Studebaker, Buick, Maxwell, REO, Jeffery, and Hupmobile. For the following model year, Ford dispensed with the rebate challenge and his sales still more than doubled, to 734,000.

9

All Power to the Farm

CERTAINLY A FACTOR that Will weighed in purchasing the Model T was the local roads. None were paved. Most would be dusty in the summer and muddy in the spring. They could be rutted, even downright dangerous at any time. And, that assumed that some kind of road maintenance was done. All of this was an endorsement for the Model T as it was designed to tackle just about any road conditions.

Still, roads were a big issue—and not a new one. Cyclists in the 1890s quickly discovered that outside the major cities, the roads were atrocious. Fortunately, the cyclists did not sit on their hands and admit defeat. A federation of cyclists, the League of American Wheelmen, actively pushed for better roads. Their efforts were fully supported by Colonel Albert Pope, the bicycle magnate. This work morphed into the Good Roads grassroots movement, with chapters in towns across the country, with the aim to push for better roads.

As the movement spread, it remained an uneasy alliance of cyclists, farmers, city drivers, and the automobile industry. Early on, federal and state bureaucracies were focused on supporting the steam railroads, but they gradually warmed to the need for better roads. More importantly, additional groups signed on to the Good Roads movement. The turn of the century brought in the US Postal Service, wanting to expand rural free delivery. Equally supportive were catalog sellers like Sears and Montgomery Ward. The American Automobile Association (AAA) was created in part to lobby for better roads. It sponsored the Glidden tours, city-to-city automobile treks that demonstrated both the use and range of the automobile as well as the lack of good roads. The most important instigator was the burgeoning automobile population. It had grown from the one car sold by Alexander Winton in 1896 to over eight million by 1918. The challenge that loomed was the condition of the roads those cars would seek to use and the cost to upgrade them. There were roughly 2.5 million miles of roads in the country in 1912, nearly all of them dirt. It cost roughly $5,000 to pave a mile whereas simply improving existing dirt roads was only $723 per mile.

By 1915, people in the area were having less and less patience with the status quo. The local farmer would usually grade the dirt roads near his farm. As more and more cars appeared from farther and farther away, farmers were less willing to handle road maintenance, especially when it was just city folks out for a drive. For an idea of the scope of the problem, Illinois had an estimated 100,000 miles of unimproved wagon roads at the turn of the century, of which about thirty miles had been surfaced.

By 1917, President Woodrow Wilson established the Highway Transport Committee to make recommendations on how to proceed. Its first chairman was Roy Chapin, that young lad who started at Olds and was by now the president of Hudson Motors. A central figure in the push for new roads was Carl Fisher. Here was an individual that was an early bicycle champion, race promoter, bicycle dealer, automobile dealer, wildly successful manufacturer of gas carbide headlights, developer of the Indianapolis 500 race track, and a major figure in the development and promotion of both Miami Beach and Long Island. Yet, because he lost his fortune in the stock market crash of 1929, he considered his life a failure.

Of course, that makes no sense. He was and remains a towering figure in the history of the bicycle and the automobile. Raised by a single mom, Fisher quit school after sixth grade and opened a bike repair shop in Indianapolis. An expert "wheelman," he traveled the country racing bicycles with Barney Oldfield. He convinced Colonel Pope to send him a railcar load of Pope Columbia bicycles, which he promptly sold—and ordered more. In 1900 Fisher traveled with Oldfield to the New York auto show and saw the future. He closed his bike shop and opened the Fisher Automobile Company, considered to be the first automobile dealership in the United

States. He sold Stoddard-Dayton, Packard, Oldsmobile, and REO cars. He rekindled his racing passion with Oldfield, but now it was with automobiles, not bicycles.

In 1904 he met inventor Percy Avery, who had developed and patented an acetylene carbide headlight system. With partner James Allison, they started Prest-O-Lite, which for a time supplied every automobile headlight in the country. Fisher timed his exit from the enterprise perfectly, preserving a fortune before electric lights replaced carbide technology in cars.

Fisher got involved in many new projects. He pulled together several local investors to build the Indianapolis Speedway. From his racing days, he knew firsthand how the cars would slide off a typical oval track. He decided to pave the new speedway with 3.2 million bricks, hence the nickname "the Brickyard."

Looking for more challenges, Fisher became interested in a roadway that would span the nation, something he first called the "Coast to Coast Rock Highway." He discussed the concept with Henry Ford, but Ford was not interested. Another Henry, Henry Joy of Packard Automobiles, was. Joy provided some initial funding and then got personally involved. He even provided a better name for the route, the "Lincoln Highway." With Fisher's tireless prodding and Henry Joy's leadership, construction of the Lincoln Highway got underway in 1914. Fisher tried to keep the route secret, knowing that contentiousness among communities might derail it. Sure enough, the concept gathered steam, and more and more communities wanted the route to come through their town.

Henry Joy favored a straight shot, one that followed a good portion of the Oregon Trail through Nebraska, Wyoming, Utah, Nevada, and across Donner Pass into California. Colorado supported the highway early on but pushed back mightily when Denver was bypassed (a "dogleg" to the city was promised but never delivered). The Lincoln Highway was eventually completed from Times Square in New York City to Lincoln Park in San Francisco, passing about fifty miles north of Williamsfield. It was a work in progress. The last stretch in Illinois was not paved until 1923.

With the success of the Lincoln Highway, or at least the concept, Fisher promoted another national route, one from Chicago to Miami. Since he had recently helped develop and promote Miami Beach, he was perhaps more intimately motivated on this project. Though he now carried more influence, this route crossed many more highly populated towns, cities, and states compared with the Lincoln Highway. Thus, it was far more factious.

One or two "doglegs" would not suffice. Hundreds of roads would need to be stitched together, eventually creating a mesh of 6,100 miles from Chicago to Miami that were labeled with the "DH" route markers: the Dixie Highway. Illinois had been one of the first states with a highway department and had spearheaded Illinois Route 1 from Chicago to Vincennes, Indiana, a distance of 250 miles. It became one of the earliest completed segments of the Dixie Highway. The northern terminus in Chicago was a couple of blocks from Vesper Shaffer's downtown office.

The Lincoln and Dixie Highways were high-profile, national successes. They relied in large part on local cities to finance construction. However, if you were not on a national highway route, the quest for financing was not as easy. Brimfield had its own Good Roads committee, and Verne's father John Reed was the road commissioner for Brimfield Township. Their focus was to work with state and local officials to fund better roads. The objective was more "hard roads" (meaning paved roads) to replace dirt roads. In the meantime, local towns did the best they could. Brimfield purchased a large steam traction engine to grade its dirt roads. And in the summer, the town would apply oil to keep the dust down.

The other issue with roads was how to get anywhere. Once you ventured out beyond your immediate township, you needed some kind of navigation. Early on, there emerged step-by-step guides for getting from town to town—at least, from major town to major town. Hopefully you had an automobile with an odometer, as every instruction would depend on the number of miles from your starting point. For example, if you wanted to motor from Bloomington to Peoria, a distance of about forty miles, the directions were along these lines: "From the Court House, go west on Washington Street with the trolley. Cross under the RR tracks and turn left at the end of the road. At mile 18, turn right on the single road. At mile 22, turn left at the crossroads. At mile 23, cross the long bridge. At mile 24, cross the trolley tracks. At mile 26 in Allentown, cross the railroad tracks." At this point, you were just over halfway to Peoria, assuming you made all the correct turns. The road guides also noted the condition of the roads. This route in 1917 was characterized as "good dirt roads."

Starting with the spring of 1915, Will and Verne had a good plan for the French Grove farm. They would cultivate grain and raise livestock. Acreage would be allocated to oats for the horses, hay for the cattle, and feed, usually corn, for the hogs. Excess grain could be sold at market. The steep hillside running from the barn down to French Creek would remain pasture.

For now, horsepower would be provided by sturdy draft horses that mixed Percheron and American breeds. For starters, this meant four to six horses. Farm implements would need to be built up. For spring plowing, Will would need an inventory that included a walking plow, Deere and Harrison gang plows, and an Emerson riding sulky plow. To prepare the soil for planting, he would have a harrow, disk pulverizer, and a manure spreader. Sowing would be done by a Deere planter. Oats would go in first, as corn required the soil to be warmer. Cultivation required single and two-row cultivators. Hay would be harvested using a Deering hay rake, binder, and International hay loader. The corn harvest would be manual, picking and tossing the ears in the wagons as the horses advanced down the row. The harvested corn would be stored in a bin using a Wenzelman corn elevator for storage. Will would soon acquire a Waterloo Boy gasoline engine to power a corn sheller and to grind feed for the hogs. The grain harvest would be contracted to a thresher outfit. The total investment in horses, implements, livestock, and seed would exceed $2,000. This, of course, did not include the Model T that Will and Verne had just purchased. Nor did it include other farm technologies now available, such as trucks and tractors.

The farm plan had to be revamped each year to maintain the soil. Oats, corn, and wheat were nitrogen-depleting. Those fields needed to be rotated with nitrogen-fixing crops such as soy beans, clover, or alfalfa. Horses were the key to success but came at a price. Acreage was lost to oats to feed the horses. And maintaining your stable of horses was not easy. The gestation period for horses was a year, capped by a 60 percent chance of a live foal. Then, there followed two to three years of maturation before the horse was field-ready. It was a big investment.

Over the next few years, Will and Verne's farm operation grew rapidly. Seventeen hog houses were constructed to support 150–200 Poland China hogs. They would typically be fattened to 200 pounds before going to market. The cattle herd grew to fifty head. And, the stable would eventually have twelve horses. Will and Verne would need some help in running the farm. Hank, a long-time local, was hired as a full-time farmhand.

In 1919 the bulk of Will's farm operation was horse-drawn. However, with the liberating experience of the Model T, he could envision how a truck could more aptly serve as a farm transport. Locally, farmers were moving to delivering grain to town in trucks, not wagons. In addition, there was a price advantage in taking farm produce, especially livestock, directly to a major shipping-and-processing center such as Peoria.

Henry Ford was well aware that regular Model Ts were being converted by the aftermarket to trucks. Enterprising owners would purchase a chassis-only Model T and have it refitted. However, this resulted in a compromise creation that fell short of a workhorse farm vehicle. Ford decided to build a proper truck. Launched in 1918, the Model TT was based on the Model T but two feet longer. It was designed with a load rating of one short ton (two thousand pounds) by including a stronger frame, heavy-duty springs, a worm gear differential, and solid rubber tires. It had lower gearing that provided for a top speed of either 15 mph or 22 mph. The engine was the same old dependable Model T engine, the L-head, four-cylinder, 20 horse-power power plant with a crank start. The result was a truck very durable for its time but quite slow and noisy. It was initially sold as only a chassis, with the buyer supplying the body. The price was $600.

Locally, the TT rapidly became the standard farm truck. Kelly Supply in Brimfield was a local dealer, and the TTs were selling quite well there. Local farmer J. L. Murdoch traded his prize mare Harriet M for a TT truck. Kelly salesman Cheever Morrissey, raised on a farm, made the swap. It seemed that a colleague had been telling him that horses were making a comeback. Also, as if to emphasize that the TT was Model T–based, another local farmer, Stuart Cady, broke his arm cranking his TT. This was bad enough, but it turned out that Cady had broken the same arm a year earlier crank-ing his Model T. Unfortunately for Cady, both episodes were covered in excruciating detail in the *Brimfield News*.

Will bought his TT truck from Kelly Supply. He arranged for a typical farm setup with a steel cab in front and a platform bed in back that could be configured either as a flatbed or with stakes, as a pickup. Moline Plow Company was one of the local aftermarket suppliers of such bodies for TT trucks.

Henry Ford had grown up on a farm a generation earlier than Will and was eager to apply his automotive skills and vast resources to reduce the backbreaking nature of farm work while at the same time enhancing pro-ductivity. One area he had been working on (let's say tinkering) for many years was a farm tractor. Early in his career (in 1880 and 1882), he had built two crude steam tractors. They confirmed his view that steam power was a dead end. In 1907, prior to the launch of the Model T, he asked Joe Galamb to build what he would call the Automobile Plow, later shortened to Autoplow. The first version used the engine from the Ford Model B and running gear from the Model K. Even in the midst of ramping up Model T production at the Piquette Avenue plant, Ford had twelve more Autoplows built. The years passed and perhaps fifty additional tractor prototypes were constructed of one sort or another, but none progressed beyond that.

Meanwhile, steam tractors were the incumbent mechanized farm power. But, they were only suitable for threshing outfits or for the very large farms farther west. They were huge, slow, and extremely heavy. A 75 horsepower Case steam tractor in 1906 weighed 20,000 pounds, and that was before you added 260 gallons of water and 1,200 pounds of coal. And, these large rigs were expensive, typically selling for $2,000 and higher. Furthermore, there were issues in use. The heavy footprint compacted the soil and prevented the seeds from germinating. They were also dangerous, with the steam boiler operating at very high temperatures and pressures. Steam traction engine sales peaked by 1910, and then rapidly declined.

As had been the case with automobiles, the availability of the Otto gas engine spurred its application in tractors. Some steam companies simply replaced the steam components with a gas engine, resulting in a machine that was still huge, heavy, and expensive. The first successful production gas tractor was the Hart-Paar, which quickly captured a third of the market in 1909. Competition developed quickly, with Allis Chalmers, Avery, Bull, Mogul, Waterloo, and Titan joining the fray.

During the same period, the Model T was being adapted in the field to perform some typical tractor operations, albeit with limited success. You could pull a rear wheel and add a pulley to the tire hub to drive a bucksaw, simple thresher, silo conveyor, water pump, generator, or corn sheller.

Will had purchased his first car, his first truck, and a stand-alone gas engine. But he was still on the fence about a tractor. The horse and buggy versus an automobile was an easy call. The horse versus tractor decision was much more difficult and would be years in the making. For a tractor, it was to be a question of not if but when.

For a medium-size farm such as Will and Verne's, horses were the incumbent power source and could ably do most of the tasks required. With horses, you had flexibility. They could work a variety of terrain, including the hills and gullies found at French Grove. Horses could work between crop rows, pulling cultivators without damaging the emerging plants. Horses could learn and apply. When harvesting corn, they would know when to pull the wagon forward as Will and his hired hand picked the ears and tossed them in the wagon. The bigger draft horses that Will was using could handle larger acreage and heavier loads. Furthermore, some of the tasks that horses had performed would now be handled by his new TT truck.

Many recent innovations, such as sulky riding implements, had already made farming less back-breaking. And, Will had amassed a substantial investment in horse-drawn implements. Those could be used with a new tractor but would require two men, one sitting on the sulky and one on the tractor. Will and Verne had started a family, but their two young boys were too young to run a tractor. The alternative would be to purchase all new implements that were designed for a tractor. Though they were amazing pieces of technology, the new tractors still had a number of issues. They remained too big, too heavy, and too expensive. With wide front wheels, they were unable to straddle the rows for cultivation. This meant that Will would still have to retain horses for that key spring function.

And then there were mixed experiences with many early tractor adopters. Though most farmers had kept some of their horses to use in conjunction with a new tractor, others tried to completely switch and ended up going back to all horses in frustration. In addition, when you really needed powerful tractor capabilities, as with threshing, there were plenty of local operators that could be engaged. Hugh Carroll and his Buffalo Pitts steam traction engine was on call just a couple of miles away from Will's farm. Possibly the primary reason for waiting was that Will already had horses and knew how to farm with horses. Of course, he was not alone in his "wait and see" attitude on tractors. In the Midwest, the tractor penetration at the time was only 5 percent. But certainly, change was in the air.

Henry Ford was not one to give up on his tractor project. His shareholders at Ford Motor Company were certainly not interested in developing a tractor. So in 1915 he formed a separate company—Ford and Sons—with the explicit mission to bring a tractor to market. Getting ahead of himself, Ford announced that he would soon bring a tractor to market for $200. A year later, he announced that he would sell a Model T automobile, a Model TT truck, and the new tractor, all three, for $600.

That same year, Joe Galamb had visited a tractor show in Wisconsin to get ideas. A tractor salesman showed him the Wallis Cub tractor, which had a unitized structure where the engine, transmission, and differential were welded together to provide strength. Joe discussed this approach with Henry Ford, and they decided to stop trying to build a Model T–based tractor and design one from the ground up using the unitized approach. Early on, Eugene Farkas was pulled off the electric car project that Ford had started with Thomas Edison and set to work on the new tractor. He came up with a frameless design that combined the engine block, gearbox, and differential as one piece. The components themselves formed the frame. A number of models were built and tested on the eight-thousand-acre farm that Ford owned.

Issues surfaced. The prototypes ran hot, too hot for a farmer to operate. Their light weight meant poor traction and weak pulling capacity. They were too high off the ground. And most importantly, they would be too costly for mass production. Ford put a team to work on each issue. He had Charles Sorensen in overall charge of production. A number of outside suppliers were also engaged. This included, quite surprisingly, the use of the Hercules engine to power the tractor (though it was later replaced with a Ford engine).

As the Ford tractor project was proceeding, a tractor manufacturer in Minnesota started using the Ford name as one of the company's principals was conveniently named Ford. This was clearly designed to play on the Ford name and brand. Henry Ford decided his new tractor would not be a "Ford" but would be called a "Fordson."

The Fordson used a four-cylinder, 20 horsepower engine that was started on gasoline and then run on kerosene. Ignition was similar to the Model T. It was started with a hand crank and the spark was generated by the same Model T–style flywheel-mounted magneto feeding a trembler coil. Like the Model T, it was fairly easy to start in warm weather but more challenging in cold. The Fordson had 42-inch steel wheels at rear and 28-inch steel wheels in front. It weighed about 2,500 pounds. By way of comparison, the Avery 30 horsepower steam traction engine weighed in at 46,000 pounds.

The first shipments of the Fordson did not go to US farmers. Instead, they were shipped to Britain in the middle of World War I. Ford's chief in the United Kingdom was Percival Perry. With the war raging, he was put in charge of Britain's wartime food program. He quickly determined they needed more tractors, quite a lot of them in fact. Perry was aware of the plans in the works for a Ford tractor and pleaded for a supply. Charles Sorensen was sent to London to discuss the request. Perry worked with the British government to secure an order for five thousand Ford tractors while Sorensen negotiated the price with Henry ($700 each, $50 above cost). The tractors were to be delivered within months, toward the end of 1917. Production got underway almost immediately at the Highland Park plant. In

Fordson tractor, with four-cylinder, 20 horsepower crank engine running on gasoline to start and kerosene to run. Steel wheels are 48" in diameter at rear, 28" in front. The Fordson weighed 2,500 pounds. (Courtesy of Living History Museum)

a dig at the futility of war, Henry Ford had the phrase "Peace-Industry-Prosperity" imprinted on the hood of each tractor. The sole-source arrangement given to Ford riled both British and US tractor manufacturers. Nevertheless, the Fordsons arrived on time and were immediately put to work, with mostly women at the wheel.

Prior to the announcement of the Fordson, farmers in central Illinois were buying a range of gasoline tractors, including Case, Avery, Bates Steel Mule, Heider, and especially International Harvester (IH). International Harvester was the clear leader and had two different tractor lines in play—the Titan and the Mogul. In 1918, Cecil and Sons, the farm equipment dealer in Brimfield, conducted an IH tractor school in town featuring the Titan. The Titan 10-20 was a 5,225-pound tractor that sold for $1,000. Charlie Savage bought a Titan and put his horses out to pasture for the plowing season. There was a larger tractor show in Peoria that year, featuring most of the tractors currently on the market. Henry Freeman bought a Heider, supplied by the Rock Island Plow Company just down the road in Moline. C. W. Porter also bought a Heider and likewise sent his horses to pasture. Gradually, the newspaper want ads filled with farmers selling horses.

In late 1918, Ford announced that the Fordson would be available for purchase in the United States. The price was initially $750 but rose to $885 due to production costs. In an arrangement that was to have longer-term repercussions, Ford decided to sell his new tractor through his automobile dealers. Kelly Supply had added the TT truck earlier and immediately picked up the Fordson. The agency soon scheduled a tractor demo in town. It featured the Rumely, Huber, and Fordson tractors but the Fordson, being a Ford and being brand new, drew the most attention.

Ford reduced the price of the Fordson in 1920 to $790, and business picked up. Edson Purcell of French Grove bought one of the first Fordsons. The City of Cuba, Illinois, bought a Fordson for road grading. Brimfield Township followed suit and also bought a Fordson for its roads. A tractor plowing demonstration was arranged at the Hartley farm north of Brimfield. It featured Rumely, Titan, Waterloo Boy, Fordson, Hart-Paar, Heider, Twin City, and Huber tractors. Shortly thereafter, Kelly Supply salesman Cliff Bundy reported eight new Fordson sales, including one to local French Grove farmer Horace Moon.

In 1921, there was a recession, with a significant drop in farm prices. Though the recession was short-lived, tractor sales were nevertheless depressed. The Fordson suffered with the others, in spite of Ford's dropping the price to $625. In January 1922 in a radio address, Henry Ford announced a further price reduction, this time to the unheard-of level of $395. Even with Ford mass production, that price was at or below cost. This precipitated a "tractor war." Competing tractor companies had to respond or perish. International Harvester decided to accept Ford's challenge and reduced its prices in line with the Fordson. The farm economy rebounded, and tractor sales doubled by 1925, with the Fordson claiming 60 percent of the market. In a sign that the more things change, the more they stay the same, Horace Moon fractured his wrist attempting to crank-start his Fordson.

Fordson's huge market share was not destined to last. There were still issues with the tractor itself. First, it was heavier in the back and had a tendency to rear up, sometimes even flipping over and resulting in injury or death to the farmer. Second, it did not do well in plowing performance. A tractor test laboratory had been established in Nebraska to rate tractor performance, particularly the ability to pull implements. The Fordson did not score well. Third—and this was a killer issue—it could not be used for cultivation. Once row crops were planted, weeds needed to be cleared in order to allow the young crop plants to emerge and thrive. But, the configuration

1924 International Harvester Farmall tractor, the first row crop tractor.
(Courtesy of the Victoria Museum, Melbourne)

of the front and rear wheels of the Fordson would not accommodate crop rows. A farmer would need to retain horses to do the cultivation.

Then there was the dealer channel. Ford agencies were car-focused, with less farming expertise than competing dealers, and they did not carry the farm implements to go with the tractor. Other tractor manufacturers, particularly International Harvester and Deere, had dealers who were exclusively farm equipment specialists.

Yet, the all-encompassing issue for the Fordson was a familiar one for Henry Ford. He focused on price and mass production and did not innovate. This became very apparent in 1924, when International Harvester came out with the Farmall tractor. This was a general-purpose tractor specifically designed for row crops. It had narrow tricycle front wheels and large adjustable rear wheels. It could straddle the rows and cultivate. The farmer could perform all the key tasks with the tractor and eliminate horses.

Ford predictably did not respond. The Farmall was wildly successful, and International Harvester grew its market share to 50 percent by 1928. Ford at that point had sold 650,000 Fordsons, swamping the competition.

Yet instead of enhancing the Fordson, Henry decided to stop production. He needed the space at his new Rouge River plant for Model A production. Meanwhile, in Britain, where the initial Fordsons had landed, the Ford tractor continued to be enhanced, sold, and it thrived. In 1929, 80 percent of the tractors in that country were Fordsons.

Will could have gone with the Fordson in 1922 when it was selling for a rock-bottom $395. Fordsons had appeared in French Grove. But for Will, it was not a good fit. The idea of running the farm with both a tractor and horses did not have much appeal. As a smart farmer, he would wait until the tractor path forward was clear.

J. I. Case Sulky plow. Will would ride the plow, which was pulled by three draft horses. (Miami University Digital Collection)

American Locomotive train arriving at the Williamsfield depot, 1892. (Photo courtesy of Caldwell House Museum)

The National Institute, 1892, home of Dr. Morton's Gold Cure and the town opera house. (Caldwell House Museum, Williamsfield)

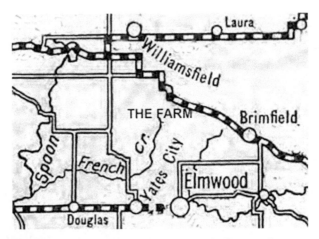

The farm country midway between Galesburg and Peoria showing the towns of Williamsfield, Brimfield, and Elmwood. French Grove and the farm are in the middle. The dotted roads are graded dirt. All others are unimproved dirt. (Adapted from a 1925 auto route map)

Westinghouse agricultural engine, portable steam engine with large boiler driving piston, which in turn rotates belt wheel. (Courtesy of vintagemachinery.org)

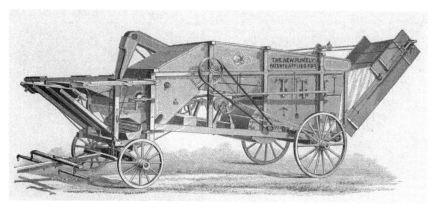

1887 Rumely Separator, driven by belt from a steam traction engine. (Rumely catalog, 1887, Rumely Manufacturing, La Pointe, Indiana)

1880 Penny Farthing high wheeler, left, and 1886 Rover safety bicycle, the first commercially successful safety bicycle invented by John Starely. (F. J. Drake and Co. catalog, Wikimedia Commons, James Stephenson)

Reeves and Co. steam traction engine, 1911. It competed with engines from Huber, Avery, Buffalo Pitts, and others. (James H. Stephenson, "Farm Engines and How to Run Them: The Young Engineer's Guide," 1911)

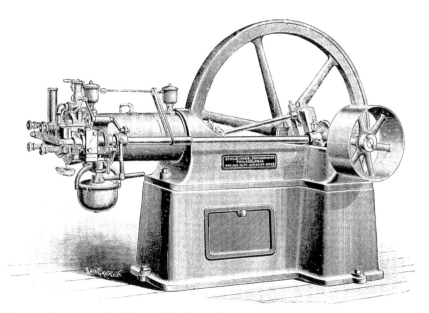

Otto stationary engine from Schleicher, Schumm, and Co., circa 1884, built under the US patent of Nicolaus Otto. (*Popular Science*, 1880)

1886 Benz Motorwagen, Model #2 with one-cylinder, four-cycle Otto engine, 1.5 horsepower. Bertha Benz drove the slightly more elaborate Model #3. (Wikimedia Commons, Daimler Chrysler, 2005)

Charles (left) and Frank Duryea with the third automobile, 1894. (Public domain image)

1899 Winton Phaeton, one cylinder, 6 horsepower, the model driven to the New York Auto Show by Alexander Winton. (Courtesy of the Crawford Museum, Western Reserve Historical Society, Cleveland, Ohio)

LEFT: Ransom Olds racing his "Pirate" racer on Ormond Beach in a 1902 time trial versus Winton's Bullet racer (Public domain image)

OPPOSITE: 1903 Curved Dash Olds, known formally as the Olds Model R, one-cylinder, 4.5 horsepower, with planetary transmission. One of 4,000 sold that year, placing Olds Motor at #1 in the US followed by Cadillac, Ford, Pope-Hartford, and Rambler. (United States National Museum)

Henry Ford and his 1896 Quadricycle posing several years later. Two-cylinder, 4 horsepower machine, with no reverse and no brakes. (Public domain image)

1902 "999" racer with Barney Oldfield at the tiller and Henry Ford standing. The "monster" machine that made both men famous. (Public domain image)

Winton "Bullet" racer (actually "Bullet" number 2, an eight-cylinder machine) after winning the Gordon Bennett trophy in Ireland in 1903 and before his October loss to Henry Ford's 999 racer. Alexander Winton is behind the wheel. (Public domain image)

Williamsfield Horse Show, 1903, with parade down Gale Street, still unpaved though now lighted with electric lights. (Caldwell House Museum, Williamsfield)

Dr. Vesper Shaffer, circa 1900.
(Caldwell House Museum, Williamsfield)

William "Will" Shaffer and Verne Reed Shaffer, circa 1913.
(Author's family collection)

1906 Ford Model N, a four-cylinder runabout that listed at $500 until runaway demand forced James Couzens to raise the price to $600. A total of 13,250 were built at Piquette, all in maroon. There were many similarities to the upcoming Model T, with three-pedal planetary transmission and brake/clutch lever. The steering wheel is still on the right side, however. (Northwestern Automobile Company catalog, from Trade Catalog Collection of the Hennepin County Library)

Ford Model N in front of the Piquette factory, circa 1906. (Public domain image)

Assembly of Model N Fords in pre–assembly line workstation format, on the third floor of the Piquette factory, 1906. (Public domain image)

Newspaper warning posted by ALAM (Association of Licensed Automobile Manufacturers) listing licensed automobile companies and threatening lawsuits if a non-ALAM car is purchased. (Public domain image)

10

Henry Does Not Change

THE MODEL T continued to dominate the American landscape in sales but not in innovation. In fact, with few exceptions, Henry Ford saw no reason to enhance his universal car. Instead, his focus remained on increasing production. Seven cars per day at Mack Avenue had grown to eighty cars per day at Piquette. Then the deluge hit, with 5,400 cars exiting Highland Park every twenty-four hours. On top of that production, Ford's manufacturing chief, Bill Knudsen, was overseeing the building of additional Ford plants across the United States and overseas. And, sales kept rising.

With the rebate-driven 1914 model year topping 300,000 Model Ts, Ford started work on his next production iteration, his "Fordism" master opus. He purchased property on the Rouge River near his estate at Fairlane and started planning the next Model T factory. Whereas Highland Park was considering sprawling at sixty-three acres, the Rouge factory would be labeled gargantuan, built on a thousand-acre footprint. The concept was raw materials in, finished cars out. The facility was 1.5 miles long with over ninety miles of railroad track. There were a total of ninety-three buildings, including separate steel, glass, tire, stamping, and power plants. Total floor area, all on one level, was fifteen million square feet. There were 53,000 machine tools on the plant floor. Ford had even purchased a fleet of ore boats that would bring raw materials from Lake Superior up the Rouge River basin to feed the massive plant. Yet despite all of this in-house production, Ford still retained over six thousand suppliers.

When it was finally operational, the plant employed 75,000 workers, a number that soon grew to over 100,000. The Rouge plant never fully assembled a Model T. For a while, it manufactured components for the Model T, but the cars themselves were still assembled at Highland Park. During World War I, the plant produced Eagle boats, boats that were designed by Ford's revered boss, Frank Kirby. After the war, Fordson tractors were built at the Rouge plant. The first automobile to roll out of Rouge was the Model A in 1928.

There was a significant backstory to the creation of the massive Rouge factory, one that had ramifications for capitalism in general and for Henry Ford in particular. The working relationship between Couzens and Ford had deteriorated, and in 1915 Couzens resigned. He had been the solid rock of the organization and was often a brake on Henry's worse impulses. With Couzens gone, Ford felt free to address one long-festering sore point—that the huge profits generated by the company continued to flow to the stockholders, particularly those that made no contribution to the company's success. He announced through his son Edsel that dividends would be significantly dialed back in 1916. Whereas the investors had been receiving 40–60 percent of the annual profits in dividends, Ford capped it at just 5 percent. With annual profits typically running $60 million or greater, that meant dividends would plummet from nearly $35 million to $3.2 million. Besides Henry's aversion to paying noncontributing owners, he also knew how much the Rouge plant was going to cost and concluded that the priority for profits must be the new factory.

One set of stockholders, the Dodge brothers, were not going to take this cut in dividends lying down. They sued. It was the height of brazenness. They had made well over $30 million in dividends in the years they had been supplying Ford. They had Ford Motor Company shares representing 10 percent of the company that were probably worth $100 million, given the estimated $1 billion valuation of the company. In addition, they had earned countless millions as a supplier to Ford, even admitting that they were often guilty of profiteering on those supplier contracts. And finally, they were two years into producing their own competitive automobile, a venture that was made possible by the millions earned from Ford. They also had an ulterior motive. The "confiscated" dividends would be going to build the largest, most efficient factory the world had ever seen. Once online, it would be that much more difficult for a Dodge automobile to compete with a Ford. They had fully supported the move to the Highland

Park plant, understanding that the sheer volume of Model T orders required such a factory. But the new plant was something else indeed. Henry Ford received the Dodge lawsuit the day after Edsel's wedding, an affair that John and Horace attended.

Their suit came to trial in 1916, and it was a highly contentious but riveting affair. At issue was the basic premise that capitalism is founded by and for the shareholders. In the courtroom, every effort was made by the plaintiff attorneys to cast Henry Ford as a country bumpkin who did not understand just how capitalism worked. They made fun of Ford's socialistic proclivities, such as the $5 day for workers and the passing of profits to customers via lower prices. Henry Ford certainly did not help his case on the stand, stating that his decision to build the Rouge plant stemmed from wanting to do "as much good as we can, everywhere, for everybody concerned . . . and incidentally to make money."[48]

The Dodge team made the case that the corporation was owned by all the shareholders. It was their money that Henry Ford was playing with. The trial ended with the Dodge position upheld. The judge ordered Ford to make an immediate $19 million payment in back dividends. He also enjoined Ford from building the Rouge plant. The plant injunction was unconscionable and was quickly invalidated by the Michigan Supreme Court, indicating that the court could not dictate company investments and strategy. However, the dividend payment ruling stood.

Ford went ahead and made the one-time dividend payment, but in his mind, that was not the end of it. The dividend decision reinforced his thinking that his 58 percent ownership of the Ford Motor Company was not enough. Years earlier, he had chafed under the direction of Alexander Malcolmson and his investors. At that time, he used the ruse of moving operations and profit to a new and separate company to cash them out and secured his current 58 percent stake. He decided to dust off the old trick and use it once again. Working through Edsel, he floated the idea that he would use the new company set up to build the Fordson tractor—Henry Ford and Son—to develop a "super" Model T. It would be priced at a half or a third of the current car and be far superior. This move would likely destroy the value of existing Ford Motor stock. Where the ruse with Ford Manufacturing was real, this was not.

Working through agents, each of the existing shareholders was contacted and offered a price for their shares. John Dodge, Horace Dodge, John Anderson, and Horace Rackham each agreed to a payment of $12.5 million.

James Couzens, who knew immediately what Henry was up to, held out and finally agreed to $30 million. Still, it was a decisive Ford victory. He had gained 100 percent of his company and at what turned out to be a bargain price. Based on a subsequent valuation of Ford Motor Company, the shares of the minority shareholders were worth at least four times what Henry Ford paid for them. It is reported that when he got word that he managed to buy out all the minority shareholders, he "danced a jig all around the room."

The total buyback came to $105 million. This amount plus the dividend award and the roughly $80 million costs of building the Rouge plant stretched even Henry Ford. At the same time, the recession of 1920–1921 had cut sharply into automobile sales. After making extensive cuts in his staff, Henry Ford was still forced to go to the banks, borrowing $75 million. As he had well learned from McGuffey readers in school years before, owing money was not a virtue. He loathed going to the banks with his tin cup. However, with the continued landslide success of the Model T, the bank loans were duly repaid within a year.

The Dodge lawsuit and courtroom circus that belittled Henry Ford had virtually no impact on his public image. He was the genius that put America on wheels. On the strength of his public image, Ford was encouraged to run for the US Senate in 1918. His opponent, Truman Newberry, spent the unheard-of sum of $176,000 on the election, though the legal limit was just $10,000. Henry, true to his McGuffey upbringing, spent next to nothing. He narrowly lost the election. In due time, Senator Newberry was threatened with impeachment for his election violations and resigned. The open Senate seat was filled by none other than James Couzens. Since leaving Ford, he had been Detroit's police commissioner and then mayor.

In an age where nearly two thousand automobile makers were jockeying for position and using innovation as a key edge, the lack of change in the Model T was nothing less than astonishing. In fact, the entire list of changes over the nearly twenty-year period could be summarized in a single paragraph. Granted, it is a long paragraph, but here goes:

The first 2,500 Model Ts produced after the 1908 debut were unique and relatively easy to identify. They were all maroon in color, had a water pump, and featured three transmission levers instead of two. With the 1910 model, all Model Ts were now Brewster green. The 1911s were completely restyled, with new fenders, a new radiator, new wheels, new bodies, and a new engine, and were now dark blue in color. The Ford emblem on the radiator no longer had wings. The bulb horn on the 1912 model had just a single twist instead of a double twist. In 1913 the cars were dark blue with black fenders. The year 1914 was the first that all Model Ts were black. The 1915 models finally eliminated the gas headlights and powered the horn and lights with the magneto. The big change in 1917 was the elimination of brass all around the car (a milestone only because early automobiles were said to be of the "brass era"). The 1919 models finally came with a battery and electric starter and lights. The dash now had an ammeter and ignition switch. The wheels finally had demountable rims like every other car. The years 1923, 1924, and 1925 saw minor styling changes and colors were reintroduced, though the final tally showed about eleven million of the fifteen million Model Ts left the plant painted black. The 1925 Model T cars also underwent a major styling revamp. The car was redesigned to look more like the Lincoln. Though this list is not exhaustive, it does demonstrate just how little Henry Ford changed the car through its nearly twenty years of production. Of course, the major change made throughout the years was in price, with an $850 car ending up costing just $290.

Meanwhile, the car industry was not standing still. Fierce competition led to a steady stream of innovations. Most automobiles had made the switch from planetary to sliding gear transmissions. Engines underwent all manner of changes, including higher compression and more cylinders. Duco paint introduced a broad array of color choices, even including a two-tone Oldsmobile in 1923. Closed bodies, balloon tires, and greater luxury appointments soon found their way into competing cars. Because of Alfred Sloan's central philosophy of constantly moving car buyers up the value chain, General Motors took the lead in making changes, starting at the top with Cadillac and filtering down to the other makes.

Solving the hand-crank problem was a major industry at the time, deploying a range of different solutions to start the engine, some quite Rube Goldberg in nature. By 1911, over sixty different automobile makes had a replacement for the hand crank, variously using compressed air, explosive gas, springs, levers, pedals, and finally, electric motors. In the compressed air approach, an air storage tank fed into mechanics that turned the crankshaft and started the cylinders. Since most cars at the time used acetylene for lights, a second method tapped into those tanks and fed explosive gas directly into the cylinders. The simplest methods were mechanical in nature, where combinations of springs and levers were deployed to mimic turning the hand crank. Some of these were so elaborate that one could sit inside the automobile and get the car running.

Though eliminating the hand crank had been an issue for years, it was a deadly accident that set in motion the eventual solution. In 1908 a woman driving a Cadillac in the Michigan winter had the engine stall. She did not have the strength to pull the crank and get it restarted. Another motorist, Byron Carter, stopped to help. When he yanked the crank, the engine backfired and the crank violently recoiled and struck him in the face. He was seriously wounded, then infection set in and he died. Byron Carter happened to be the founder of the CarterCar Company as well as a close friend of Henry Leland.

With the news of Carter's death, replacing the crank became an immediate priority with Leland. He had heard of Charles Kettering's work with electric motors and sought him out. Kettering was a prolific inventor and engineer who had gotten his start at National Cash Register (NCR), where he developed a small electric motor that provided automation for the cash registers. He left NCR and founded Dayton Engineering Labs (Delco) in 1909. Working with Leland, he developed the modern starter system, with an electric motor that doubled as a generator. When starting was activated, it drew current from the battery and turned the crankshaft. When the car was running, the motor switched to generation and recharged the battery. The Kettering electric starter debuted on the 1912 Cadillac. Electric starters would become widespread within a few years. They would also hasten the death of electric automobiles. It should be noted that Billy Durant purchased all of the companies involved in the first electric starter—Cadillac and CarterCar in 1909 and Delco in 1918.

After Charles Kettering sold his company to Billy Durant in 1918, he assumed overall charge of General Motor's engineering work. In an early project, he teamed up with DuPont to develop Duco paints, formulations that provided a wealth of hues and, more importantly, dried fast and thus sped up car production.

In another project, he sought to find an additive that would eliminate engine knock when using the available low-octane gasoline with GM's higher and higher compression engines. He could have potentially used ethanol for the purpose, but ethanol could not be patented. Instead, he decided on a unique lead compound called tetraethyl lead. GM and Standard Oil formed the Ethyl Corporation in 1921 to sell it, subcontracting the production to DuPont. Though the lead compound was dangerous and led to a number of deaths in its handling, GM and Kettering were undeterred. In fact, Kettering hired a medical expert to declare it safe for automotive use. Unfortunately, fifty years of leaded gasoline left a very painful legacy.[49]

Despite the rapidly shifting automobile landscape, Henry Ford resisted. He was not adverse to certain kinds of innovation. When safety glass came out, Ford adopted it immediately. Even so, Ford ignored most other calls for changes. His dealers continually pressed for enhancements to the Model T. They knew it was becoming an outmoded design, with no shocks, water pump, oil pump, gas gauge, or demountable tires. It had the awkward planetary transmission with just two forward gears. Until very late in the Model T's run, a person was still required to run back and forth between the hand crank at the front and spark lever at the wheel in order to start and smooth the engine.

Ford was not even amenable to simple changes. His thinking was that if he set the price low enough, he could still sell millions, so "why change"? But, with the continued pace of innovation of other automobile companies, the genie was out of the bottle. Tastes had changed. Huge swaths of first-time car buyers were ready for more style, more color, easier starting, and easier shifting. Most ominously, existing Model T owners were simply not going to buy another Model T, regardless of price. This was especially true after they got a look at their neighbor's far superior new car.

Two influential individuals who tried to change Henry Ford's mind about the Model T were his son Edsel and Bill Knudsen. Knudsen had moved with the Keim Company to Detroit in 1913 and soon became the master builder of Ford plants. One of the designers of assembly lines and the "Fordism" mass production concept, Knudsen had grown increasingly irritated at Henry's countermanding of his decisions. While his fellow Dane Charles Sorensen was much more accommodating with Ford, Knudsen was not. In 1921 he resigned. He was just one of many larger-than-life individuals that had made the Ford Motor Company successful. Yet Henry Ford was used to being in charge and, most importantly, receiving all the credit for the company's success. This inevitably led to the resignations or firings of key people. Ford admitted as much by saying that Knudsen was "too good" to keep around. That "too good" label could be applied to a long list of key individuals that included Knudsen, Couzens, Wills, and even the Dodge brothers.

Knudsen did not mope after he left Ford but made sure that Henry paid the price. He was hired almost immediately by Alfred P. Sloan of General Motors. Big Bill set to work on building up Chevrolet as the superior brand to Henry's Model T. He became president of the division in 1924 and succeeded in unseating Ford as the number-one car brand by 1928, although he had an assist from Ford with the delays in launching the Ford Model A.

Whereas Ford had outsold Chevrolet by a margin of thirteen to one in 1921, Knudsen's Chevrolet division sold over a million cars to Ford's 600,000 for the 1928 model year. Knudsen continued to drive GM excellence. From 1927 to 1937, Ford lost a total of $100 million while Chevrolet earned $692 million. Henry Ford may not have even been aware of the extent of his losses, forgoing accountants and auditors as he did. The depths of the losses were not clear until Henry Ford II took over and had the wartime "Whiz Kids" do an analysis on Ford's profit and loss during the Depression years.

The "too good" label did not apply to Edsel Ford. If anything, Henry thought that Edsel was never good enough. Edsel was born in 1893, an only son, named after one of Henry's schoolmates. He was clearly groomed early on to take over the company, becoming president at age twenty-seven. But, he was president in name only. Most decisions remained with Henry. Edsel was a car guy and a very able one, knowledgeable about the latest styles and innovations. When Lincoln Motors ran into financial trouble in 1921, Edsel convinced Henry to buy the company. It was a win for Edsel though Henry may have acted on the idea simply because Lincoln was Henry Leland's company, and this was payback for Ford for Leland's treachery back in 1902. Other Edsel moves did not fare as well. When Edsel had ground broken for a new administrative building, Henry abruptly canceled it. And, when Edsel produced a prototype replacement for the Model T, Henry cruelly destroyed the car with a sledge hammer. It was hard to understand the sheer malevolence of Edsel's treatment by his father.

Yet, Edsel did finally convince Henry to move on from the Model T. He was instrumental in the design of the 1926 Lincoln and used many of the styling touches there with the Model A. Edsel was essentially the entire styling department at Ford, as a styling department was not needed when one produced the exact same automobile for twenty years.

When William Knudsen resigned in 1921, Ford still sold 57 percent of all automobiles in the United States. By 1926 the car market has seemingly passed Ford by. Buyers were looking for closed-body cars, annual models, the latest technologies, and most of all, choice. Henry Ford finally came to the realization that the universal car had reached the end of the road in August 1926. Working with Edsel, an all-new Ford was designed and produced within just sixteen months. Since Henry Ford spurned accounting, he had no idea how much was spent on the development of the Model A. A later estimation pegged the investment at $250 million, or roughly $2 billion in today's dollars.

Called the "Baby Lincoln", the Ford Model A featured everything that the Model T was missing—a closed body, a powerful four-cylinder 40 horsepower engine that moved the car at 65 mph, a three-speed sliding gear transmission, four-wheel hydraulic brakes, hydraulic shocks, battery start, and of course, Lincoln styling. *Automotive Industries* commented, "Ford has done what many doubted he would be able to do—he has brought out a really modern car, involving a complete rebuilding of his production organization, at a price scarcely exceeding that of the Model T." That price was just $495! The Model A was announced in December 1927. It was estimated that a quarter of all Americans saw the car in the first week. There were 400,000 orders (with 50 percent cash down) in the first two weeks. By January, that number had grown to 600,000 orders on the Ford books. The Model A could be ordered in four new colors — Niagara Blue, Arabian Sand, Dawn Gray, and Gunmetal Blue. You could still go for black, though.

The plan to shift from Model T production to Model A was not handled well. No, it was downright catastrophic. The Model A was to be produced at the Rouge River facility. Many of the machine tools at Highland Park were specific to the Model T and had to be rebuilt or replaced for the new car. In addition, the Model A was a dramatically more complex vehicle. Besides the massive retooling effort, assembly line changes were required at Rouge to change it from a plant making components to a plant producing finished automobiles. Rouge was down for six months. That was six months without producing a single car while there were 600,000 buyers waiting for delivery. It was estimated that the cost to Ford in retooling, lost sales, and idle workers exceeded $100 million.[50]

In contrast, Bill Knudsen was able to roll out a new Chevrolet featuring a completely new six-cylinder engine the following year with only a six-week hiatus in production. Ford did finally get Rouge running smoothly, and 1929 was Ford's year, selling 1.5 million Model As to Chevrolet's one million.

11

Trading Up to Buick

S HORTLY AFTER MOVING to the French Grove farm, Will and Verne started a family. John Reed Shaffer was born in 1915, delivered by Dr. David Morton.[51] Of course, Dr. Morton made the house call in his 1911 Maxwell automobile, the Doctor Maxwell model. Two years later, he was back, this time delivering another boy, Paul Franklin Shaffer. A third trip to the farm in 1921 produced Margaretta Louis Shaffer, who was forever known as Detta Lou.

Additional help was secured for Verne with the hiring of Mabel Clinch. Born in Kent, England, and settling in Elmwood with her parents, Mabel helped with the chores and the family. She would later marry Ralph Mott, who owned the neighboring farm, and continue to be a friend of the family until she died, never having lost her English accent.

The farm operation was going well, and in 1922, Will and Verne decided to expand the acreage. They purchased 73 acres across Elmore Road south and west of the farmhouse. The purchase was from William C. Reed, Verne's uncle. The price was $10,500, or $144 per acre. This was a Reed family bargain as farms in earlier years had sold for well over $200 per acre. The purchase brought their farm to 233 acres.

The Reed school was a mile south of the farm at the corner of Elmore and Forney Roads, a slightly shorter distance than the French Grove School to the north. Brimfield Township had nine schoolhouses across its thirty-six square miles, with the Reed school in the northwest corner. The original schoolhouse was built in 1869 in the Tucker farm orchard, constructed out of rough-hewn logs. It had poor lighting and was hard to heat. Miss Eliza

Tucker took the first turn as schoolhouse teacher. A new building was put up in 1884 that would last over sixty years.

Six-year-old John Shaffer started walking to the Reed school in 1921. Younger brother Paul tried to tag along, but teacher Marie Cole made sure that did not last long. As with most one-room schoolhouses, there were eight grades and one teacher. Average attendance at the time was about thirty students. The school teachers were mostly women, mostly young and unmarried. They generally did not last for more than a couple of years. It was a very demanding job.

The layout of most one-room schools was standard: a cloak room in the back, near the entry, and a wood or coal stove at the front of the room near the teacher's desk. The front of the room had a large blackboard and a pull-down map of the United States. All the students packed lunches, usually in pails. There were separate outhouses for boys and girls. A flag pole was set in front of the building. The only play equipment was a swing set.

The school day was 9 a.m. to 4 p.m. The syllabus leaned toward character and citizenship in addition to the basic subjects of English, math, history, and geography. McGuffey readers were still typically used. The youngest students were called "abecedarians" because they were still learning their ABCs. The group that the teacher was currently instructing would move to the front desks. The older students were expected to help the teacher by working with the younger ones. Boys were usually absent during spring plowing and fall harvest. Graduation was a big deal. There was an entrance test to continue on to high school, and it was not easy.

Paul started at the Reed school in 1922, one of only two students in his grade. The other student was also named Paul—Paul Reed, his first cousin. Della Perrill was the new teacher. She was only eighteen. The local schoolhouse was also a community center, and the Reed school was no exception. There were school events—recitations, plays, commencements. There were also monthly social events such as potluck suppers. The teacher leaned on the local parents to organize most of the social events.

Will's Model T was not going to survive a growing family. It had served Will and Verne well at first but was too small to handle a family of five, besides being more and more outmoded thanks to Henry Ford's obstinacy. Verne was pregnant with Detta Lou when Will began looking for a replacement car. By 1921, the field of automobiles had seriously thinned out. The leading brands in 1920 were Ford, Chevrolet, Dodge, and Buick. The timing was not good, at least for the car companies. A recession started in

1920 and lasted well into the next year. Chevrolet was still focused on going toe-to-toe with the Model T while GM positioned Buick as a step up.

But, when Will compared the Buick with the Ford, it seemed more like a giant leap than a simple "step up." The Buick was powered by a six-cylinder, 242 cubic inch engine generating 60 horsepower with a top speed of 55 mph. The Buick had all the current mechanicals: sliding gear transmission, mechanical brakes, electric start, and electric headlights. It had a modern driving layout with clutch, brake, and accelerator pedals along with the three-speed stick shift. Most of all, it was a much larger car, 3,000 pounds versus the Model T's 1,200 pounds, that could handle the larger family.

To combat the economic slump of 1920–1921, Buick announced price reductions in June 1921. The five-passenger touring car that Will was interested in went from $1,795 to $1,495. At the same time, the Model T was selling for an unheard of $319, and Kelly Supply had recently announced that it had sold nearly fifty Model Ts in the last six months alone. But, it was a measure of the strength of Will and Verne's farm operation that they were seriously looking at a car at roughly five times that price. Will and Verne went ahead with the purchase of the 1921 Buick. His decision, along with countless similar ones across the country, laid bare the folly of Henry Ford's having the Model T overstay its welcome.

The original force behind the Buick car was its namesake, David Dunbar Buick. Born in Scotland, he came to the United States at age two with his family, who settled in Detroit. He left the city at age eleven to work on a farm but quickly came to the same conclusion about farm toil as Henry Ford. He returned to the city and secured an apprenticeship at Alexander Manufacturing, a maker of brass plumbing fixtures. Buick left for a brief spell to work at the James Flower and Brothers Machine Shop, rising to foreman. This was roughly a decade before Henry Ford walked in the door at the same shop.

Buick returned to Alexander Manufacturing and proceeded to develop a number of innovations. The most lucrative one was a process to bond porcelain to cast iron, paving the way for white bathtubs. When the company experienced a financial downturn in 1882, Buick and a partner (William Sherwood) acquired the assets and renamed the company Buick and Sherwood.

Despite his early success, Buick grew bored with the business, sold his interest in the plumbing company for $100,000, and started tinkering with L-head gasoline engines. He formed the Buick Power Company with the goal of making gasoline engines for farm and marine use. About the same time, he also started working on an automobile.

In 1898, in what would prove a stroke of good fortune, he met Walter Marr, a former bicycle mechanic and self-taught engineer. Together, they completed a first automobile a year later in the shed behind Buick's house, and deemed it the Buick Model A. It was a basic buckboard carriage powered by a single-cylinder engine and steered via a tiller. Buick and Marr were frequently at odds, and Marr eventually left. Buick then hired Eugene Richard to replace him. Between the collaboration of Buick, Marr, and Richard, a "valve-in-head" engine was developed, or what would come to be called the overhead valve engine. With the valves repositioned at the top of the cylinder, the engine provided greater horsepower for equivalent cylinder displacements.

During this time, Buick and his small team had been building and perfecting cars but not selling any. He had run through his small fortune and needed additional financing to continue. He received an infusion from the Briscoe Brothers in exchange for a controlling ownership stake. Buick continued to plod along, producing just two Model A cars. The Briscoes got cold feet and sold the company to a carriage maker, James Whiting of Flint Wagon Works. Buick's team completed the first Flint Buick, the Model B. It was a pretty conventional two-cylinder automobile with a planetary transmission and right-hand steering. Those two "valve-in-head" cylinders produced an amazing 22 horsepower, showing the value of the engine design. Walter Marr and Buick's son James drove it to Detroit and back. Yet, with no James Couzens on hand to prod him on, Buick was only able to manufacture thirty-seven Model B automobiles in all of 1904.

Whiting threw in the towel and sold the Buick Company to another Flint wagon maker, William "Billy" Durant, certainly one of the most colorful and consequential of all the automotive pioneers. Though small in stature—he was called "Billy" throughout his life—he loomed large in automotive history. What he lacked in height, he made up for in vision, drive, work ethic, stock "inventiveness," and most of all, salesmanship.

Durant's maternal grandfather, Henry Crapo, had made fortunes in New England whaling and then in Flint lumber. His father was the Flint mayor before becoming governor of Michigan. Durant left school at age sixteen and worked a string of jobs before becoming manager of Flint Water Works at just twenty. Quickly becoming bored there, he moved on to insurance, an industry that was split into many small agencies spread all over the state.

Here, Durant applied his selling skills and honed his stock skills, buying agencies and stitching them together to produce the largest insurance operation in the state. It was his first lesson in the value of bigness. A chance encounter with an individual who had designed a new buggy led Durant into the carriage business. With partner Dallas Dort, he formed Durant-Dort in 1885.[52] Durant handled sales, Dort handled the finances, and they contracted out most of the manufacturing. By 1900, the company was the largest carriage maker in the country, selling 500,000 buggies a year.

Being in horse-drawn carriages, Durant was initially unimpressed by the automobile. Yet, his view changed when a fellow carriage maker approached in 1904 with the opportunity to acquire the Buick operation. Durant and Dort jumped in. Durant immediately pushed David Buick and his team to complete the Buick Model C. With the new car ready, Durant attended the 1905 New York auto show, returning to Flint with over 1,100 orders. He proceeded to push the factory to build 750 cars. And, he was just getting started. He signed up his carriage dealers as Buick dealers and rapidly ramped up sales—1,400 in 1906, 4,641 in 1907, and 8,820 in 1908. That put Buick at number two in the country, just behind Ford.

David Buick got lost in this flurry of activity and his health was declining. By 1909 he conceded that he was no longer in control of the company he created. He accepted $100,000 in cash, shares of stock, and a promissory note to pay his salary ($100,000 annually) for the rest of his life from Durant, and left. His later years were not kind. He sold his GM stock to finance Buick Oil, an investment in California that went bankrupt. Durant and his new General Motors Company reneged on the salary agreement, stopping payment after several years.

By 1923 over a million Buicks had been sold. David Buick had been around for only the first 120. The GM stock he received would have been worth well in excess of $20 million had he kept it. Though a towering pioneer of the American automobile, he completely disappeared from view. As this was somewhat of a mystery, the journalist Bruce Catton (later a renowned Civil War historian) decided to track him down. This was not an easy task as Buick was by then in Detroit, penniless, and with no listed address or phone, living in a rundown apartment. Buick sat down for an interview with Catton in 1928. He was just barely making it, living month to month. He had approached many of his friends from the early automobile days, most of whom were millionaires many times over, for any kind of job. He received no response. He was currently an instructor at the Detroit

School of Trades, who proclaimed in a *Popular Mechanics* advertisement, "Let BUICK HIMSELF train you quick for big pay auto jobs." Buick died the following year at age seventy-five.

Meanwhile, Durant continued to grow Buick with the Model 10, a car very similar to the Model T. The four-cylinder car continued to feature the "valve-in-head" design for superior performance. It was marketed for "men with real red blood who don't like to eat dust." It reached sales of thirty thousand in 1910. Durant had not forgotten the lessons learned with insurance and carriages. He aimed to get big and get big fast. He incorporated General Motors in 1908 and went on a buying spree, acquiring a slew of car companies (Cadillac, Olds, Oakland, CarterCar, Elmore, Ewing, Marquette, Ranier, and Welch) and truck concerns (Rapid, Reliance). He also expanded up the supply chain into automotive parts, buying Champion, Dayton Engineering (Delco), and Hyatt Ball Bearings. The latter addition made its owners, Alfred P. Sloan and his father, millionaires. It also brought young Sloan on board as a General Motors employee. Most of these companies were acquired with stock. For example, Durant bought Olds for $3 million but only supplied $17,000 in cash. The lone exception was Henry Leland, who held out for $4.4 million in cash, plus GM stock and an agreement to keep running Cadillac. This arrangement only lasted until 1918, when Leland wanted to produce Liberty aircraft engines for the war effort. Durant refused; Leland left Cadillac, formed Lincoln Motors, and proceeded to build the Liberty engines.

Billy Durant was not one to linger over a business issue. When the newly acquired Oldsmobile team was looking for help in creating a new model for 1909, Durant had a Buick Model 10 sent from Flint to Lansing. He arrived at the Lansing factory and had the wood-framed Buick sawed in quarters crosswise and lengthwise. A few inches were shaved off both dimensions, the frame was reassembled, and what emerged was the 1909 Olds Model 20.

By 1910, Buick and Cadillac were doing well. General Motors had secured 25 percent of the US car market. But, with the breadth of his holdings, Durant was woefully overstretched financially. The banks finally forced the issue. They would supply emergency financing only if Durant resigned—which he did. Durant, by the way, did not leave empty-handed. He had a pile of GM stock and more grandiose plans.

Durant's head at Buick, Charles Nash, was promoted to run GM, and another very famous automotive pioneer was tapped to take over Buick:

Walter P. Chrysler. A surprising figure among car pioneers, Chrysler was not involved in bicycles, gas engines, or even wagons. Instead, he was a steam man. His forebears had emigrated from Germany in 1710, part of the second wave of Palatine emigrations. His father, Henry, moved to Kansas when the Homestead Act opened up the territory and began work as an engineer for the Union Pacific Railroad. Walter grew up in Kansas working odd jobs until he secured an apprenticeship with the railroad at 5 cents per hour. He was very mechanically minded. As a teen, he had read *Scientific American* cover to cover, which included features on the new Otto and Daimler gasoline engines. Yet, he continued with the Union Pacific Railroad, becoming an expert in repairing steam engines. He also happened to have charismatic people skills and rose through the ranks quickly, culminating in 1906 with the position of superintendent of the Chicago Railroad. His earnings had gone from 5 cents an hour to $2,000 a year.

While stationed in Chicago, Chrysler attended the city's 1908 auto show on the streets of Automobile Row. He spotted a beautiful Locomobile touring car, ivory with red leather interior. With only $700 in the bank and a wife and two kids to support, he should have taken a pass. But, he took out a loan and purchased the $5,000 automobile (roughly $145,000 in 2020 dollars). Chrysler drove it home and proceeded to disassemble and reassemble the car at least eight times in order to understand how it worked. Still in debt, he bought a second car, a Stevens-Duryea (this was pioneering engineer Frank Duryea's company).

Walter Chrysler was torn between his steam past and his new passion for automobiles. Wanting to get into manufacturing, he quit the Chicago Railroad and was hired by American Locomotive in Pittsburgh as its manufacturing manager at a salary of $8,000 per year. It turned out that American Locomotive had dabbled in automobiles. The company had secured a license to build the French Berliet automobile in its Providence, Rhode Island, factory. Its engineers soon thought they could build a better car, and they proceeded to design and build the most expensive car in the country, selling for more than $7,000. Called the Alco, each car was hand built. It was a point of pride that the assembly of each car took nineteen months. Unfortunately, after producing five thousand cars, management realized that they were losing nearly $500 on each one. In 1913, they wisely went back to building steam locomotives.

Chrysler was managing the manufacture of the company's steam locomotives in Pittsburgh. Here, he grew his formidable engineering and people skills with the addition of manufacturing know-how. Keeping detailed notes on the manufacturing process, he developed his own system of continuous improvement.

In 1912 James Storrow, who happened to be on the board of both General Motors and American Locomotive, suggested Chrysler as a manufacturing manager at Buick. Jumping at the opportunity, Walter took a 50 percent pay cut to move to Buick. It was his chance to get into the automobile industry. Relocating to Flint, Chrysler applied his manufacturing system to Buick production, dramatically boosting efficiency and profit at Buick plants. Car production went from 45/day to 560/day. His salary was raised to $25,000 per year. Buick continued as the number-three or number-four carmaker throughout the teens.

Billy Durant was not gone from the automotive scene for long. He formulated a plan to get back, and get back in a most surprising way. His first step was to start a new automobile company. Durant had used a Swiss racer named Louis Chevrolet to promote his Buick cars. Durant enticed Chevrolet to join him in developing a new car, even agreeing to name the new car the Chevrolet. Durant was leery about the upscale, high-performance car that Chevrolet designed. In 1911 he opted to release two new car brands at once, the Chevrolet and the Little, the latter based on a Flint friend's design. The Chevrolet was big and sturdy and sold for more than $2,000. The Little was cheap, of very poor quality, and would not last very long on the road.[53] Neither car sold well.

Durant quickly realized his mistake and modified his approach. His revised thinking was simple. The Model T was the most purchased US automobile but was not aging well. Durant would use the cachet of Chevrolet's name and go directly after the Model T's price point but with a superior car. He combined the best attributes of the Little and the Chevrolet and launched the Chevrolet Series H in 1914. Initially, he offered the Chevrolet Baby Grand touring car at $875 and the Royal Mail roadster at $750. This was purely an intermediate move. The following year, he stripped down the H models to create a true Model T fighter he called the Chevrolet 490. The 490 happened to be the current price of a Model T, a not so subtle dig at Henry Ford. Launched in 1915, the Chevrolet 490 was an immediate success. It featured a three-speed sliding gear transmission, a bigger engine, full dash instrumentation, and electric starter and lights. Other manufacturers such as Maxwell had tried to go toe-to-toe with Ford but forgot they needed to offer something over and above just price. Of course, Louis

Chevrolet was appalled that his name was attached to a low-end Model T competitor. He promptly returned to Switzerland.

Developing a successful car was only the first part of Durant's game plan. Enlisting the financial clout of the DuPonts, he offered five shares of the new but rapidly rising Chevrolet stock in exchange for one share of GM stock. Along with DuPont GM investments, he surreptitiously amassed over 50 percent of the General Motors stock—and suddenly he was back in control. He offered Charles Nash, his old associate and current president of GM, $1 million a year to stay on, but Nash had had enough of Billy Durant and resigned.

One of Durant's first actions was to promote Walter Chrysler to general manager of Buick at $500,000 per year. He also threw in a significant slice of GM stock. Chrysler continued his good work at Buick, growing annual sales from 40,000 to 120,000. Durant raised his salary to $600,000 the following year. Yet, working for Durant was tough, and Chrysler quit in 1919 amid disagreements. He left, however, with $10 million in GM stock and the budding thought to have his own automobile company someday.

Meanwhile, Durant reverted to his old reliable playbook and went on another buying binge. Perhaps because Henry Ford had just announced his Fordson tractor, Durant bought two tractor companies to get into the action. Those ventures rather quickly lost $30 million. By 1920, the banks led by the DuPont consortium paid $23 million for his GM shares, with the now familiar stipulation that he immediately walk out the door.

This amazingly was not the end of the Billy Durant story. Within weeks, he floated a large stock offering for a new company called—what else—Durant Motors. Buoyed by his reputation, the stock was wildly successful and he was right back in the car business. He set about creating another GM-like automobile giant with each of the car segments covered. For his top of the line, he purchased Locomobile, a once-proud, high-end company that was now on its last legs. For the Buick slot, he announced the Flint automobile. For the Olds and Pontiac slots, he rolled out the eponymous Durant car. In this frenzied buildup, Durant had spent $5.2 million to outbid Walter Chrysler for the former Dusenberg and Willys factory in Elizabeth, New Jersey. Walter Chrysler had been busy with an engineering team developing a new six-cylinder car. Durant did not acquire the engineers but purchased their initial plans for the six-cylinder car. This became the Durant.

As for his entry car line, a Model T and Chevrolet competitor, he announced the Star. This automobile, though a completely assembled car, was an immediate success. This was evident even locally in Brimfield when Cliff Bundy, formerly a salesman at Kelly Supply, opened a Star agency. Meanwhile, Durant, as usual, had overextended himself for yet a third time, with too many car lines, too many factories, and too many companies. The Star, Locomobile, and Flint only survived until 1928, when Durant pulled the plug on those car lines. With the stock market crash in 1929, Durant pumped $90 million of his own money in an attempt to save what was left of Durant Motors, but his timing couldn't have been worse. Auto sales heading into the Great Depression plummeted. The Durant motorcar lasted until 1932, at which time Durant Motors was liquidated. Billy Durant filed for bankruptcy in 1936. At age seventy-five, he opened a supermarket in New Jersey. Four years later, he was back in Flint opening a bowling alley with typical expansive "Durant" plans to expand to thirty locations. He dabbled in cinnabar mines and hair tonic before declining health forced him to spend his waning days with his wife in a New York City apartment. He died in March 1947.

When Durant was forced out in 1920, the DuPonts struggled to find the right team to run GM. Alfred P. Sloan, who was a supplier for Henry Ford when he was with Hyatt Ball Bearings, was a General Motors vice president. He conducted an extensive study of GM and put together an analysis that described in essence his conception of the modern corporation. The DuPonts were impressed, and Sloan was promoted to GM president in 1923. Sloan continued the multiple-division approach started by Durant but avoided Durant's scattergun management style. Each brand had to address a precisely defined price segment and be held accountable for success in that segment. Chevrolet was the entry point, with cars priced at $600–$795; Pontiac was next, at $900–$1,200; then Olds, at $1,200–$1,700; Buick, at $1,700–$2,500; and finally Cadillac, at $2,500-$5,000.

Besides structuring GM's product line, Sloan also introduced a stream of innovations in running the car business. Among these were trade-ins, buying on credit, and, most insidious of all for Henry Ford, the annual model change. An essential ingredient to the annual model change was styling. Of course, Henry Ford had gone nearly twenty years without a whiff of a styling change. Sloan, in contrast, was completely open to styling changes and in fact, institutionalized them.

A key tipping point for GM styling occurred when word reached Lawrence Fisher, the head of the Cadillac division, of an order for a hundred Cadillacs from a customizing shop in California. Fisher traveled to

Hollywood and saw firsthand the expensive restyling treatments being given Cadillacs, Marmons, and Chandlers for the Hollywood elite. He met with Harley Earl, a 6' 6" former track athlete at USC, who was running the design operation in his father's shop. Suitably impressed, Fisher returned to Detroit and encouraged Sloan to hire Harley for an upcoming project, designing the new LaSalle automobile. This was a new brand designed to fit in the widening slot between the Buick and Cadillac. Sloan agreed, and in January 1926, Harley was on a train to Detroit. General Motors styling would never be the same.

▷ ▷ ▷

Heading into 1923, things were going well for Will and Verne on the French Grove farm. The golden age of agriculture had only slightly dimmed due to the mild recession in 1920–1921. On Christmas Eve 1922, Dr. Morton motored up the hill to the farmhouse and assisted as Verne delivered the fourth member of the family, a son. He would be Will's namesake—William Caldwell Shaffer Jr.

In midwinter, Will was working on expanding his Poland China hogs for the coming year. There was a hog sale in Brimfield put on by H. E. "Cap" Chichester, a local dealer and master breeder. Will was especially interested in Cap's prize-winning boar named Rainbow Master, which had sired a litter of young boars and sows that were up for sale.

On Monday, February 5, 1923, Will cranked up the TT and headed into Brimfield. It was early in the morning, with a low sun glinting through the dirty windows of the truck. Even with clean windows, the cab had limited visibility. The noise of the TT engine drowned out most other sounds. The Burlington railroad came straight into town, crossing Knoxville Road at Adams Street. The road crossing was at an angle and unlike the main lines in Williamsfield and Elmwood, this was a spur line with very infrequent trains. As he motored down Knoxville Avenue into town, Will neither saw the train approaching to his left nor heard the whistle. The oncoming train struck the truck broadside and carried it down the tracks. The truck's cab was mostly intact and Will had very few scratches. But, he had been killed instantly on impact by massive head trauma.

Trains and automobiles did not fully coexist in the 1920s. Virtually all crossings between the train line and the road were at grade. Will was very familiar with train crossings in Williamsfield, as the farm was south of the

Santa Fe line and required crossing the tracks just to get into town. But, the Santa Fe was a major line with double tracks, not a spur. Trains passed each way many times each day at high speed. You were constantly aware and thus careful. Despite this, there were accidents even here. George Gipson was killed by a passenger train in Dahinda, just west of town. And several years later there was a horrific accident at the crossing where a family of four proceeded to cross the tracks after a train passed in one direction, not seeing another train barreling down at 60 mph coming from the other direction. This led to the conversion of the Williamsfield crossing to an underpass.

The Burlington railroad had improved the crossing in Brimfield in 1921, but there was still no crossing gate or signals. By 1923, Illinois had nearly a million cars. And, these were vehicles that traveled far faster than horse-drawn wagons, and had far less time to react at crossings. In addition, drivers in cars had a smaller field of vision than someone on foot or sitting high on a wagon. And in an enclosed car, they were much more insulated from the train's whistle. The Model TT truck was significantly worse in this respect.

Both the railroads and public officials were slow to react to the impending conflict. Will's death in a train collision was tragic but not unique in these times. That same year in Chicago, a new crossing signal that illuminated a "Stop" sign when a train was approaching was being tested. Such a system, if widely deployed, might have saved Will's life. The previous year, an entire family was killed crossing a train junction in Galesburg. The Burlington line then surveyed that particular crossing, finding that of a total of 1,500 automobiles that crossed, only two stopped before proceeding. Shortly after, the Sidney Beamer family of Laura was killed when their Studebaker collided with a Burlington train near town.

The bottom line was that the railroads lacked motivation to change. It was easier to make payments to victims than revamp all of their grade crossings. The Burlington railroad paid $1,000 to each surviving member of the Shaffer family. But that did not bring back Will. He was gone.

12

Dealing with Adversity

WILL'S DEATH WAS a shock to the community. The *Brimfield News* lauded Will as "one of the best young farmers," one who was "held in high esteem" and "known for his genial nature, upright character, readiness to help others, and ability." The Elmwood paper wrote that Will "was much loved by all who knew him. He had a smile for everyone. His love for his splendid young family was very evident."

A young family indeed. Verne was left with four young children. The youngest, William, was just six weeks old. And there was the farm to manage, a farm that Will and Verne had only just recently expanded. BF took Will's death especially hard. He was in Fairhope, Alabama, for physical therapy when Will was killed. He died the following year. Much like his wife Sarah before him, he was unable to cope with the loss of a child.

Without Will, Verne had little option but to rent the farm and move into town. First she had to arrange for an estate auction. And, it was a sizeable auction. There were thirteen horses, ten averaging 1,400 pounds plus two colts and a mare with a foal, along with three sets of work harnesses for the horses. They had forty-five head of cattle plus two milk cows, a Jersey and a Swiss. There were sixty-five hogs, a mixture of Poland China and Hampshire, doubly treated for cholera, along with the seventeen hog houses, a hog waterer, and several galvanized tanks. There were two horse wagons and two truck wagons. An extensive array of farm implements including single, gang, and sulky and walking plows, harrow and disk pulverizers, a manure spreader, seed planters, and five different cultivators. Harvesting tools included a hay rake, hay binder, hay loader, and corn elevator. There was a 4 horsepower Cushman gasoline engine and a gasoline storage drum. Finally, the auction list included seed, grain, and hay that had been recently bought and stored, ready for the upcoming season.

The auction at the farm, held on February 25, 1923, was a financial success.[54] The Brimfield newspaper described it as "one of the largest sales of the season" with an "immense crowd." The auction dramatically illustrated what Will and Verne had accomplished in their short time farming at French Grove. Yet, it had to be very tough on Verne to see the fruits of their enterprise carted off at the end of the day. And to be constantly reminded with each bang of the gavel that her life partner was no longer there.

Given the high price of farm acreage, there was no shortage of local farmers looking to rent land. The farm was quickly rented and the family moved into Elmwood. Verne borrowed against the farm to purchase a Victorian house on the corner of Butternut and Magnolia. The price was $3,500. With rental income coming in she was able do extensive remodeling, adding a large bedroom for the boys, a sewing room, a tornado cave in the basement, and a wrap-around front porch. When completed, the house represented quite a contrast with the 1850 farmhouse at French Grove. It was relatively new, spacious, and most importantly, had indoor plumbing. In addition, it was not isolated. It was right in the middle of town.

Parked in front of the house was the 1921 Buick touring car. Verne did not drive, but that would have to change. She enlisted her first cousin Dan McCoy to teach her how to drive the Buick. Dan, a stout young man, had inherited the large French Grove farm that straddled Millbrook and Brimfield Townships from his father, Joseph McCoy. Both Joseph and Dan were early automobile enthusiasts. His father had purchased a Studebaker in 1916, by which time Dan was already attending automobile races in Peoria. Dan liked Studebakers and was looking to buy a new one in the near future. Dan schooled Verne in operating the Buick. She finally felt somewhat comfortable running the car, though it was not an easy car for a woman to drive.

Elmwood was in 1923 a town of about two thousand residents halfway between Peoria and Galesburg. It was an attractive town with a leafy central town square. First settled in 1831, the area initially had limited prospects. It was not even allowed to keep its original name. The settlement was called Newburgh but soon discovered that there was already a Newburgh in Illinois (much like Brimfield's naming experience). The town became Elmwood in 1838. Two prominent stage lines bypassed the area, with one line running north through Brimfield and the other south through Farmington. It appeared that the new town was destined to be a backwater.

All that changed when William J. Phelps walked into the township, having traveled all the way west from Connecticut. He liked the area, put down roots, and immediately went to work. He became a significant landowner, helped plat out the town in 1852, and then, crucially, worked to get the railroad routed through town. When coal was discovered (so close to the surface that it was strip mined), he formed a coal company to exploit it. He also organized the first bank.

With this new footing, Elmwood quickly became more prosperous than most surrounding towns. Besides the coal mine, it added a paper mill, a canning factory, and at least sixty retail merchants. Then, there was the railroad. The Peoria and Oquawka Railroad arrived in 1854. It soon became part of the much larger Chicago, Burlington, and Quincy system. People took to the train immediately. You could, for instance, ride into Galesburg in 1860 to see the Lincoln-Douglas debates at Knox College. Later, you could take the train into Galesburg just for the day to shop at O. T. Johnson's "Big Store." Or, you might head all the way up to Chicago. The train timetables were printed in the local newspaper, which had started life as the *Gazette* in Brimfield but moved to Elmwood in 1879.

By 1880, the population was 1,500 and growing. The main street was dirt, but it was oiled in the summer to keep the dust down. As with Williamsfield, the first automobile in town was the Winton that toured in 1899 advertising O. T. Johnson's department store. The main city streets were paved in 1925, and the main roads to Peoria and Galesburg were paved three years later. That same year, the sculpture "The Pioneers" was dedicated in the central park. It celebrated "the Pioneers who bridged the streams, subdued the soil, and founded a state." It was done by Lorado Taft, who had grown up in Elmwood and rose to be a famous sculptor.

Verne and the children settled in to town life. Elmwood had a large brick school building with grades 1–8 on the first floor, the high school grades on the second, and an auditorium on the third. The basement held the agriculture department and a recreation room. The school day started at 8 A.M. and ended at 4 P.M., with an hour for lunch. John and Paul had just a half mile walk to school and typically came home for lunch.

The first years in Elmwood were good years. Farm prices had rebounded and the farm was generating good rental income. There were band concerts every Saturday during the summer in the park at the square. The Palace Theatre ran movies as well as community events. Movie tickets were a dime. Until talkies arrived, the theater employed a band to provide background music for the silents. You could saunter by the Waible Electric Shop and listen to Cubs games on the radio. High school sports were big and well-covered. Both John and Paul joined teams, though John had a bit more success than Paul. John was shorter and stout whereas Paul was tall and gangly. Paul was not amused when John received a pair of boxing gloves for Christmas and anointed his brother as his sparring partner.

When Verne took the family on a trip to Missouri, the Buick proved uncomfortable and difficult to drive for longer stretches. Determined to replace it, Verne turned once again to her cousin Dan McCoy. He was, as usual, up on all things automotive and had recently purchased a 1925 Studebaker Big Six Brougham car for $2,500 (when a Model T was selling for $260). He knew that car would not be a good fit for Verne but was familiar with the new Chrysler that had debuted the previous year and recommended it. He helped her sell the Buick and purchase the Chrysler. The Auto Sales Company in Brimfield was the local agent for Chrysler, and the cars were selling briskly, including one to O. E. Root of Williamsfield (Big Joe Shaffer's former buddy and later nemesis).

If Dan McCoy recommended a Chrysler, then we know that Walter Chrysler must have been very busy since he left Billy Durant and Buick in 1919, walking away with $10 million in General Motors stock. In fact, he was not on the automotive sidelines for long. John North Willys came calling. Willys-Overland had started to drift downward after reaching number-two in sales in the mid-1910s. Like Durant, John Willys had overextended his company. In 1919 he bought the former Dusenberg World War I engine plant in Elizabeth, New Jersey, in order to develop a new six-cylinder car. He hired a brain trust of engineers from Studebaker—Fred Zeder, Owen Skelton, and Carl Breer—who had just finished revamping the Studebaker line in 1918. This trio came to be called the "ZSB" team or the "Three Musketeers," and they were tasked with designing Willy's six-cylinder car. No sooner had they completed a design prototype than Willys-Overland was forced into receivership and the plant was put up for auction. Though Walter Chrysler bid for the plant, Billy Durant came away as the winner.

As the dust settled from receivership, Chase Bank, the new owner of Willys-Overland, turned to Walter Chrysler to revive the company. The bank hired the former railroad apprentice at the then unheard of salary of $1 million per year for two years. Chrysler started to work his turnaround magic but financial trouble resurfaced again in 1922, resulting in bankruptcy. Chrysler considered buying the company and so did Studebaker.

Studebaker wanted to "retrieve" its wayward engineers and the new automobile design they had been working on. John Willys, seemingly cast adrift from his own company, orchestrated a stock reorganization that put him back in the driver's seat. He proceeded to turn the company around, growing sales to 215,000 by 1925.

After leaving Willys-Overland, Walter Chrysler learned through a back-channel source that the car design that the ZSB team had been working on and was now in the hands of Billy Durant was not quite what he was looking for. He decided to engage the ZSB team himself and have the men work on a brand new car using his own money. He funded ZSB plus a whole cadre of engineers working in the ZSB shop. Studebaker lost its star engineers a second time.

Though Walter Chrysler had left Willys-Overland with unfinished business, he left with his reputation intact. It was not long before another down-on-its-luck car company came calling; this time it was Maxwell. When Dr. Morton of Elmwood bought his Doctor Maxwell runabout in 1911, Maxwell was the third leading car company. The Maxwell brand was in a sense a rebound from Buick. Benjamin Briscoe had financed David Dunbar Buick early on but quickly lost faith that he could ramp up production. Instead, Briscoe teamed up with Jonathan Maxwell to create the Maxwell-Briscoe company and roll out the Maxwell automobile. While the Maxwell took off, Briscoe continued work on an automotive conglomerate he called US Motors. It was centered on the Maxwell line but included a number of other car acquisitions.[55] This was two years after Billy Durant started pulling together the car companies to form General Motors.

Walter Flanders, the machine tool salesman who had started Henry Ford on the path to efficient manufacturing, was hired as Maxwell's president. By 1912, Briscoe's US Motors was financially overextended and collapsed. Flanders took over Maxwell. He added the Chalmers line, providing a six-cylinder companion to the four-cylinder Maxwell.

Flanders was a salesman who understood the manufacturing process. He was not an engineer. Poor engineering led to a dwindling reputation for both cars. By 1920, Flanders was gone and both the Maxwell and Chalmers brands were struggling. In addition, there was a large "sales bank" of unsold Maxwells at the factory, in part because of the rapid decline in the mechanical quality of the cars. Chrysler went to work on a turnaround. In 1923, facing multiple lawsuits from suppliers, he forced the firm into bankruptcy to protect what was left. As the company emerged from bankruptcy protection, Studebaker made a bid for control. The latter still coveted the engineers that it had lost, but the ZSB team had no interest in working again for them and Studebaker withdrew the bid. Seizing the opportunity, Walter Chrysler bought a controlling interest in the reorganized company and renamed it Maxwell Motors, dropping the Chalmers brand.

Meanwhile, Chrysler continued to fund the ZSB team as well as up to thirty-five additional engineers. The original plan to design a new Chalmers car was scrapped. The team would start with a blank slate and work on what would become the Chrysler automobile. As an engineer himself, Walter wanted nothing less than the best automotive engineering available at the time. His vision was an automobile with high performance coupled with a quiet and smooth ride that could be produced with low enough manufacturing costs to price out at the mid-market.

Zeder, Skelton, and Breer focused a good part of their efforts on a new six-cylinder engine. They completely redesigned engine cooling, bearings, and combustion to create a power plant that produced 68 horsepower at 3,000 rpm. A prototype was completed in July 1923. Chrysler wanted a sleek roadster version ready for the New York auto show in January 1924. A member of the ZSB team, Oliver Clark, did the styling on the roadster and then added what he called "King Tut" colors to create a stunning look.[56]

The new Chrysler car was ready, but was the auto show ready for the new car? Because of a large increase in the number of brands to be displayed, the New York show had been moved from Grand Central Palace to the Bronx Armory, nine miles north. Even with the larger building, there wasn't sufficient space for every automobile. The auto show had a rule that a car must have survived a year of production to quality for a slot. The Maxwells were welcome. The Chrysler was not. Fortunately, Walter's sales manager had the foresight to book some additional space in the expansive lobby of the Commodore Hotel.

With harsh winter weather during the show, attendance at the Bronx venue was sparse. However, that was not the case at the Commodore. The display of the new Chryslers drew big crowds, and the resulting press went a long way toward helping Chrysler sell nearly twenty thousand Model B Chryslers in the first year, and many, many more the following year.

Interestingly, the new Chrysler was not alone in the Commodore Hotel lobby. The Stephens automobile was also on exhibit there, created by the Moline Plow Company, the same company John Willys bought in 1919 to get into tractors. Production of the Stephens car ended shortly after the show, and Moline Plow went back to concentrating on farm equipment. Also on display was the Wills Sainte Claire car. Yes, this was the same Wills—Childe Harold Wills, who had started with Henry Ford in 1899, contributed so much to Ford's early success, but left in 1919 amid disagreements with Henry. The Wills automobile would only survive until 1927, in part due to Wills' penchant to constantly tinker with designs instead of focusing on production. Wills subsequently went to work for Walter Chrysler as a metallurgist, a nod to his extensive experience with vanadium steel and other alloys.

The Chrysler Model B (the prototype was the Model A) was a thoroughly modern car, a comprehensive redesign that stood head and shoulders above other automobiles of the period. Besides the new engine, it featured four-wheel hydraulic brakes, shocks, aluminum pistons, an air filter, oil filter, tubular front axle, and full pressure lubrication.

The engine was the crown jewel of the new car. The six cylinders ran at a relatively high compression (4.7 to 1, versus a more normal compression of 4 to 1), turning a new seven-bearing crankshaft. The crankshaft was one critical but expensive addition. It had been precisely engineered for the compression and then bench tested by driving the engine at 3,000 rpm for fifty hours without complaint. The higher compression enabled the ZSB team to get 68 horsepower out of an engine with displacement of only 201 cubic inches.[57] This yielded a top speed of 80 mph on the high-end model. Also, despite the high compression, it could use lower octane gas (50–55) without knocking. The ZSB engineering team wanted to ensure that silence and smoothness were also key characteristics of the power plant.

The Chrysler car had a three-speed floor-mounted transmission and central one-piece instrument panel under glass containing the ammeter, temperature gauge, speedometer, tachometer, and odometer. All of this, including the King Tut colors and superior fit and finish, was priced at $1,395 to go head-to-head with the Buick.

Dan McCoy clearly recognized the innovation of the new Chrysler automobile. It was faster, more nimble, and seven hundred pounds lighter than the Buick. Certainly, none of these details were important to Verne Shaffer. The combination, however, produced a car that was much more drivable, with smooth power, firm and controlled braking, and low noise. It was a car designed for real comfort—with long, soft springs, extra size tires, overstuffed cushions, and wide doors. This meant that a woman could drive in comfort for long distances, including, maybe, all the way to Missouri and back.

It was an easy recommendation for Dan and a quick decision for Verne. It was out for the Buick and in for the Chrysler. Verne selected the five-passenger enclosed sedan, priced at $1,825. She did not opt for any of the King Tut colors but took delivery of a black Chrysler Model B70.[58] It was a significant step up, an exciting car. What she did not know at the time was this car had to last quite a bit longer than the Ford or the Buick had. Verne's purchase of the Chrysler helped put Illinois to over one million automobiles—more than the total number of cars in Great Britain or in France. The US car population stood at 17.5 million. The worldwide car inventory was 21 million.

13

The Great Depression

T HE RELATIVELY GOOD TIMES in Elmwood ended in 1929 with the
coming of the Great Depression. Rental income from the farm declined. Times were tough. Everyone pitched in. Paul had a paper
route, delivering the *Galesburg Register-Mail*, with an assist from John and
Detta Lou. There were lawns to mow at 25 cents to a dollar each. The family
had a garden and raised chickens. Paul won a $5 gold prize for the best
garden in town. Verne had plenty of help around the house. Even so, there
was ample time for the kids to be kids and enjoy life in Elmwood.

As the Depression wore on, however, Verne was no longer getting sufficient income from renting the farm, and continuing to live in Elmwood
was not sustainable. By 1933 she decided to move the family back to the
farm. She notified Ed Daily, the current renter, of their plans. The family
would join an exodus of 1.5 million people who left the cities for farms
during the Depression.

On March 4, 1933, the day that Franklin Delano Roosevelt was inaugu-
rated as president, Verne, John, Paul, Detta Lou, and Billy moved back to
the farm. Stanton Moore and Dan McCoy provided hay racks to help in
moving the household goods. John had graduated from Elmwood High in
May. Paul was a junior, and Detta Lou and Billy were still in the first level.
Back at the farm, Paul would go to Brimfield High School while Detta Lou
and Billy would be walking the mile down Elmore Road to Reed School.

Whereas life in Elmwood had been comfortable, the years ahead would
be very tough. The farmhouse, now seventy years old, was filthy and cold.
The family had enjoyed indoor plumbing in Elmwood but now had a two-

hole outhouse out back. Water had to be pumped from a cistern in the front and lugged into the house.

Getting the farm up and running was no easy feat. Through a series of renters, the land had been over-farmed without proper crop rotation.[59] The soil was depleted and would need to be enriched before crop yields even reached average. The drainage of the swale running down to French Creek would need to be tiled, and the same with a similar area in the new field across the road. The bulk of Will's farm equipment had been sold in the 1923 auction. And then there was the big overriding question: where would the farm power come from? There were no horses and no tractor.

John had not yet turned eighteen when they arrived back at the farm. He was 5' 6" tall, 145 pounds, with blue eyes, blond hair and a stout build. He had been a good athlete at Elmwood High, even running the eight miles from town to the farm at one point. Now, he would have to be the man of the farm, and yet he was totally inexperienced. The prior summer, he had helped Stanton Moore and Dan McCoy with farm work. But he had grown up in Elmwood, not on the farm. His father, Will, had worked on a farm from an early age and farmed during the golden age; John, in contrast, was thrown into farming in the midst of the nation's worst depression. Luckily, John was not alone. Paul was just a couple years younger and would be another strong back. Verne, Detta Lou, and Billy would also help run the farm. And there was no shortage of local farmers, many of whom were relatives who would be ready to pitch in.

The first order of business was power. The farm was 220 acres, of which 198 were farmable. Will had run the farm with upwards of fourteen horses. That was simply not possible at this time. John elected to try a combination of horses and a tractor. For the horses, the timing was actually quite good. The horse population had declined by 25 percent, or six million horses, from 1920 to 1930. The 1930 Census report was actually concerned about the decline, noting that the eighteen million acres of oats freed from feeding horses would simply increase cash crop production and further depress already low Depression prices. Further, the mechanization replacing horses would eliminate hired help and increase unemployment. However, the key result for John was that horse prices were at their lowest level since the turn of the century.

He was able to buy a couple of colts at a bargain price, as one was blind and the other lame. They were twins, one red and one white, bred to the same stallion and delivered only days apart. The family christened them

Bill and Bob. For the first year, they were left to the pasture to grow into their frames. The second year they were harnessed and grew to be big, strong draft horses, the pride of the neighborhood. Bill and Bob became part of the family. They were not afraid of road traffic or the deafening roar of the threshing machine. And they were intelligent, knowing how to tread when cultivating the corn rows and when to move the wagon forward when John and Paul were harvesting corn. They were a great team for ten to twelve years, until Bill was struck and killed by lightning, and Bob was no longer effective and was put out to pasture.[60]

The other power need was a tractor. By 1930, about 30 percent of Midwest farms had tractors. But in a 1938 survey of 847 Midwest farms, there were no farms that used tractors exclusively. Over half used a combination of tractors and horses, and the rest relied completely on horses. Locally, companies like Kelly Supply were selling both new and used tractors. A used International Titan 10-20 could be had for $900. Even that was not affordable for the family. Shortly after relocating to the farm, John bought a used steel-wheel tractor that had a bent crankshaft. Because of the extraordinary heat that summer, he worked on repairing the tractor during the day and then used Bill and Bob early or late in the day when the hot temperatures had abated.

Farm prices had been trending down since 1920 but fell off a cliff after 1929. Farmers kept producing, but the demand was not there. This in turn drove prices even lower. The worst years were 1930 through 1932, with 1932 being the nadir. Corn prices fell to 12 cents a bushel, a far cry from the price level of $1.55 a bushel in 1920. With an average yield of 46 bushels per acre and 160 acres planted in corn, the net earnings would be $883—not enough to even cover costs. In the depths of the Depression, Verne would fire the furnace with corncobs. It simply did not pay to store the corn or ship it to market. When corn prices finally rebounded to $1.60 in 1937, the net earnings on those 160 acres rose to $11,776, which would more than cover costs.

The downward spiral of demand also affected livestock prices. With hog prices plummeting from $14 per hundred pounds to just $3.25, it did not pay to feed the corn to the hogs. Raising hogs had been the cornerstone of the farm operation that Will and Verne had built up. When money was needed, Will would take several hogs to market. That was no longer an option.

As the Depression wore on, overproduction and falling demand drove prices further down. Then, as conditions started to minimally improve, the great nationwide drought of the mid-1930s rolled in. These were the Dust Bowl years. Harvests plummeted. At the farm, the drought produced unbearable heat and little rain. The heat was especially challenging for all-horse farms. In Illinois, the heat also produced an ongoing plague of chinch bugs, which were attracted to grain crops like wheat, barley, and corn. Many techniques were tried to eradicate them, including planting a "trap" crop to attract them and then destroying them when they clustered. John and Paul elected to plow a furrow around each field, roll the trench with a log to pulverize the soil, and pour a strip of crankcase oil and creosote in the trench. This was repeated every week or so until the bugs disappeared.

The farm toll was merciless. Roughly two million farms out of a total of six million were foreclosed by the banks. Farm income cratered, from $14.5 billion to $4.5 billion, in 1932. All was not totally grim, however. On the plus side, having a farm enabled you to feed yourselves. And movie tickets at the Palace Theatre in Elmwood were still just 10 cents and no longer silent. *Speed Demon* and *Animal Kingdom* were the films showing that first March.

FDR came into office during the depth of the Depression with the attitude that he would try anything to help climb out of the abyss. A barrage of initiatives were passed, many in the first hundred days he was in office. The core issue, one that Herbert Hoover little understood at the time (despite his stellar record as "food czar" in the wake of World War I and his stint as secretary of commerce under President Harding), was the total collapse of demand. Americans were out of work and had no money to buy products, which led to more companies failing and subsequently more people out of work, and even lower demand. As farmers continued to produce crops and livestock without customers to buy it, prices crashed.

The Roosevelt administration passed the Agricultural Adjustment Act (AAA) in 1933, which paid farmers to cut back on acreage in production in order to support prices. This proved to be a significant help. Though AAA was struck down by the Supreme Court in 1936, it was improved and reinstated in another form in 1938.

There were also actions to address the demand side of the equation, through job creation and wage support. The National Recovery Act (NRA) aimed to expand and protect jobs by setting minimum wages and, in some cases, setting prices. The Civilian Conservation Corps (CCC) provided young men with public works jobs. The National Youth Administration

(NYA) aimed to provide a combination of work and education for Americans between age sixteen and twenty-five.

There was improvement, but progress was very slow. Prices started to climb. Corn hit $1.22 a bushel in 1936, a price that had not been seen since 1925. With the increase in prices and thus farm income, farmers started buying tractors again. By 1936, John had several years of farming under his belt. The years of subsistence farming gave way to years with reasonable income. Verne and John decided to move forward on a new tractor. Bill and Bob were still going strong, but the new tractor would complement their power and then step in to perform full time when they were gone. The new tractor would have to be a general purpose or row-crop machine, one that could handle the critical task of cultivation. John would be leaving behind steel wheels, as the new tractors sported large pneumatic tires.[61] John surveyed the field and decided on a Case tractor.

Fortunately as we have seen, Case got out of the car business in the 1920s and focused solely on farm equipment. The company introduced its first row-crop tractor in 1929, a response to the revolutionary International Harvester Farmall tractor. Its Model CC, or "C Cultivator," was a row-crop version of its Model C. It had an adjustable rear axle to change rear tread width from 48 to 84 inches, narrow for plowing and wide for cultivation (corn rows were typically 30–40 inches apart). It had an unusual "chicken roost" steering mechanism that snaked control rods around the side of the tractor, connecting to the narrow tricycle front wheels. This reduced vibration at the steering wheel. It had dual fuel tanks, gasoline to start the engine, and kerosene to run. It used a crank to start the engine, driving a magneto to spark the cylinders, with a choke and spark advance to smooth the engine. All of this was very much like the Model T, right down to the danger of breaking your arm when cranking.

John purchased the Case CC in 1936 from dealer and local auctioneer Howard Beeney in Peoria. Though he did not know it at the time, this was the first of many Case tractors he would buy through the years. And, he pretty much went back to Howard for each new Case.

The Depression took its toll on automobile sales. From a 1929 production high of 5.3 million cars, the industry tumbled down by over 75 percent by 1932, with sales just breaking one million. As of 1929, there were only forty-four car companies left. Among those that did not survive the Depression were Stutz, Dusenberg, Auburn, Cord, Peerless, Pierce Arrow, Franklin, Durant, Marmon, and Locomobile. The Big Three automakers—GM, Ford, and Chrysler—had secured an 80 percent share of the market, leaving the major independents (Studebaker, Hudson, Nash, Packard, and Willys) with what was left. In the first year of the Depression, a third of the automobile dealers went out of business.

General Motors, with its modern corporate management system deployed by Alfred P. Sloan and executed by capable executives like Bill Knudsen, made it through the decade very profitably. Chrysler had risen miraculously from the near-ashes of Maxwell and Chalmers into a full-fledged member of the Big Three. With strong management headed by Walter Chrysler, the company did well during the Depression.

Ford was another story. It lost money throughout the 1930s, but due to the total lack of administrative control, this was not fully apparent until much later. The Ford Model A put Henry Ford back in the number-one position in 1929. Over its first five years, four million Model A cars were sold, but the company was barely profitable. While Henry Ford continued to drive down manufacturing costs through large-scale operations, he had no use for administrative "overhead" and laid off many in those departments. When Ford was a near-monopoly this was not a serious problem. But as competition grew and automotive operations became more complex, control by one man no longer was feasible.

The Model A ran out of gas in 1931. Chevrolet was quickly back on top, and Chrysler, with the addition of the Plymouth brand, slipped into the second slot. Henry Ford decided to develop a V-8 engine, leapfrogging his two arch competitors, who were running on six-cylinder models. Henry decided to reprise his approach to the Model T, developing the new engine in secrecy. He actually used Thomas Edison's workshop, which he had moved from Menlo Park, New Jersey to Dearborn. The Ford V-8 automobile debuted in May 1932. It was ranked as one of the best cars of the decade, but the engine under its hood was very expensive to develop in the midst of the Depression. And continued poor cost control meant losses even in the face of good volumes for the car.

Ford still lacked the brand scaling that his competitors had crafted. General Motors buyers would start with Chevrolet and then move up to Pontiac, Oldsmobile, Buick, and Cadillac. Walter Chrysler had built a similar progression with Plymouth, Dodge, Desoto, Chrysler, and Imperial. Ford had nothing between the top-of-the-line Ford V-8, priced at $750, and the entry Lincoln, priced at $4,200. In 1938, the Mercury brand was added, slotted against the mid-priced competitive makes—Studebaker

Commander, Dodge Deluxe, Pontiac Six, Olds Six, Buick Special, Packard, Nash Ambassador, and Chrysler Royal. And in 1939, the Lincoln Continental was added to top off the Ford line.

In aggregate, auto sales were on the upswing by 1936 and reached 3.6 million in 1937. There was a severe recession in 1937 and 1938, after which car sales tracked up again.

Even as the Depression years eased, there would not be a new car for Verne and the family. Farm equipment was the first priority. The 1925 Chrysler had to last.

For the first two years that Detta Lou and Billy were at Reed School, Bertha Pierson was the teacher. At graduation time, Mrs. Pierson would treat the kids to ice cream and a movie in Elmwood. Erma McKinty took over the school in September 1935. She was a lifelong Elmwood resident and taught into the 1950s in town after her stint at the Reed School. Detta Lou was a part-time cub reporter for the *Brimfield News* when she reached eighth grade, reporting on French Grove happenings. As a community social center, something was always happening in French Grove. Through 1935, there were monthly potluck suppers with entertainment afterwards.

In 1936, both John and Billy contracted scarlet fever. The feared disease still could be fatal, particularly for young children. The farmhouse was quarantined for a period of fourteen days.

Detta Lou graduated eighth grade and started at Brimfield High in the fall of 1935. Billy graduated from Reed School two years later and joined her at Brimfield. Detta Lou graduated high school in 1939 with a "large" class of twenty-two girls and seven boys. Verne kept up a presence in Elmwood. She leased out the house in town, not selling it until 1940. She also conducted the 1940 census for Brimfield Township.

The 1925 Chrysler had been like a member of the family. It was still going strong after fifteen years. The family had quite a scare in the fall of 1937 when the car was stolen while parked in Laura. Fortunately, it turned up the next day, twenty miles west in Knoxville.

One major change was the local roads. Real progress was at hand. Main routes 91 and 78 were paved in 1928. Route 150 linking Galesburg and Peoria was completed in 1934. It was a little shocking that in 1914, the Brimfield town supervisors still thought dirt roads were just fine. But, the Brimfield Good Roads club disagreed. They organized, lobbied Springfield, and finally their efforts as well as others paid off. With the major routes paved, the local paper announced, "At last Brimfield is out of the mud. Her long cherished dream has come true. Her citizens can back the old bus out of the garage, climb up on the cement and head north, south, east or west on real honest to goodness hard roads." Of course, Elmore Road in front of the farm did not make the cut. It was not paved until 1954.

As the eldest son, John took the reins of the farm in 1933, with Paul helping. Paul graduated from Brimfield High the following year and enrolled at Knox College in Galesburg in the fall of 1934. He had virtually no money and worked odd jobs to pay for room, board, and tuition. He was a full-time waiter in his dorm and had a National Youth Administration (NYA) job feeding the lab rats and alligators in the science building at 35 cents an hour. He often made the short commute back home to help John with the farm. He carried a full load his first three years and was the sports editor for the Knox College paper. A decision to live in the Phi Gamma Delta fraternity house as a senior was ill-advised. Though he dialed back to a lighter course load, his grades still took a nose dive.

Paul graduated from Knox in June 1938 and moved back to the farmhouse. He was hired by Caterpillar in Peoria, a well-paying job. The commute from the farm to work was over thirty miles on Route 150. Initially, Paul would walk up Elmore Road to the highway and thumb a ride into Peoria. But this got old quickly.

In the summer of 1940, a new factor had surfaced. Paul's roommate at Knox, Bob Thompson, was dating a Williamsfield girl, and she had a younger sister. Bob set up a blind date, and Paul asked her to a softball game in town. When they first met, she looked vaguely familiar. Her name was Lucile Daub. Her father, a World War I veteran, was the stationmaster in Williamsfield for the Santa Fe Railroad. At that time, 30–40 trains passed through town daily, mostly freight but also through-passenger service from Chicago to Los Angeles.

Lucile's mother, the former Gertrude Wesner, was the town postmaster. She was also the younger sister of Floyd Wesner, the star athlete from Will's 1906 Williamsfield High class. Lucile attended many of the 1906 class reunions with her mother, and she and Paul crossed paths many times there as youngsters. But, this was long before either had any interest in the opposite sex. Lucile graduated with honors from Williamsfield High in 1938. She was also a noted classical pianist, winning several local competitions. She went on to Knox College, four years behind Paul. After graduation, she got her teaching certificate and started teaching history, English, and performing arts at Williamsfield High School.

The date at the Williamsfield softball game led to more dates. And very quickly, a new car suddenly became a priority. Given the long service provided by the 1925 Chrysler, a Chrysler would be the first brand that Paul would consider.

What were Chryslers like in 1938? And, what had Walter Chrysler been up to in the intervening years? After its impressive debut at the 1924 auto show, the Chrysler was off to a respectable start. Yet, even after combining the falling Maxwell volumes, that only put the company in 27th place in US sales. But Walter's first car then took off in sales, and three short years later, the company (now renamed the Chrysler Corporation) had climbed to fourth place, just behind Ford, Chevrolet, and Willys-Overland.

Walter Chrysler knew he had to move quickly to build out a car company broad enough to compete with the Big Two. For openers, he re-badged the four-cylinder Maxwell as a four-cylinder Chrysler. That was a start, but he would need to have multiple marques designed for different segments, much as Durant and Sloan had done with General Motors.

In 1928 he purchased Dodge. The company was available because John and Horace Dodge were no longer around. They had attended the New York City auto show in early January 1920. The influenza pandemic of 1918–1919 that had infected an estimated 500 million people worldwide and killed an estimated fifty million had continued into 1920. By that time it had morphed into a slightly less lethal form; however, this did not matter for John Dodge. Having previously survived tuberculosis, his damaged lungs could not fight the pneumonia that set in, and he died within a week in his Manhattan hotel room.[62] For Horace, the Spanish flu initiated a series of health setbacks, ending in his death the following December. The official cause was cirrhosis (both John and Horace were hard-charging, hard-drinking individuals), but the influenza was the knock-out punch. Both were in their early fifties and on top of the world with the success of the company and the recent court victory over Henry Ford. The Dodge Company passed to their widows, who sold it to a bank consortium for the then record figure of $145 million. By 1928, Dodge volumes were down due to mismanagement and the bank group was looking for a buyer. Walter Chrysler needed both more factory space and another brand to complement his eponymous automobile company.

Chrysler moved quickly. After buying Dodge, he added the DeSoto and Plymouth nameplates the same year. At the start, both cars were simply warmed-over Maxwells. The Plymouth would be positioned as the low-price entry car geared to compete with Ford and Chevrolet. The new lineup now started with Plymouth and worked up to Dodge, DeSoto, Chrysler, and Imperial at the top. Having single-handedly pulled together a formidable member of the now Big Three in just four years, Walter Chrysler was named *Time*'s Man of the Year in 1929. The following year he finished the Chrysler Building in midtown Manhattan, an Art Deco landmark that was the tallest building in the world (but just for eleven months, when it was surpassed by the Empire State Building).[63] Sales of the new stable of automobiles elevated Chrysler to second place in 1933 just above Ford, with the tremendous volumes of Plymouths leading the way.

The Three Musketeers team continued to lead Chrysler engineering. Despite unbridled success, Walter was already looking down the road. He wanted to repeat the experience of 1924, to come out with another revolutionary car in 1934, on the tenth anniversary of his landmark first car.

Carl Breer began toying with the idea of a more aerodynamic car while continuing to work on the current Chrysler lineup. In 1927 he took the aero concept to Walter Chrysler and received the go-ahead. Breer's objective was not a streamlined automobile for design impact but a practical aero design from an engineering and efficiency perspective. The first step was to understand how a car moved through the airstream.

Breer was able to meet Orville Wright through a mutual friend and took some prototype models to the Wright facility in Dayton for wind tunnel testing. The results were interesting enough to convince Walter Chrysler to fund an in-house wind tunnel. Through many test models, Breer determined that the ideal aerodynamic shape for an automobile was a blunt but streamlined front end coupled with a tapered rear. Making this happen meant moving the front and rear seats forward. This, in turn, meant moving the engine forward and having it straddle the front axle instead of being positioned behind the axle.

Breer's work went beyond the normal bounds of engineering and essentially dictated a certain external aerodynamic styling look. If Walter Chrysler had any reservations about the path that Breer was taking, he could turn to famed designer Norman Bel Geddes. Bel Geddes, an early proponent of streamlining, had put down his aerodynamic principles for automobiles in his 1932 book *Horizons*.[64] The book was influential with both Chrysler and his engineering team. Bel Geddes was a major critic of contemporary automobile design, which continued to be based on the horse-drawn buggy. This was fine when you were poking along at 4 mph but made less sense at 65 mph. He felt that automobile manufacturers were too conservative, thinking the public was never really ready for change. Nothing moved forward until someone took a risk. As an example, Bel Geddes cited Erret Cord. Cord had bought the Auburn Automobile Company (former wagon builders) in 1927 and proceeded to introduce an iconic streamlined car, the Cord, with front-wheel drive, a lower profile, and even hidden headlights.[65] Cord was willing to step far out in front of accepted automobile mores. In 1933, Walter Chrysler hired Bel Geddes to fine-tune the exterior design of the emerging tenth-anniversary car and add some Art Deco touches to the interior, even taking some cues from the Chrysler Building's extensive use of the new Bakelite plastics formulation.

The new car, to be branded as Airflow, would be the first American production car to use aerodynamic styling. As the new car's new layout dictated wholesale changes in many other areas, Breer and his team decided to be even more ambitious. With a completely new body, they took the opportunity to replace the current body-on-frame structure with unibody construction. And, as the aerodynamic effect would enhance efficiency, they added an automatic overdrive, engaged at speeds over 38 mph to further improve mileage. And they converted the windows to safety glass.

In testing, there were some unintended but very positive additional benefits of the Airflow design. The sleek profile raised the top speed from 83 mph to 98 mph. The reduction of weight over the rear axle meant a smoother ride. And the change in the weight distribution from front to back improved the car's handling. Walter Chrysler was impressed. He wanted a statement car, a car for the future, a car to show off at the 1934 New York auto show, much as he had done ten years before. It appeared that he had it.

Breer and his team delivered on schedule, and the Airflow cars were front and center at the New York show. There were three Airflow models— Chrysler, Imperial, and DeSoto—and they attracted huge crowds. The cars were voted the best-looking automobiles at the show. Unfortunately, they were also voted the worst-looking cars at the show. Still, Chrysler came away with more orders than any other car company, and Walter Chrysler felt the team had hit the target. But it would soon become apparent that the design strayed too far from conventional tastes, even leaving the perception that the cars were ugly.

Still, competitors, and in particular General Motors, were so concerned about the impact of this potentially revolutionary new car that they

cranked up a smear campaign. In full-page ads, GM touted its own approach as "mature refinement," compared with "ill-timed or dubious ex-
periments" not so subtly alluding to the Airflow. They also implied that
the new unibody construction was unsafe. This latter charge was just too
much for Walter Chrysler, who handled it in grand style. An Airflow was
taken to a 110-foot-high cliff in Pennsylvania and pushed off the side. The
unibody held, the doors opened and closed cleanly, and the car was driven
away.[66] Just to be sure that the public got the point, Chrysler added a second demonstration at the Chicago World's Fair that year, where the company had built a seven-acre pavilion complete with a test track. Chrysler
hired Barney Oldfield and his team to perform rollover demonstrations in
the Airflow. Barney's drivers would accelerate to high speed, roll the car,
get out, dramatically inspect the fit of the doors, and then get back in and
drive off.[67]

The Airflow's startling look and aggressive smear tactics against it
weren't the only problems. The design's unibody required many changes
in the tooling and manufacturing process for construction. This led to a
critical delay in getting early cars produced to respond to the initial high
demand. Moreover, there were defects in some of the early cars, including
loose engine mounts. Thus, more rumors surfaced that the car was unsafe.
The manufacturing processes were quickly smoothed out, but the lost time
in getting cars on the road was costly. The car's look remained a problem,
but a self-inflicted issue was the price. The Airflow models were priced
20–25 percent higher than the models they replaced.

Though disappointed, Walter Chrysler moved quickly to limit the damage. He retained Bel Geddes to design some changes in the grille's appearance. In addition, he asked Ray Dietrich, the head of his styling department,
to soften the Airflow look for the 1935 and 1936 models. Dietrich, a close
friend of Edsel Ford, had done design work on the Packard, Franklin, and
Erskine automobiles before coming to Chrysler in 1932. His team was also
tasked with designing a new line called Airstream that reverted back to
more conventional styling.

However, the die was cast. Airflows did not recover, and the entire Airflow line—Imperial, Chrysler, and DeSoto—was canceled after the 1937
model year. To further add insult, Ford announced the new Lincoln-Zephyr
in 1936. Like the Airflow, it was a streamlined, aerodynamic automobile.
Likely because of the Airflow experience, its styling was done by designers
and not dictated by engineering. The car was perceived as beautiful and

was a great success. This must have been tough to take for Walter Chrysler. The Lincoln-Zephyr was the statement car that he wanted to make.

Viewed in the rear view mirror of history, however, the Airflows were way ahead of their time. The repositioning of the engine and passenger compartment toward the front predated Chrysler's 1993 LH "cab forward" cars by sixty years. Walter was able to take some solace in the fact that Chrysler was very profitable for the rest of the 1930s, driven in large part by Plymouth sales.

In October 1937, Chrysler introduced the Chrysler Royal as the entry point for the company's top brand. The Airflow design was nearly completely gone. The neat flush-mounted headlights of the Airflow were jettisoned in favor of the old style torpedo headlights. In addition, it had external fenders, running boards, and a decidedly non-aerodynamic grille.

However, Paul Shaffer was focused on getting wheels, not style. He did not need to spend much time surveying the current automobile scene. He didn't even need to consult with Dan McCoy. The family's experience with the 1925 Chrysler was more than enough. He borrowed money from his brother Bill and bought a 1938 Chrysler Royal. There was no notice of this big investment, his first car, in the local papers. The novelty of automobiles had finally run its course and they were just part of the landscape now.

The Royal was a four-door sedan with a high-compression engine, hydraulic brakes, and three-speed floor shift with automatic overdrive. Compared to the old Chrysler, compression had increased sharply from 4.1 to 6.2, horsepower was up from 68 to 95, and the top speed had increased from 75 mph to 95 mph. The car was priced at $1,010 from the factory. Paul's assessment said it all: "What a car and what a joy to own and drive." To break it in, he took it on an auto trip to Minneapolis and Duluth. It performed flawlessly. He now had a car for the work commute, but much more importantly, he could race from the farm to the Victorian house on South Elm Street in Williamsfield where Lucile lived in no time.

14

War Clouds

T HOUGH THE DEPRESSION had substantially eased by 1940, another dark threat was looming on the horizon. The rise of Adolf Hitler and the Nazi Party, German rearmament during the 1930s, and the German annexation of the Sudetenland in 1938 made it clear that another European war was likely. The civil war in Spain in 1936, aided by German dive bombers supporting General Francisco Franco, and the Japanese invasion of Manchuria in 1937 further darkened the war clouds.

In the meantime, American isolationism was in full bloom, thanks in part to the efforts of Henry Ford and Charles Lindbergh. US military preparedness was at low ebb. In 1940, the United States was ranked 19th in armed capability in the world, after Romania and just ahead of Holland. Hitler struck Poland on September 1, 1939, with an overwhelming force that was to shatter any remaining confidence among the European Allies that war could be averted.

Franklin Roosevelt was painfully aware of both the weakness of the European partners and the lack of US readiness. In May 1940, he asked Bernard Baruch, a close advisor, to locate the best production man in the country. Not needing to spend much time researching that question, Baruch told him the clear answer was "Big Bill" Knudsen, who had by then risen to be president of General Motors. FDR immediately requested that Knudsen come to the White House for a chat. Feeling that when the president calls, you come, Knudsen arrived at the White House the next day. He listened as FDR described the depth of America's war readiness and his desire to have Knudsen lead a massive rearmament effort to turn it around. Specifically, FDR wanted Knudsen to head the newly formed War Production Board, a group that would be in total charge of all military production—tanks, planes, ships, trucks, engines, everything. He also announced that $3 billion in defense spending had already been approved.[68]

Alfred P. Sloan, the chairman of GM, discouraged Knudsen from taking the job. Sloan was staunchly and actively anti-Roosevelt. And like Henry Ford, he had the resources to press his case. He had financed the American Liberty League, which had worked to defeat FDR in 1936. He was now lending his support to the National Association of Manufacturers, whose aims included defeating the president in 1940. GM also had substantial investments in Germany.

Knudsen felt otherwise. The country had given him everything, and here was a way to pay it back. Taking no salary, Knudsen jumped into his new role. He spent a significant amount of time on the road with defense contractors both large and small. Given his background, he worked closely with the automobile industry. He set Chrysler to work building tanks and Ford to build bombers, Jeeps, trucks, and engines. He enlisted GM for trucks, tanks, and aircraft engines. Studebaker signed up for trucks and radial aircraft engines. Willys-Overland, REO, Nash, and Packard would all come aboard for the effort. Edsel Ford committed early, negotiating a contract to build six thousand Rolls Royce Merlin aircraft engines for British airplanes like the Spitfire. Though true to form, Henry Ford interceded and canceled the contract because Ford's own engine design had been spurned.

With this running start, FDR made his "Arsenal of Democracy" speech in December 1940. He explained to the American public the need to provide armaments for those fighting the Axis powers while keeping America neutral. In an earlier address to Congress, he had set the bar at producing 50,000 planes per year. Given that the Army Air Corps had only twelve hundred planes total at the time, this figure seemed outlandish. Roosevelt's challenge turned out to be pretty conservative as the "arsenal" would produce nearly 300,000 planes during the conflict.

➤ ➤ ➤

Detta Lou graduated from Brimfield High in 1939 and was now a junior at Western Illinois State Teachers College in Macomb. She had returned home for Thanksgiving in late 1941. The Palace Theatre in Elmwood was playing a double feature—*Dive Bomber* with Fred MacMurray and *Dr. Jekyll and Mr. Hyde* with Spencer Tracey and Ingrid Bergman. John's harvest was in and silo'ed. The market prices for corn, wheat, oats, and hogs had substantially recovered from Depression lows.

However, the situation overseas was dire. Europe had been overrun by Germany. Though Hitler had failed in his attempt to invade Britain, the battle was now joined in North Africa. In the Pacific, Japan had broken the international naval pact, joined the Axis powers, and brutally invaded China. The man responsible for the aggression, Hideki Tojo, had been elevated to premier by the emperor. The United States had been a major supplier of oil and steel to Japan but now moved to embargo those commodities. At the same time, it moved to support the Chinese resistance. Talks were ongoing in Washington between the United States and Japan, aimed at resolving the stalemate.

Paul, Verne, and John decided to go for a Sunday drive in the '38 Chrysler and visit Detta at school. It happened to be Sunday, December 7, 1941. They met Detta Lou in a common room at the college. There was a large, wood-grained Philco radio in the corner playing background music. At around 4 p.m. local time, the music was interrupted with a news bulletin. The Japanese had attacked Pearl Harbor, in the US Hawaiian Territory. It may not have been clear at that moment, but life had completely changed for the Shaffers, for the automobile companies, and for the country. Theirs was a quiet and somber drive back to the farm.

Auto production came to a halt on February 1, 1942, by order of the president. Auto sales had been strong the two previous years, averaging 4.5 million cars. The car companies were in the midst of the 1942 model year when production was halted. There remained only seventeen automobile makers still standing—GM's five divisions, Chrysler's four, Ford's three (Mercury had been added in 1938 on Edsel's recommendation), and the five independents—Hudson, Packard, Studebaker, Nash, and Willys-Overland. With the factories quiet, there was a scramble for munitions contracts from Bill Knudson and his War Production Board. Dan McCoy, ever the local car maven, had been able to secure one of the last automobiles off the line, a 1942 Studebaker Commander. It was one of only 3,500 cars that Studebaker produced before switching to wartime contracts.

In 1940, Selective Service legislation had been enacted requiring all men ages 21–35 to register for the draft. John and Paul drove to Peoria that October and registered, two of the more than fifty million men that registered during the war. They were each given a draft number from 1 to 9,000. A lottery would determine the order of the numbers.

Earlier in the year, on July 4 no less, John had married Georgia Stevens. Paul was his best man. Georgia had grown up in Knox County and received her teaching degree from Illinois State Normal University. Her sister, Eleanor, happened to be married to a farmer next door—Stanton Moore. She joined the household with Verne and Bill. Paul was working in Monmouth and Detta Lou was still at school at Macomb. That September, Georgia started teaching at Nightingale School, a one-room schoolhouse a couple of miles northeast of the farm.[69]

John had persevered through the 1930s and was clearly on top of his game, charting the fields, managing the business, and continually upgrading his equipment. The farm was in good shape and very productive when the war came. Farm production was essential to the war effort, but there was a bit of bureaucracy required to qualify your farm and, in turn, receive a deferment from the draft. The rules sought to gauge the scope of the farm's production while stressing certain crops and livestock deemed critical. The rules were administered with a somewhat arcane unit system that assigned point values to the number of livestock raised and the amount of acreage in production.[70]

Actually farming during wartime was another story. If you needed to buy a tractor, you had to deal with the War Production Board, which was more interested in steel for tanks than steel for tractors. But the war accelerated the need for tractors as there were fewer and fewer men available to work on the farms. Then, come harvest time, there were regulations on shipment to be met from the Office of Defense Transportation. Farm labor problems were handled by the War Manpower Commission, and the prices farmers received were set by Congress and the Office of Price Administration. These were all hurdles specific to the farmer. They did not include the other home-front regulations, such as limits on gasoline, tires, and parts. And, of course, with all automobile production stopped, John, Verne, and Georgia were left with an aging car.

Since graduating from Knox in June 1941, Paul had worked for the Brown-Lynch-Scott hardware store in Galesburg, and then secured the position with Caterpillar in Peoria. In the summer of 1941 he became engaged to Lucile. The draft began in October 1940. Paul received his draft notice the month before the Pearl Harbor attack, with instructions to report in February 1942 to Camp Grant in Rockford, Illinois, for one week of orientation. Most of the Army basics and drills were familiar to him because he had participated in ROTC at Knox.

At the completion of the Camp Grant week, Paul received orders to report to Sheppard Field in Wichita Falls, Texas, where the Army Air Corps was stationed. He was to start a twenty-two-week course in aircraft maintenance, joined by twelve thousand other recruits. The first step was to sew the insignia of the 9th Army Air Force onto his uniform. This would be the first of many different unit insignias he would wear.

Due to his ROTC service at Knox, Paul was assigned as team leader for the forty students in his barracks. This translated into running the exercise period and marching the group to and from class, and to and from the mess hall. The aircraft maintenance course took one week for each phase of aeronautics, including wheels, hydraulics, electronics, and aircraft engines. Upon graduation, Paul taught aircraft engine concepts and maintenance to several following classes. At Sheppard Field, the engine work included the Wright R-2600 Twin Cyclone engine (a 14-cylinder twin radial producing 1,600 horsepower) on the B-25 Mitchell bomber and the Pratt and Whitney R-2800 Double Wasp engine (18-cylinder twin radial producing 2,000 horsepower) on the B-26 Martin Marauder bomber. The Double Wasp was manufactured by Ford and several other automobile companies. It had also been selected to power the new Grumman F6F Hellcat fighter plane.

One new bomber that was not handled at Wichita Falls was the B-24 Liberator, newly designed for heavier bomb loads and higher cruising speeds. After Bill Knudsen joined the War Production Board in May 1940, one of his first calls was to Edsel Ford, the president of Ford. He knew that Ford would bid for a number of defense contracts, but he had one in particular in mind—the B-24 Liberator. Consolidated Aircraft, the plane's developer, would not be able to produce the volumes envisioned, and he felt that some application of Fordism techniques to building the plane would expedite things. He was thinking of having Ford mass-produce select components and shipping them to Consolidated. He felt the job was too complex for one company. Where an average car had 15,000 parts, the bomber had upwards of a million parts, required 400,000 rivets, and weighed 36,000 pounds.

After the discussion with Knudsen, Edsel sent Charles Sorensen to San Diego to tour the Consolidated Aircraft plant to see how the B-24 was currently being built. He was shocked to discover that workers were constructing each bomber by hand, in place, and producing only one per day.

Returning to his hotel, he broke down the entire process and sketched a plant layout with the goal of producing one bomber per hour. He designed two enormous plants built side by side, one for component manufacturing and the other for final assembly. Attached to the plants would be a thousand-acre airfield. The Liberators would come off the line, one per hour, roll directly onto the airfield, be checked out, then fly off for deployment.

Sorensen had his plans reviewed and approved by Edsel Ford, and presumably by Henry. Knudsen had to be skeptical of the one plane per hour objective, but intimately knowing the Ford reputation for mass production, agreed to let the contract. Albert Kahn, as usual, was retained to design the facility. Edsel and Sorensen would be responsible for directing the venture. Henry would supply the land.

Years earlier, Henry Ford had purchased farmland near Ypsilanti, about thirty miles west of Dearborn, Michigan, that abutted the Willow Run creek. He noticed an abandoned one-room schoolhouse nearby—the Willow Run School—and decided to repair and reopen it. He invested a significant amount in recapturing the one-room school of his own experience, down to the 1860s-style desks and McGuffey readers. It was akin to a field version of his idealized Greenfield Village. The school reopened in 1931 with thirty students. Later in the 1930s, he established a camp for young boys on the property that used farm tasks to teach skills such as self-reliance and teamwork. The camp was called Willow Run.

Ground was broken at Willow Run for the bomber plant in 1941. The plant was completed in less than a year, and the first plane rolled off the line onto the tarmac in September 1942. Charles Lindbergh, who had been hired by Henry Ford, was one of the test pilots for the initial Liberators. Many of the former Camp Willow Run boys became workers at the plant, joining some 42,000 others. Given the scope of the undertaking, there were many ramp-up issues. Knudsen considered dialing back on Ford's ambition and let them concentrate solely on mass-producing B-24 components. Given the slow progress in meeting its stated target of one bomber per hour, the press started to refer to the bomber plant not as "Willow Run" but as "Will It Run."

The issues at Willow Run were gradually ironed out, and the plant hit its stride in 1944, with 650 Liberators produced that April alone. It had reached the rate of one bomber every sixty-three minutes, or nearly twenty-four each day. There was a continuous line of one hundred bombers in the plant at any time. As the plant finally fulfilled its promise, Charles Sorensen was dubbed the "Wizard of Willow Run" in the press. As expected, this did not sit well with Henry Ford, and he sacked Sorensen in March 1944.

In spite of the problems, the payoff was huge. The completed B-24 was 110 feet long, 67 feet from wing tip to wing tip, and weighed in at twenty tons. It was powered by four 1,200-horsepower Pratt and Whitney radial engines, many of which were built at a new Buick factory in Chicago. The plane could carry four tons of bombs up to three thousand miles at 300 mph. Willow Run built 8,865 Liberators during the war.

Paul's work at Wichita Falls was interrupted in June 1942 when Lucile traveled from Williamsfield and she and Paul were married in the base chapel. Lucile's father, Isidor Daub, was on hand as well as members of Paul's Army Air Corps squadron. The newlyweds spent the summer in Wichita Falls, at which time Lucile returned to Williamsfield to continue teaching at the high school.

In August 1942, Paul was sent to the Army Air Corps base at Chanute Field in Rantoul, Illinois, for advanced aircraft training. Rantoul was close enough to Elmwood to allow him to spend several weekends at the farm. That fall he returned to Sheppard Field to continue aircraft work and conduct classes for new recruits. Paul may have wondered during this time why a college graduate with ROTC training was being groomed for aircraft maintenance. The answer came that November. He was tapped for Officer Candidate School and ordered to report to Fort Knox. The "Fort" was definitely not Army Air Corps. It was the center of the US Army's armored training. He would be stripping off the Army Air Corp insignia and replacing it with an armored division insignia.

As with most areas of armed readiness, the Army's tank program was woefully inadequate. At Fort Knox, tank maneuvers in the early years of the war included supporting soldiers on horseback. These cavalry units had no problem keeping up with the slow tanks the Army currently had in the field. This concept of an armored unit changed dramatically in 1940.

The Allies in Europe were first stunned in late 1939 when the Germans struck Poland with swift tank-led motorized divisions. The Germans called this *blitzkrieg,* or lightning war. Poland was overwhelmed and surrendered within weeks. This was followed by a lull lasting six months, during which time the German and Allied armies faced each other along the German border from the Low Countries to the Alps. The French expanse of the border was protected by the heavily fortified Maginot Line. But these fortifications did not extend into Belgium and Holland. Plans had been floated to extend the line, but both countries wanted to remain neutral. When it was clear that war was imminent, most of this open border region was frantically blocked by the nearly 1.5 million Allied army mustered by the French, Belgium, Dutch, and British. The six month "Phony War" ended on May 10, 1940, when the Germans attacked, again at blitzkrieg speed.

The Germans used their fast, mobile Panzer divisions to race through defenses. In particular, one of three army groups moved through the Ardennes, a dense forest area that straddles Belgium and Luxembourg, and one of the sections without fortification. The German armored units emerged at Sedan, and then raced behind Allied lines to reach the English Channel on May 17. This effectively trapped the Allied armies in a small coastal pocket centered at Dunkirk. Only the miracle of Operation Dynamo, the British evacuation effort, enabled a majority of the soldiers to escape. The Germans then consolidated their army groups and drove south against the retreating French divisions. They were in Paris on June 15, 1940.

The message of the Allies' swift defeat in Europe would not be lost on the US Army. It would be fielding sixteen armored divisions comprised of seventy tank battalions. This would require a lot of tanks, presumably in excess of fifty thousand. It would also require a lot of officers to lead those tank battalions. Tanks became a top priority for the US Army, for the War Production Board, and for the Armored Center at Fort Knox. This was the grave sense of urgency that awaited Paul when he arrived in late 1942.

Bill Knudsen made the call to Chrysler in June 1940. Walter Chrysler had semi-retired in 1935, and K. T. Keller had succeeded him as head of Chrysler Corporation. Knudsen proposed to Keller that Chrysler build tanks. In addition, because of his manufacturing background, Knudsen suggested building a dedicated plant for the purpose. Keller agreed, and ground was broken in August 1940 in a cornfield in Warren, Michigan, ten miles north of Henry Ford's Piquette plant. The factory, called the Detroit Tank Arsenal, was designed by Albert Kahn and was ready in just seven months. The first tank, an M3 General Lee, rolled out of the building in April 1941. The Detroit Arsenal would eventually have ten thousand employees, working three shifts, while assembling the roughly 4,500 parts to make a tank.

The Detroit Arsenal was the biggest of eleven tank factories. Knudsen had split the contracts among eleven major firms and over a hundred subcontractors. These included the Fisher division of GM (11,000 tanks built during the war), Ford (1,700), American Locomotive (2,300), Baldwin

Locomotive (1,250), Lima Locomotive (1,700), Pressed Steel Car (8,000), Pullman (3,300), and Pacific Car (900). KT's Detroit Arsenal added 22,000.

The M3 General Lee medium tank was the only tank already designed, tested, and ready to build as the United States entered the conflict. It was a given that the M3 was a stopgap solution. It was slow, lacked sufficient armor plating, and was cramped inside for a crew of five. But its main deficiency lay in the fact that its main gun was mounted on a small side turret that only rotated 180 degrees. To attack a target on the other side, the tank driver would have to swing the tank around. Even knowing this, the US and Allied tank commanders still lobbied for all the M3s they could get, and as quickly as they could get them. The priority was on getting equipment onto the battlefield.

The Army had already been working with the tank contractors on the replacement tank, the M4 General Sherman tank. The centerpiece of the new design was a massive turret with complete 360-degree rotation. It also featured heavier armor, a higher top speed, and more crew space. In addition, the new tank was easier to produce and maintain than the M3. Unlike the Germans, whose factories were near the battlefield, Allied tanks needed to be shipped across the Atlantic or Pacific and could not be recycled back to the factory for refit or repair.

Since it was clear that the American medium tanks would be at a firepower disadvantage to the German heavy tanks, the gap would have to be made up both in speed and in raw numbers. The tank engine needed to power the nearly 40-ton M4 at close to 30 mph. There were four competing engines for this role.

The incumbent tank engine, the one designed into the M3 General Lee, was the Wright Whirlwind radial aircraft engine. It was built by Continental under license from Wright and designated the R-975. Its huge footprint resulted in space and cooling issues within the confined crew cabin.

The troubles with the Continental engine led to an interesting approach at Chrysler. Its automobile engineers somehow took five six-cylinder engines from the Chrysler Royal automobile and mounted them in a star pattern around a common crankshaft. This resulted in a very large thirty-cylinder power plant. It was quite a wonder that this was even possible. And, the engineers put it together in just four months. As might be expected, it was not simple to maintain and was even more difficult to drive. The gears did not easily mesh, so the tank driver had to double clutch each shift.

This led the Army to look at another engine, one from Ford. Early in the negotiations with the War Production Board and the Army Air Corps, Ford developed a radial twelve-cylinder engine to replace the Rolls Royce Merlin engine deployed in the British Spitfire. The V-12 was built around a solid cast-aluminum engine block designed and built to aircraft standards. But, this was the contract that Henry Ford did not get. It was, instead, awarded to Packard, which licensed the Merlin engine and manufactured it for both the British Spitfire and the American P-51 Mustang.

Ford did not throw in the towel, however. Ford engineers cut off four cylinders from the V-12 to create a V-8 tank engine. It was a lightweight, compact 500 horsepower engine with huge torque that would easily propel the Sherman at the rated speed. In addition, it was simple to build, easy to maintain, and a snap to drive with its meshed gearing.[71] By the summer of 1943, it was the preferred engine for the Sherman.

One other tank engine was produced and proposed to the Army, a purpose-built diesel from GM. While it was certainly adequate as a power plant, its diesel fuel requirement was a liability, one that would complicate logistics in the field. It was not pursued.

The M4 entered production in October 1941. On the battlefield, the Shermans proved reliable, fast, and mobile. Their weaknesses were armor protection and inferior gun power against the German heavy tanks. This was more than offset by their speed, maneuverability, and sheer numbers. By 1943, one Sherman rolled out a factory door every thirty minutes. A total of 88,000 tanks were produced during the war, with the Chrysler Detroit Tank Arsenal building 22,000 of them.

Paul arrived at Fort Knox as one of eleven thousand officer candidates that would go through the armored program. The commanding officer at the time was Lt. General Jacob Devers, one of the architects of the new Army tank strategy. Unbeknownst to Paul at the time, he would later serve directly for General Devers on the battlefield.

The officer training program was seventeen weeks in duration, split into two segments. The first segment focused on two major areas—leadership and tank warfare. The officer syllabus included Army norms and administration, leadership, and command responsibilities. The tank syllabus included operations, gunnery, maintenance, communications, and tactics. Of course, central to armored training was operation of the tank itself. Fort Knox had extensive grounds for large-scale tank training. As an officer destined for a tank battalion, Paul was expected to learn the

Sherman from the ground up. The tank had a five-man crew. The driver sat in the front left seat and the backup driver and machine gun operator in the front right seat. Crammed into the turret were the gunner, loader, and tank commander. Space was tight, and Paul at over six feet would have a tight fit for any position except for tank commander, who could stand on his seat and ride above the turret. The driver had standard accelerator and clutch pedals, and two levers to steer the tank left and right. The Sherman powered by the Ford engine with meshed gears was easy to drive, if you could consider maneuvering the massive vehicle at up to 30 mph as "easy."

At the successful completion of the officer training, Paul was commissioned as a second lieutenant and was assigned to the 8th Armored Division (the Thundering Herd), newly mustered at Camp Polk, Louisiana.[72] This would require yet another insignia sewn on his shoulder, featuring a tank and lightning bolt. He was the executive officer in charge of maintenance, gunnery, and training for Company D of the 18th Tank Battalion.

Located in north-central Louisiana just east of Texas, between the Sabine and Red Rivers, the area for Camp Polk was chosen for its vast stretches of open territory—some 3,400 square miles. Three major war games maneuvers were conducted in these sprawling Army grounds. "Red" and "Blue" armies totaling up to 350,000 men and their armored vehicles participated. Both Generals George Patton and Dwight Eisenhower were among those who came to the camp to sharpen their armored skills. In the vast marshy areas of these war games, a new vehicle proved its mettle. It was called the "peep," and it was a new reconnaissance car the Army was testing, built by Ford and Willys-Overland.

Camp Polk would prove to be a tough slog. It was hot and humid in summer and damp and chilly in winter. Eisenhower heard it simply described as "mud, malaria, mosquitoes, and misery." This description does not include the snakes and alligators that were common in the area. On the plus side, the size and prominence of the camp during World War II attracted top entertainment. Cary Grant and Bob Hope visited. Frances Langford also came and posed atop a Sherman tank. In the summer of 1943, Paul was sent back to Fort Knox for advanced training. Lucile joined him there for the balance of the summer, and then returned to Williamsfield for her second year teaching at Williamsfield High School.

Paul was on leave again for Christmas in 1943, returning to the 8th Armored in time to participate in another round of full-scale maneuvers in

Texas, this time in freezing rain. In late May 1944, Paul was assigned to an officer pool for reassignment, likely to take an officer's slot in an armored division already deployed in Europe. He received orders to travel by troop train to Fort Meade, New Jersey, and then on to Boston. He sailed on the luxury liner USS *Mariposa* with another armored division.[73] The *Mariposa* zigzagged solo across the Atlantic at close to thirty knots, carrying over four thousand soldiers. For Paul, this Atlantic crossing was noticeably quicker than the one endured by his great-great-great-great grandfather Heinrich back in 1771.

The *Mariposa* docked at the port on the River Clyde in Scotland, arriving on D-Day, June 6, 1944. Paul then transferred by train to Frome, in Somerset County west of London. Frome had been set up as one of many marshaling areas for American troops arriving from the United States and preparing for the massive invasion of Europe. Paul settled into the Frome barracks, expecting to ship out with an armored unit. While there were drills and exercises to keep in shape, there was also a lot of card playing and trips to the USO.

After several weeks at Frome, Paul received his orders. To his surprise, he was not bound for the Southern ports and a trip to Normandy. He was ordered to report to the US Embassy in London. He did not know it at the time, but his vehicle was about to change from a Sherman tank to a Jeep, the new name for the "peep" he saw at Camp Polk.

The US Embassy was located at the east end of Grosvenor Square in the Mayfair section of London. Directly across the square on the west end was Eisenhower's Supreme Headquarters, American Expeditionary Force (SHAEF). At the north end of Grosvenor Square was the Grosvenor Hotel, whose huge dining room became the officer's mess hall for the Americans. In fact, the entire Grosvenor Square area was called "Little America" for its concentration of American soldiers and facilities. And just off the square was the main NAAFI (Navy, Army, and Air Force Institutes) location, the British equivalent of the American USO.

Initially Paul was billeted with a barrister family in the north of London, after which he was moved to a house closer in town owned by Lord Mountbatten. He was issued British ration cards and took meals at the Grosvenor Hotel. The great mess hall at the hotel was dubbed Willow Run after the B-24 bomber plant for its vast meal production. The dining room seated over one thousand servicemen and served fourteen thousand meals a day at its peak, totaling 5.5 million meals over the course of the war. Generals

Eisenhower, Marshall, and Patton were seen frequently at the dining room prior to D-Day.[74]

Reporting to the US Embassy, Paul learned that he had been selected for a role in the highly secret Allied program called Ultra, the British effort to break the German war code. The British and American governments had negotiated how to share this "ultra" sensitive information with the American armies in the field without compromising the secret to the Germans. The agreement specified that the British would train specially selected liaison teams in the use of Ultra communication intercepts, and those teams would be inserted into each of Eisenhower's army groups. Paul was tapped for this role because he was older, an officer, a college graduate, and someone who had leadership experience with both his aircraft and armored assignments.

His selection was done some time after he arrived at Frome by intelligence specialists with the Office of Strategic Services, the US precursor of the CIA. The American Ultra teams would be part of a counterintelligence group with the OSS called X2. Once Paul reported to the US Embassy in late June, he was directed to OSS headquarters in a nondescript building at 14 Ryder Street, several blocks from the American Embassy. The training would be conducted by British counterparts to the OSS, the MI-6. The American OSS counterintelligence agents were formally called X2 intercept officers. The first step for the American liaison teams was to sign documents that made them subject to the British Official Secrets Act.[75] Once the confidentiality documents were signed, the new X2 teams were trained in the background of Ultra and given an idea of what their role would be.

The Ultra saga had its start in 1923 when a German engineer built an encryption machine and promoted it as a business communications tool. In use, two identical machines were set up, one sending and one receiving. Each machine had a typewriter keyboard with twenty-six letters. As the sending operator depressed a letter on his machine, the selected key would connect via a rotor to one of twenty-six letters in lights. The illuminated light represented what encrypted letter had been selected. The selected light, and thus the selected encrypted letter, would change with each depress of the same letter key. This was the result of the rotating assembly. At the receiving end, a machine with an identical setup would decipher each letter, and hence the message. Adding additional rotors within the machine would increase the potential combinations of input keys and output lights exponentially. Though originally designed to encrypt business

German Enigma machine, with machine settings at top, light section in middle, and keyboard at bottom. (Wikimedia France)

communications, the machine was adopted by the German army in the 1920s for field communications. The machine was called the Enigma.

In 1929 an Enigma machine fell into the hands of Polish intelligence. Immediately understanding the value of breaking the Enigma's code, the Polish army selected twenty outstanding math students, schooled them in in cryptography, and set them to work decoding the Enigma machine. At the same time, the French determined that the Germans had, in fact, adopted the system but had enhanced it by upgrading their machines from one rotor to three. The Polish team proceeded to crack the new three-rotor machines. They were aided by the German army field units' tendency to use repetitive sequences in messages, which the cryptographers called "cribs." For example, it was pretty obvious what the content of messages would be on April 20. That was Hitler's birthday.

In addition, an army major who worked in the German cryptographic section sold several Enigma code books to the French, who passed them on to the Poles. Since the Enigma machine settings were changed every twenty-four hours, the code books were an aid, not a solution. Needing a system to speed up daily decoding, the Polish team set up a rudimentary mechanical device to mimic the action of the rotors and help devise the settings quickly. However, in 1938, with Germany gearing up for war, the German army increased the number of rotors to five.

With both Poland and France in danger of being overrun by the Germans, the British were pulled into the secret in 1940. British intelligence set up an enormous cryptographic organization at Bletchley Park, about fifty miles north of London. They assembled a large staff of math experts and savants. And, as had the Poles before them, the British developed a more advanced mechanical device, called a bombe, to semi-automate the decryption process. In 1942 the German navy enhanced its machines to nine rotors, again raising the number of possible solutions to each depressed key.

At this point Alan Turing, one of computing's most famous pioneers, got involved. He oversaw the construction of an early electronic computer to crunch the Enigma possibilities. This computer was called the Colossus. He also added the important insight of having the computer identify all the possible combinations that were not solutions, leaving a much smaller pool of possible combinations for the cryptographers to deal with. When combined with cribs and intercepted code books, the teams at Bletchley Park were able to get the process down to a twenty-four-hour cycle. The cryptographer Dillwyn Knox is credited with breaking the Enigma code. This led to Enigma intercepts being called ISKs (Intelligence Service Knox).

It would be hard to overestimate the importance of the Enigma breakthrough. It provided a detailed picture of German military movements and foreshadowed German strategies and intentions. Should there have been any inkling that Enigma was compromised, the Germans would have undoubtedly changed to a completely different system. All the work would be lost, not to mention the great strategic advantage that Ultra conveyed.

Given this, the British and Americans decided to create highly trained intelligence field teams that would be responsible for receiving Ultra intercepts, assessing their significance, and combining that knowledge with other types of intelligence to present a picture of German plans. The composition of these teams was thus critical. Each core team would be assigned to an American army group and would be comprised of four members: a chief intelligence officer, an assistant intelligence officer, an engineer, and a specialist in interrogation, who was usually a lawyer. They would be part of OSS but would wear the insignia of their assigned army group. They would be officially known as Special Security Officers, or SSOs, and would report directly to the commanding officer of their army group. Eisenhower decided, perhaps wisely, to keep the team members at fairly low rank so as not to attract undue attention.

Paul was in London training for X2 deployment for about two months. In his new role, he was promoted to first lieutenant, a rank that would not create much suspicion that he held the knowledge of one of the most important secrets of the war. In mid-August, he boarded a ship along with all British units for Normandy. The "lawyer" part of his team was filled by Frank Richardson, who became a lifelong friend as well as rising to be chief justice of the California Supreme Court. The intelligence team was a self-contained unit. It landed at the makeshift harbor at Omaha Beach and was briefly stationed at a seaside villa just south of Mont Saint-Michel. The unit was assigned to the 6th Army Group, which had landed earlier in Southern France and raced northward. It was composed of the US 7th Army and French 1st Army and headed up by General Jacob Devers, the same Devers from Fort Knox and the Sherman tank. Now, however, the vehicle of choice for Paul's team was the Jeep.

Paul had left the 1938 Chrysler Royal with younger brother Bill, moved up to a 1942 Sherman tank, and now traded that for a 1943 Jeep. That Jeep had come a long way in a very short time. In 1940, one of the priority items for Bill Knudsen's War Production Board was producing a new scout or reconnaissance car for the Army. For Knudsen, coming from Ford and GM, it must have been quite a surprise when he was told where some National Guard units were getting their current scout cars. The Pennsylvania National Guard was using a small open sedan made by the tiny car company American Austin under license from the British Austin company. This car had debuted in 1930 and was sixteen inches narrower and twenty-eight inches shorter than any other American car at the time. Given that this was in the midst of the Depression, it was thought that such a small car would do well. That did not turn out to be the case. The company was reorganized in 1937 after selling only ten thousand cars and was renamed American Bantam. The Austin engine was revamped enough to avoid licensing issues, and a somewhat similar small car was announced. It fared no better. The company was near bankruptcy and had let go all of its engineers. It then received a request for a bid from the War Production Board for the scout car. The Army had compiled its specifications and sent them out to 135 manufacturers, including Bantam.

The Army's bid requirements would prove to be slightly wishful. It wanted a rugged four-wheel-drive vehicle that weighed less than 1,300 pounds, was powered by an engine of at least 40 horsepower, and could haul up to six hundred pounds. In addition, bids were due back within a matter of days. The Army received only two bids, one from near-death American Bantam and another from Willys-Overland. Bantam viewed the proposed scout car bid as a possible lifeline. A contract engineer, Karl Probst, was enlisted to design a car for the bid. He was to be paid only if his design actually won the bid. Probst wavered but on July 15, 1940, received a call from Bill Knudsen, who asked him to do it out of patriotism. To meet the Army's specifications, Probst could not rely solely on current Bantam components. He had to find another engine, transmission, and axle just for openers. Yet, he completed his design in five days and sent it to Bantam. In his notes, he estimated the weight of his vehicle, at 1,850 pounds, would significantly exceed the specifications.

The other automotive company responding, Willys-Overland, was not in much better shape. John Willys had returned and rescued the company when it was in receivership in 1933. But Willys died in 1935, and by 1940, Willys-Overland was still making automobiles but with a total annual volume of only twenty thousand cars.

Only American Bantam, Willys-Overland, and Ford were in attendance at the Army's bid meeting. Bantam had a complete bid, down to the design blueprints created by Karl Probst. Willys-Overland had just rough information, no design specifications. And Ford attended without any response at all. Bantam was awarded a preliminary contract and given just forty-nine days to build a prototype. Working in Butler, Pennsylvania, Bantam sourced a four-cylinder 45 horsepower engine from Continental, axles from the Studebaker Champion, and a transmission from Warner Gear. Probst drove the completed prototype 250 miles to Camp Holabird, near Baltimore, Maryland, arriving on the deadline date, September 23. The Army immediately put the vehicle through preliminary testing, and it was quite impressed.

Yet, just as Probst had predicted, the car was way over the Army's weight limit. He was very up front with the Army, indicating that little could be done to shed weight. At that point, a burly Army captain walked to the rear of the vehicle. He lifted the back wheels off the ground and said,

"Feels like 1,300 pounds to me!" And that was that. The US Army ordered a large group of test cars from Bantam and continued putting the little scout through the paces at Fort Benning.

Upon further consideration, likely with Knudsen's input, the Army asked Willys-Overland and Ford to also build test cars using Bantam's design. All three companies received contracts for 1,500 cars. The Willys model (code names "MA" and "MB"), featuring its powerful 60 horsepower Go-Devil engine, arrived at Camp Holabird weighing in at 2,520 pounds. The Ford model (code name "GP") weighed 2,150 pounds. In rigorous testing, the Army rated Willys-Overland number one, Bantam number two, and Ford number three. Willys-Overland was also the low bidder.

Despite how far it had come in the procurement and testing process, the Army was still concerned about the size and financial condition of both Bantam and Willys-Overland and wanted to give the entire scout program to Ford. Knudsen intervened, and the first volume contracts were issued to Willys. Quite soon, the number of scout cars needed soared, and a second contract was awarded to Ford. Bantam was frozen out except for a contract to build trailers for the scout car (Harry Truman, a watchdog on military contracts during the war, launched a Senate investigation as to why Bantam received next to nothing, but it was to no avail).

Willys-Overland ended up building 363,000 cars while Ford manufactured 280,000 more at its Rouge River factory. The new reconnaissance car was not called the MA or MB after Willys designations, or GP or GPW (General Purpose Willys) after Ford designations. It quickly became the "Jeep." And, the little "go anywhere, do anything" Jeep became one of the stars of the Allied war effort. The completed open car was a rugged four-wheel-drive vehicle with a four-cylinder engine capable of a top speed of 65 mph. Despite the Army's initial weight restriction of 1,300 pounds, the finished Jeep ended up with a gross vehicle weight of 3,650 pounds.

➤ ➤ ➤

After arriving in Normandy and linking up with Dever's army at Mont Saint-Michel, Paul and his X2 team moved with the 6th Army Group to Versailles, shortly after the liberation of Paris. In October 1944, an OSS major with knowledge of Ultra was captured near the front lines by the Germans. Fearing the loss of Enigma, General Eisenhower immediately ordered that no Ultra personnel could be closer than thirty miles from the front lines to avoid capture and possibly divulging the Ultra secret. Paul must have mused that as a tank officer he would not have been thirty miles from the fighting but right on the front lines. In November, the 6th Army Group advanced 400 miles across France to secure the eastern front. Paul and team were billeted first at Vittel and then in Phalsbourg in northeastern France.[76]

General Devers and his divisions captured Strasbourg and were poised to be the first Allied army over the Rhine. In December, Paul and the Ultra team stopped getting Ultra intercepts. The Germans had gone silent, dropping Enigma and substituting couriers. On December 16, they launched a full-scale attack on the western front. The Battle of the Bulge was on, concentrated on the Western sector in Belgium. Once again, German armor came crashing through the Ardennes forest. On New Year's Eve, they launched a sweeping second attack called Operation Nordwind on the eastern front, centered on the 6th Army Group's position at Strasbourg. There had been some Ultra intercepts in this area, so the attack was not a total surprise.

Paul's X2 unit moved back the thirty miles to Phalsbourg. With the status of the Allied hold of Strasbourg in the balance, an additional armored division was put on alert, ready to join the fray. That happened to be Paul's former unit, the 8th Armored Division.[77] Heavy winter fighting followed. In March, Devers, working with General George Patton and the 3rd Army Group, broke out of the Rhine bridgehead, through the Siegfried Line, and on to Heidelberg.[78] The German resistance crumbled. Within weeks, the 3rd Army Group had overrun Nuremberg and Stuttgart and liberated the concentration camp at Dachau. By late April, it had captured Munich and proceeded to link up with the US Army advancing from Italy at Brenner Pass. The German surrender came on May 8, 1945. The 6th Army Group was deactivated that July.

Paul flew back to Washington with senior officers on a C54 transport. A memoir of the flight was a "short snorter" dollar bill that was autographed by all the passengers.[79] After stops in Ireland, Newfoundland, and Boston, Paul landed in Washington, DC. He was given leave and took the overnight Capitol Limited train from Union Station in Washington to Chicago.[80] As a result of all his Army pay going to a home bank account, he boarded the train without any spending money. Come dinner time, he went to the dining car to see if he might arrange a sandwich or coffee. Seeing Paul in uniform, the chief steward sat him down and treated him to a very nice steak dinner.

Paul met Lucile at the train station in Chicago. She had money. They spent two days at the Palmer House in Chicago before taking the Santa Fe train to Williamsfield. There, he had the first glimpse of seven-month-old daughter Jane. Paul returned to Washington two weeks later on the Capitol Limited. He ran into the same steward. This time he had money, but the steward still refused to take it and treated him to a second steak dinner.

Paul was assigned to the Siam intelligence unit and told to prepare for possible Pacific duty. He underwent training on Magic, the US deciphering of the Japanese war code, as well as the basics of the Japanese language. Yet, the war with Japan ended in August and he was discharged from his intelligence post before Christmas.

15

War in the Air and at Home

BILL SHAFFER GRADUATED from Brimfield High in May 1941, one of a class of twenty-seven. He was an athletic young man, a multiyear letterman on the basketball team. Everyone liked Bill. He was energetic and popular, "a prince of a guy." But his class graduated as war raged in Europe and tensions were on the rise in the Pacific. His commencement included a call to address "a changed and startled world, find work for your hands in helping to shape a new America, a new democracy, and a new world."

Through the summer and fall, Bill helped John on the farm. He was with Paul when they drove out to see Detta Lou on December 7. Returning to the farm, he knew that any plans he had for the future would have to be put on hold. Paul was drafted in early January and was gone two months later. Bill was still too young to register for the draft, but like most men his age, he wanted to be part of the war effort. He talked with Charleston Dow, a second cousin who was among the Elmwood "expatriates" living in Glendale, California. The nearby Lockheed aircraft factory was gearing up and was desperate for workers.

Bill's interest in naval aviation had grown during the summer. The local newspaper had run full-page ads each week extoling the benefits of a naval enlistment. The Navy's pitchman was none other than "Popeye the Sailor Man," Popeye joined the US Navy in 1941, at least in the cartoons, and held forth on the free meals, free board, free training, and free travel that came with the Navy. He also stressed that you would look good in a naval uniform and get paid very good money.

With the Chrysler falling to him, Bill took four leisurely days to drive out to California and seek work. He secured a job with Lockheed in its Burbank plant, building P-38 Lightning fighters and B-17 Flying Fortress bombers. After a couple of months, Verne joined him in Glendale and they rented a place together.

Bill was just one of the 98,000 employees that worked there during the war. Prior to the war, the Lockheed Burbank factory had signed on to build Vega transports, Hudson bombers, and the P-38 twin-tail Lightning fighter. Securing an additional contract to build 2,750 B-17 Flying Fortress bombers under license from Boeing required that a new plant be constructed at the north end of the complex (this building would later gain fame as the assembly area for the U-2 and SR-71 spy planes, and the stealth F-117 aircraft).

At about the same time in early 1942, a Japanese submarine surfaced offshore of an oil field near Santa Barbara and lobbed a few shells. Although damage was minimal, it raised the fear of more attacks while stoking concerns about Japanese Americans in California. The Lockheed facility took advantage of set designers in nearby Hollywood and had its entire manufacturing plant area covered with a camouflage of burlap tarps. The tarps were painted with a complete and intricate scene of homes, false trees, and even fire hydrants. To a Japanese pilot it would have appeared as simply another large tract of suburbia. Bill would park the Chrysler in the parking lot under the tarp and clock into the plant. By war's end, Lockheed had built 19,278 aircraft, about 6 percent of the total American aircraft production. The site is now known as Bob Hope Airport.

In June 1942, the Selective Service lowered the draft age to eighteen and Bill registered. He was listed at 5'11" and 180 pounds, with brown eyes and brown hair, tall like Paul but stocky like John. His experience at Lockheed building airplanes, especially the P-38 fighter, whetted his appetite to fly. In December 1942, he enlisted in the Naval Reserves Cadet Program, geared to dramatically increase the pipeline of Navy pilots. Those selected would receive extensive pilot training, ending with gold wings and a commission as a Navy officer. As an added enticement, those who enlisted were not subject to being drafted by another service. Candidates were called up as the Navy built up the training program and determined the number of pilots needed.

Before accepting any young men into the program, the Navy conducted a barrage of tests. For openers, there were the general physical requirements. You had to be of average height, have 20/20 vision, and be in good shape. You were tested on color perception and then placed in a spinning chair apparatus to check for stability under different motions and head positions. There was a psychiatric exam and an FBI security check. And finally, there was an aptitude test. Ironically, many of these qualification hurdles had been developed by the Japanese and adopted by the US Navy. Bill passed all of the tests, was certified as qualified, and continued to work at Lockheed. In June 1943, the Navy notified him of his acceptance into the program and ordered him to report to the University of Texas in Austin for the initial cadet training school.

When the Navy program was instituted, it took about eighteen months to complete. By the time that Bill entered the program, the Navy had slowed the transit rate to two years in order to match the deployment needs. This was done in part by adding an additional school at the front end, the Flight Preparatory School. This was a twelve-week school with classroom aeronautical training and flying in Piper Cubs. This training was set up at several universities around the country. Bill was assigned to the program at the University of Texas at Austin. While he was there, Verne and John drove from the farm to visit.

In October, Bill proceeded to Kerrville, Texas, for the Wartime Training Service (WTS) flying school. This was another school added to keep cadets in the pipeline a little longer. It was also a twelve-week program with a heavy emphasis on flying, conducted at the private Kerrville Flying Service in Piper Cubs.

The next step was Preflight School. Bill arrived on the campus of the University of Georgia in Athens in December 1943. This was the main ground education and fitness school. The fitness part was rigorous and was meant to be selective to the point of driving a 5 percent dropout rate. College football coaches were enlisted to conduct the physical drills. Somewhat surprisingly given normal allegiances, Paul "Bear" Bryant from the University of Alabama was there in Athens to run Bill and his fellow recruits through the drills. Being a Navy program, a swim test was included—but it was not just any swim test. The cadets were loaded in a plane fuselage and dumped upside down into a pool. Bill managed to get out and swim to the surface.

His reward was Primary Flight School in Ottumwa, Iowa, starting in May 1944. He spent fourteen weeks in Ottumwa, logging over a hundred hours of flight time in a Stearman biplane called the Yellow Peril, so named for obvious reasons. A welcome side benefit to being in Ottumwa was proximity to the farm. Bill was able to take leave and drive home.

By mid-1944, the Navy had determined the pilot pipeline was still too big. This was primarily the result of a lower pilot loss rate in Pacific action. Early in the war, American fighter planes were not as competitive against enemy combat planes such as the Japanese Zero. Now, the F6F Hellcat fighter was deploying in large numbers and was building a 19:1 kill ratio. This meant more Navy pilots were surviving for more and more missions. Starting in 1943, the Navy started raising washout objectives, eventually targeting as many as 50 percent of cadets.

Yet, Bill kept rolling along and was promoted in August 1944 to Intermediate Flight School in Corpus Christi, Texas. Here, the classroom was mostly left behind. It was fourteen weeks of more rigorous flying that included formation flying, landing, gunnery and dogfighting, and instrument flying. In addition, cadets were upgraded from training aircraft to the North American SNJ, a single-wing, heavy aircraft very similar to the Hellcat. This school was an important milestone in the cadet program, as successful completion got you your gold wings and a commission as an ensign in the Navy. For Bill, this ceremony was conducted in April 1945.

With his wings and commission in hand, the next step was operational school. Since Bill had requested deployment as a Navy fighter pilot, he received orders to report to the fighter pilot training base at the Naval Air Station in Melbourne, Florida. The Navy had constructed seven bases on the east coast of Florida, each specializing in a different type of aircraft (fighters, bombers, transports). The bases were at Banana River, Miami, Ft. Lauderdale, Daytona Beach, Deland, Sanford, Key West, and Melbourne. The latter was operational in late 1942, and flight operations peaked in 1944 with over 150 Hellcats and a full complement of a thousand enlisted men. As the base mission was training carrier pilots, a satellite base called Valkaria had been built five miles south, close to the Indian River, and set up to practice carrier landings.

Bill had one small detail to attend to before traveling to Florida. Since graduating from Brimfield High, Bill was not completely focused on flying. While at Lockheed, he had met Charlotte O'Brien. She had grown up in Glendale, California, went to Glendale High, and had started work at the plant. Through all of the flight schools around the country they somehow managed to keep the romance going. As deployment to the Pacific loomed larger and larger, Bill proposed and Charlotte accepted. They set a date between the end of training at Corpus Christi and Bill's start date at Melbourne. For just a few short days, it was back to the farm. They were married on April 29, 1945, at First Presbyterian Church in Peoria. John was Bill's best man and Detta Lou was Charlotte's bridesmaid. Bill was in his dress blues with the newly acquired gold wings. Charlotte wore a pastel-green dress with pink accessories. Charlotte's parents, Stacey and Blanche, traveled from California. The "honeymoon" as it were would be in Florida. Bill was due at the airfield by May 4.

When Paul went into the service in February 1942, the 1938 Chrysler passed to Bill. Before heading to Florida he was able to trade the '38 for a newer car. The "new" car was only slightly newer: a 1939 Chrysler Royal. Ironically given the painful Airflow experience, the 1939 Chrysler had eased back in some of the aerodynamic features of the Airflow cars. The torpedo headlights were now flush with the fenders. The running boards were slimmed down, and the grille was less blunt to the wind. The gearshift was mounted on the steering column for the first time.

As a serviceman, Bill had a higher allotment of gasoline through ration cards. Bill and Charlotte loaded the "new" car and drove to Melbourne, arriving on the second of May. They rented a house and immediately hit the beach. Reporting to the Naval Air Station, Bill would be exchanging the Chrysler for a Hellcat fighter plane. The Hellcat had an eighteen-cylinder 2,800 cubic inch radial engine generating 2,100 horsepower for a top speed of 380 mph. The Chrysler had the inline six-cylinder, 241 cubic inch engine generating 102 horsepower for a top speed of 95 mph. It was quite the step up.

The Hellcat (formally designated the F6F) was developed by Grumman Aircraft in Bethpage, Long Island, New York. Grumman was a long-time builder of Navy carrier deck planes. The company had pioneered the wing-folding mechanisms that increased the total number of planes that could be carried on the carrier deck. The Hellcat was the replacement for the Grumman Wildcat (F4F), which, in turn, had replaced a Grumman biplane used in the 1930s.

The Wildcat was a good fighter, but early battles with Japanese Zeros showed the Zero was more maneuverable and could climb faster whereas the Wildcat had better armament and a much better ability to absorb damage and protect the pilot. Understanding the reasons for the high loss rate with the Wildcat was a core challenge in the design and development of the Hellcat. To that end, the Army Air Force and Grumman would have loved to have a Zero available for comparison. As luck would have it, during the June 1943 Japanese attack on Dutch Harbor in the American Aleutian Islands, a Zero crash-landed on a nearby island. The pilot was killed on impact and thus unable to destroy the plane. The plane was retrieved and sent to San Diego, repaired, and put to extensive flight tests, all of which were helpful in the design of the Hellcat.

Grumman intended to keep the positives of the Wildcat, such as its heavy armor protection of the pilot, while addressing the shortcomings. The real key was the new engine, the Pratt and Whitney R-2800 Double Wasp. Its beefed-up horsepower enabled the new plane to be heavier and sustain more damage while still being faster. The R-2800 engines came to Grumman from several automobile plants—Studebaker's Los Angeles plant; Chevrolet's Tonawanda, New York, plant; and Ford's Dearborn plant.

The Zero and Hellcat were dramatically different. The Zero weighed in at 5,200 pounds versus the Hellcat at 9,050 pounds. The Zero's fuselage was paper thin. It didn't take much to kill the pilot and thus down the plane. In contrast, the Hellcat could sustain grievous wounds and still limp back to the carrier, safely returning the pilot for future action (which the Navy had invested over two years in training). The Zero's lightness did have the advantage of making the plane more maneuverable. The weight difference also affected stall speed. The Zero would stall out at the very slow 69 mph while the Hellcat had one of the highest stall speeds, at 84 mph.

The Grumman contract for the Hellcat was signed in June 1941. General Motors was given a contract for the ongoing F4F Wildcat program to free up the Grumman factory. The first Hellcat flew in June 1942, and mass production commenced that November. Grumman built 12,274 Hellcats. GM added about 6,000 Wildcats.

The arrival of the Hellcat immediately reversed the fighter equation in the Pacific. It became the US Navy's dominant fighter plane, with the most aces (305) and most kills (5,200).

Bill reported to the Melbourne air base on May 4. This final school in the Navy training sequence would prepare the pilot for actual combat. It would stress tactics, dogfighting, and, in particular, carrier operations. But the first phase was to learn an entirely new aircraft, the Hellcat. This started with a flight simulator. Here, Bill was first exposed to the complexity inside the cockpit. While there were the standard throttles and flight pedals, the dash was crowded with switches, levers, and gauges. There were controls for ignition, carburation, landing gear, wing lock, and flaps. There were gauges for airspeed, rate of climb, tachometer, attitude gyro, altimeter, directional gyro, bank indicator, ammunition rounds, counter, oil pressure, fuel pressure and fuel status, manifold pressure, cylinder head temperature,

The cockpit of the F6F-5 Hellcat. (Courtesy of Yanks Air Museum, Chino, California)

and much more. Then, right in the center of the cockpit was the gunsight. It dominated the view directly ahead and looked somewhat like a submarine periscope. Adapted from the gunsight in the British Spitfire, the unit illuminated the target ahead in cross hairs on the cockpit windshield with guides to optimal firing of the six machine guns mounted in the wings.

Once seated in the cockpit and ready to start the engine, the pilot needed to lock the wings, check and adjust the gas mixture, set the blower, set the propeller, switch the fuel pump on, set the cowl flaps and tabs, and unlock the tail wheel. Then and only then, he would signal the ground crewman to fire the shotgun capsule that would explosively start the engine.

After several weeks of flight time to acclimate to the new plane, there would be practice on gunnery, flying in formation, and fighter tactics. Then came the most critical and difficult skill: carrier landings. This was done at the remote Valkaria Field. The airstrip was marked like a carrier deck so that both the pilots and instructors could gauge if the landings and take-offs were successful. The training was done in a racetrack approach, where each pilot would approach the "carrier" and land, then immediately take off and return to a loop of Hellcats. Sticking the landing was difficult to master. In order to land successfully, you had to approach at an airspeed just seven knots above stall speed and at an altitude of just one hundred feet. At that position, there was virtually no chance to recover if you stalled out.

It was July 1945, and the carrier landing drills were Bill's last phase at Melbourne. His next stop would be the Naval Air Station at Glenview, Illinois, on the outskirts of Chicago, where landing practice would continue on real carriers. Well, they would be real carriers dimension-wise but nothing more. Termed the "Corn Belt Fleet," these were two former Frank Kirby steamships, the *Wolverine* and the *Sable,* that had been converted into carrier practice ships.[81] After several weeks and the completion of at least five successful landings, the pilot was cleared for deployment to the Pacific.

Friday, July 13, 1945, was another hot summer day in Melbourne, with afternoon temperatures in the high eighties. If he didn't have carrier landing practice, Bill would be down at the beach with Charlotte, working on their tans. Instead, he drove to the base. Bill checked out his Hellcat, took off from the main field, and headed south for Valkaria Field. He slipped into formation with several other Hellcat pilots. Once in the racetrack line for the practice field, he completed two touch-and-go landings, had completed the grand loop, and was in the approach for his third landing of the day. He descended to about one hundred feet and slowed for the landing.

His airspeed must have slipped, and the plane momentarily stalled. He pointed the nose down and recovered, but the plane stalled a second time. This time, Bill was unable to recover, and he plunged straight down into the Indian River. On impact, he was thrust forward into the Hellcat's gunsight.

The pilot immediately behind Bill radioed the base, and within minutes an ambulance arrived. Bill was pulled out of the cockpit and hustled to the ambulance. He was alive but in a coma. He was transferred from the base hospital to the US Naval Hospital in Jacksonville. Verne and Paul traveled by plane to the hospital, joining Charlotte at Bill's bedside. He did not regain consciousness and died on July 18, 1945. He was just twenty-two years old.

Verne, Paul, and Charlotte drove back to the farm. It was a long, sad trip. Bill's body was transported to Elmwood, and he was buried next to his namesake father with full military honors at Elmwood's cemetery. Charlotte stayed at the farmhouse for several days, along with her mother, who had come out by train for the funeral. Charlotte then drove the '39 Chrysler back to California and started a new life.[82]

Bill was one of sixty-three pilots who were killed in training at Melbourne, Florida, during the war, including at least one other who had died at Valkaria Field in the same manner. Bill's commanding officer, Captain Devere L. Day, wrote an extensive letter to his widow Charlotte, describing the accident and ending it in sadness that such a fine young man had been lost. Verne talked with a fellow pilot of Bill's who said that the pilot harness on the Hellcat was poorly designed, making the plane more difficult to control when cinched tight, especially in critical situations like carrier landings.

Bill's father had been killed for the lack of a seatbelt in the TT truck. Bill had the harness fastened but fastened loosely. Had he had the harness fastened tight he might not have been thrust forward into the Hellcat's gunsight and very likely could have survived the crash. Bill was one of the last casualties of the war. The war in Europe had been over for two months. Japan would surrender in less than a month.

Interestingly, it turned out that the author's father-in-law had virtually the same wartime experience as his Uncle Bill, except for the tragic ending. Charles Ward Erwin, known as "Ward," was born in 1924 in Chicago. He was just over a year younger than Bill and in September 1942 was just starting freshman year at Carleton College. Two months into college, he enlisted in the same Navy cadet program and was called up in mid-1943. He attended the Flight Preparatory School in Monmouth, Illinois (the school that had been added to slow the pilot pipeline). He went on to his primary flight school at Minneapolis, with the flying done in Piper Cubs. Then, it was out to Iowa City for preflight school at the University of Iowa that included the same physical regimen that Bill had endured at the University of Georgia.

In 1944 Ward reported to the Naval Air Station in Pensacola for intermediate flight school, training in the Hellcat-like SNJ trainer. He received his commission and wings at Pensacola. In early 1945, Ward was at Naval Air Station Sanford, near Orlando, a second operational school created for Navy fighter pilots. They used an outlying field called Osceola for carrier landing practice. In April 1945, he was promoted to Naval Air Station Atlantic City, where he had five good carrier landings on a real carrier stationed offshore. He was set to be deployed and scheduled to join an air group forming for duty on the new Essex-class carriers USS *Champlain* or USS *Antietam,* but the war ended before he saw any action. He was separated from the Navy in November 1945 after roughly 98 weeks of schooling.

➢ ➢ ➢

With Paul and Bill off to war, John, Georgia, Verne, and Detta Lou remained on the home front. The war effort reached every corner and every person in America. In May 1942, the Office of Price Administration (OPM) issued Ration Book No. 1. This was the first of many ration books and the primary vehicle for the extensive rationing to support the war effort. A ration book was issued to each man, woman, and child not in the armed services. The OPM had enlisted 245,000 elementary schools as centers to administer the books locally. Each book contained twenty-eight stamps, one for each rationed item. The list of items was long. It included sugar, coffee, meat, canned goods, and much more. Stamp No. 17 in the first book was good for one pair of shoes. And if you needed a pair of shoes, you needed to act quickly, as the all of the stamps had end dates and there was no flexibility with ration books.[83]

At the start of the war, there were twenty-seven million automobiles in the country. Those cars would have to last the duration of the war. There would be no more new cars until late 1945. Use of existing automobiles was, of course, a prime rationing target. Gasoline, tires, and replacement parts were all rationed. There was a separate system for gasoline, a card with a letter from A to E. Letter "A" holders were pleasure drivers while letter "E" holders were for emergency vehicles. Associated with each letter was the number of gallons you could purchase at a time. Service members on leave could purchase one gallon of gasoline per day. Regardless of letter, driving was severely constrained. Biking made a comeback, but only if you already had a bicycle. You could not buy a bicycle, as the steel was going into essential war goods.

Not all of the home-front rationing was administered out of Washington. There were local committees. Mrs. William Carter of French Grove was on the Brimfield sugar rationing committee. All members were required to take an oath of office before assuming their duties. The committee would issue sugar certificates for the purpose of canning. This was limited to ten pounds per person. Food rationing led to Victory Gardens. Henry Tully was the local Victory Garden chairman. As the war progressed, the programs changed. Coffee rationing ended in 1943. The value of gasoline cards was raised in June 1945 after VE Day.

One purchase that did not require a ration stamp was a ticket to the movies. The Palace Theatre in Elmwood provided a brief respite from the total focus on the war. The film *Casablanca* came to the Palace in March 1943. The magazine *Movie-Radio Guide* had changed its ratings system from 1–5 stars to 1–5 "V"s. For some reason, *Casablanca* only rated 3 V's, though it is now ranked #3 by the American Film Institute among all American movies.

Aside from rationing, there were other programs to help the war effort. A Brimfield group was formed to run a scrap metal drive. They noted that an old clothes iron recycled would make two steel helmets or thirty hand grenades. There was also a series of war bond drives to help finance the conflict. One home-front program that the Midwest (luckily) missed out on was air-raid drills.

For John, running the farm during the war was a mixed bag. Farming was deemed a critical industry with the mission to feed the home population, the military, and Allied partners. Farmers were subsidized with price support of key crops (corn, wheat, soybeans, cotton, and livestock) in order to ensure adequate supplies. Prices were also calibrated to match the farmer's buying power with that of the industrial workers.

Yet, John faced two major obstacles in getting the crops out—manpower and equipment. Over ten million men had been drafted. And, most of the men who were not drafted wanted to fight in the war, not work on the farm. Thus, what used to be a minor challenge to get hired help turned into a near impossibility. So, there was full employment in the country but not on the farm.

The answer lay in productivity. Farm yields continued to rise during the 1940s. Average corn yields grew from forty to fifty bushels per acre. John had already been using Case tractors for nearly a decade. The number of tractors increased from 1.5 million to 2.4 million over the course of the war. Tractors, tractor parts, and implements were being produced, but the supply was limited. If you needed a part, a Peoria county committee would hear your request and, if approved, would issue a certificate to take to a dealer. The dealer may or may not have the part you needed. In 1943, tractor production was limited to 40 percent of the 1940 volumes. By 1944 this was relaxed to 80 percent, along with complete relaxation of tractor parts.

The other looming challenge was the Chrysler. It had survived the Depression, but despite John's best efforts, it was on its last legs. Enter Dan McCoy once again. McCoy had retired from farming the old McCoy homestead in French Grove in 1927, shortly after buying the 1925 Studebaker Brougham. He moved to Peoria and started work as a representative for a milling company. In late 1941, he bought another top-of–the-line Studebaker, a 1942 Commander Skyway. The Commander line had replaced the Dictator line, the name changed for obvious reasons. Ever on top of the automobile scene, McCoy had moved fast when it was clear that automobile production would be halted and was able to buy one of the last Studebakers off the assembly line. When the Chrysler could not be patched together any longer, McCoy sold the Studebaker to John.

John and Georgia anchored the French Grove home front. The old farmhouse saw plenty of comings and goings. When Bill was drafted into the Navy cadet program in June 1943, Verne moved back to the farm for the summer. Detta Lou graduated from Western State Teachers College that June with degrees in home economics and chemistry. She secured a teaching position at Oakwood High School in Sibley, Illinois, starting in August. Verne joined Detta Lou in that farm town for the school year. They both returned to the farm for the summer of 1944, and then back to Sibley for the following school year.

Meanwhile, back at the farm, John and Georgia started a family, adding Eleanor in 1942 and Reed in 1943. While this filled a couple of empty bedrooms, it would not be enough to save the one-room schoolhouses. For the 1944–1945 school year, there were ten students with Mrs. Leila Bodinus teaching. John was a trustee of the school. Though reformers had pushed for school consolidation for years, rural parents, comfortable with agrarian traditions and learning with McGuffey readers, had continually resisted. Yet, when it was clear that there would only be nine students for the next school year, the decision was made to close the school. And with that, the local tradition of one-room schoolhouses, embodied at French Grove, Reed, and Nightingale schools, passed into history.

16

Post-War Scramble

DR'S SPEECH IN 1940 introduced the term "Arsenal of Democracy" with a challenge to produce fifty thousand airplanes a year. Actual aircraft production during the war was over 300,000, with nearly 100,000 planes produced in 1944 alone. And, aircraft numbers were only part of the story. American industry had turned out over 100,000 tanks, two million trucks, over 600,000 Jeeps, 87,000 ships and countless other war munitions. FDR's billion-dollar request in 1940 eventually turned into $337 billion. The automobile industry was the behemoth of the war effort, producing roughly a quarter of all material, including 75 percent of all aircraft engines, 80 percent of all tanks, and 100 percent of all vehicles. Of course, the American war effort came at enormous human cost, with over 400,000 deaths, including that of Ensign William C. Shaffer.

In April 1945, with victory in Europe only days away, the War Production Board announced that automakers could resume limited civilian production of automobiles on July 1, 1945. Quotas were set for the second half of the year, with limits of 184,000 cars for the Big Three and 57,000 cars for the seven independents (Studebaker, Nash, Hudson, Packard, Crosley, Kaiser, and Frazer). The quotas were removed in August with the surrender of Japan, though there was one unusual caveat: new cars could not include a spare tire.

After five years of profitable war production contracts, the automotive companies were flush with cash. Likewise, the war years of full employment and extensive rationing meant that virtually everyone else was also holding onto a lot of cash and long shopping lists. The wartime restrictions on gasoline, tires, and parts meant existing automobiles had to be nursed through the war. Old cars and plenty of cash spelled a seller's market for automobiles. Just about anything on four wheels would sell. The auto makers had their 1942 designs and machine tool dies already in-house. There was really no need nor time to change. Rather, it was a time to start producing new "1942" automobiles. With the quotas removed, auto sales ramped up from 200,000 in 1945 to 2.2 million in 1946, 3.3 million in 1947, and 5.2 million by 1949. The hot market induced a number of new companies to jump in, including Crosley, Kaiser-Frazer, Tucker, and Jeep.

Going into the war, the Ford Motor Company remained a fiefdom run by one man. Edsel Ford was nominally the president, but, as always been the case, Henry Ford continued to call the shots. Chrysler had overtaken Ford in the 1930s to claim the number-two position. Ford's market share, once over 60 percent in Model T days, had tumbled to 19 percent. Even more concerning, the company had consistently lost money during the Depression. Ford did not have even the most basic of controls to track how the company was doing. Despite the fact that James Couzens had saved Henry Ford from himself in the early years, Henry continued to believe that administrative and financial employees were a waste of money. There had not been a single financial audit done for the entire decade. The success in numbers of the Model A and Ford V-8 had masked the real situation. Meanwhile, both GM and Chrysler had come through the Depression in good shape.

In addition, Henry Ford's health was deteriorating. He was nearing eighty, had suffered several heart attacks, and was increasingly frail as the war set in. He seemed to lose the attributes that made him great while falling back on the dark traits that caused many of Ford's problems. He continued to be suspicious and distrustful of everyone, thinking that all were out to steal his money or shadow his glory. As his health declined, he turned increasingly to Harry Bennett, a street thug, to be his enforcer and run roughshod over the entire Ford operation. Bennett had been originally hired to blunt efforts at unionization, but his influence had grown to such an extent that he thought that one day Henry might tap him to take over the company.

Nevertheless, Edsel and his team, and in particular Charles Sorensen, stepped up. The war production at Ford was nothing short of incredible. Just a partial list would include 8,684 B-24 Liberator bombers, 57,000 Pratt and Whitney R-2800 aircraft engines, 278,000 Jeeps, 93,000 trucks, 1,690 M4 Sherman tanks, 27,000 V8 tank engines, and 4,200 wood gliders. Edsel and Sorensen worked long hours managing the breadth and depth of the company's war effort. Sorensen was responsible not only for the Willow Run plant but also for the Jeep and aircraft engine contracts. Henry Ford seemed to step in at inopportune times, such as his veto of the proposed Merlin engine contract.

Edsel's health declined precipitously from overwork and the mental toll of years of his father's abuse. His condition then worsened, and he died in May 1943. Henry Ford stepped back in as Ford's president. The nation's war leaders, and particularly Secretary of the Navy Frank Knox, were aghast. They could not live with the nation's second-leading armaments producer being run by a weak and ornery Henry Ford. There were discussions about brokering a sale of Ford to Studebaker, though calmer heads prevailed. It was the Ford family women, including Edsel's widow Eleanor and Henry's wife Clara, that resolved the crisis. They threatened to sell their Ford stock unless Henry stepped aside and let Edsel's son Henry Ford II take over.

Henry Ford II had joined the Navy in 1941 after graduating from Yale and working in the lower reaches of the Ford Motor Company. He went through Officer Candidate School and was promoted first to ensign and then lieutenant. Shortly after his father's death, he was discharged from the Navy (thanks to Frank Knox) and returned to Ford as a vice president. Henry II was considered by some as too inexperienced to take over such a large and sprawling operation. At the start, he was tutored by Charles Sorensen. When Sorensen was not offered an ongoing role in the company, he retired to Florida (Sorensen quickly unretired, as he was hired as president of Willys-Overland, managing wartime Jeep production and the subsequent transition to peacetime).

Once Henry II took full control of Ford, he moved quickly, taking two important actions. First, he personally fired Harry Bennett (carrying a gun with him just in case) and Bennett's entire department of enforcers. Then, he hired noted automotive executive Ernie Breech, formerly of GM and currently president of Bendix. His goal was to learn the ropes from Breech while working on his central priority, moving Ford from a one-man company to a modern corporation.

As the war ended, Henry II had a visit from Tex Thornton, formerly of the US Office of Statistical Control. This was a wartime organization that hired select individuals based on their innate smarts and set them to do analysis of various Allied operations with an aim to increasing effectiveness and efficiency. One project Thornton's team worked on was an analysis of

the B-29 sorties in the Pacific under General Curtis LeMay. They delivered
a set of recommendations on how to increase results.

At war's end, Thornton handpicked ten of the brightest individuals
from his statistical group and offered them as a package to Henry Ford II.
Ford agreed and hired them. The group came to be known as the "Whiz
Kids" and included Robert McNamara and Arjay Miller, both of whom
rose to the Ford presidency. The first project for this team was the analysis
of Ford operations during the 1930s, which confirmed the Ford losses.

With some semblance of an organization in place, Henry Ford II turned
his attention to building automobiles. His objective was to chase down
Chevrolet and General Motors. Ford was in a good cash position from war
contracts but had ignored its plants for years and would need to make huge
investments in improving manufacturing capacity. Still, he was the first
out with a post-war car, coming off the line in July 1945. Granted, it was
just a 1942 Ford, but that was all that was really required. At the same time,
he set in motion the development of a brand new Ford. Sales of the "old"
Fords for 1947 and 1948 averaged 500,000. His new Ford, the sleek 1949
model[84], took the numbers off the chart, exceeding one million in sales for
the first time since 1929 and the Model A. Even more importantly, Ford
topped Chevrolet for the year. The two brands would go at it neck and neck
throughout the 1950s. Over the next few years, Ford market share climbed
steadily, up to 31 percent.

In sharp contrast with Ford, General Motors was in great shape when
automobile production was halted in 1942. Despite lower volumes, it had
made money throughout the Depression. In 1941, four of the top six car
brands were GM divisions (Chevrolet, Buick, Pontiac, and Olds), and most
importantly, Chevrolet was number-one in sales, with a significant lead
over second-place Ford.

All seventeen GM divisions were active in the war effort. As a company,
GM built 854,000 trucks, over 200,000 aircraft engines, 38,000 tanks and
tank destroyers, and a huge list of other armaments. By value, GM produced 41 percent of the total munitions produced by the automotive industry. The Chevrolet division produced 60,000 Pratt and Whitney R-2800
radial engines and over 500,000 trucks. Buick built M-18 tank destroyers
and radial engines for the B-24 Liberator. Cadillac built the M5 Stuart tank,
including the V8 engine that powered it. The Olds division produced can-
nons and the millions of shells needed to outfit them. Pontiac took on the
complex Bofors antiaircraft gun that was manufactured by hand in Sweden

and produced thousands in assembly line fashion. The Fisher Body division built 11,000 Sherman tanks.

General Motors transitioned to car production in the fall of 1945. Across all five divisions, the "new" cars were 1942 models that had been gussied up with bits of chrome here and there. There was almost a cottage industry in grille redesign. There was no new Chevrolet until 1949, yet it remained the best-selling automobile brand, even if pretty stale. There were no new Pontiacs until 1949 and no new Buicks until 1950.

The high-end Oldsmobile 98 and Cadillacs were restyled in 1948. Harley Earl, chief of GM styling, had paid a visit to Selfridge Air Base and marveled at the look of the P-38 fighter planes. He was particularly enamored of the twin tails on the plane. These became modest tail fins on the new Olds and Cadillac models, ushering in the fin age.

GM's market position dipped slightly in 1947, though it still had four of the top seven brands. However, upstart Studebaker was nipping at GM's heels, at number eight.

K. T. Keller had guided Chrysler through the war. He had built the Detroit Arsenal tank plant in record time, and then proceeded to produce over 22,000 tanks. Chrysler built another dedicated plant, this one in Chicago, to produce the Wright R-3350 aircraft engine. This engine was destined for the B-29 Superfortress bomber, which turned out to be the largest and most expensive American program of the war, costing even more than the Manhattan Project. The plane, weighing over three times the B-24 Liberator bomber, was powered by four of the Wright engines. Virtually all of the automobile companies were involved in some aspect of the B-29. The rear fuselage section was constructed by Hudson, the front fuselage by Desoto, the rear tail turret assembly by the Fisher Body, and the bomber nose by Chrysler. Chrysler also worked on the Manhattan Project, making the diffusers that were used in Oak Ridge to separate fissionable uranium-235 from uranium-238.

Having been stung by the failure of the revolutionary Airflow cars in the mid-1930s, Keller had moved the company back to conventional designs. The last Chrysler rolling off the line in 1942 was downright dumpy. Keller had started in automobiles as an engineer and was naturally conservative where Walter Chrysler was not. If anything, the Airflow fiasco pushed him even further away from any styling deviations. He liked tall, boxy cars where men could wear their hats while they drove. He would show up at styling reviews and sit in the car with his hat on. If the hat touched the ceiling, the roofline had to be raised. Keller poured resources into engineering and let the styling departments limp along. Chrysler styling was on life support for nearly twenty years after Airflow.

Of course, the first Chrysler post-war models were pre-war cars. Like the other automobile companies, there was a focus on restyling the grilles so there was just enough differentiation to call it somewhat new. Though the Chrysler cars from 1946 to 1948 were those slightly altered pre-war designs, sales were robust. Plymouth sold a million cars over the period, which allowed Keller to keep pace with Chevrolet and Ford. A new design was not ready until the 1949 model year, and it was equally boxy and boring. Meanwhile, Ford, GM, and Studebaker were all charging forward with streamlined looks—or, in other words, imitations of the Airflow.

Willys-Overland was saved by the Jeep contract. Despite not submitting a valid response or building a prototype, the company received a huge contract and built 350,000 Jeeps during the war. The inventor of the Jeep—Bantam—was essentially shut out of its own design. Karl Probst, the engineer that Bill Knudsen asked to design the scout car out of patriotism, was paid a paltry $200 for his efforts. Moreover, a concerted effort by Willys-Overland to claim credit for inventing the Jeep pushed Probst's central role further into the mists of history. As early as April 1942, Willys-Overland started an ad campaign that claimed it had created the Jeep. It then took it a step further, trademarking the "Jeep" name with an idea to build a new future around the most successful new vehicle of the war. Ford sued Willys-Overland over the trademark filing but failed.

In 1945 Charles Sorensen was hired as president of Willys-Overland. Sorensen looked to create a full range of vehicles based on the military Jeep. Those designs included a civilian Jeep, panel truck, pickup truck, and a woodie station wagon. Though anything on four wheels would sell, the Jeep was something special. Millions of servicemen returned from the conflict with fond memories of it. There was a program to sell surplus war materials, but Jeeps disappeared quickly, much to Sorensen's satisfaction.

Despite the civilian Jeep's potential, Sorensen was not successful in signing up a car body manufacturer. They were not interested in what was perceived as a small-time player. However, the simple, flat-panel construction of the Jeep led Sorensen to a solution. He signed up appliance manufacturers as body suppliers. They were experts at stamping sheet metal into flat shapes like refrigerators and ovens. This limited the curves that could be designed into the new Jeep models, but of course, that was just fine.

What was not fine was the price. He set the civilian Jeep price at $1,136, which significantly cooled reception.

For Studebaker, the timing of the war was not ideal. New leaders Hoffman and Vance had steered the company back from the brink and into eighth position in sales. The company had regained its status as the top independent. The pre-war years 1940 and 1941 had been especially strong, buoyed in large part by finally introducing a successful low-priced model, the Champion. It was Studebaker's third try at the segment and a winning one. The Champion was designed by Virgil Exner, working for the design firm of Raymond Loewy.[85]

Yet, despite the inopportune timing, the company immediately set to work on wartime contracts. It built three new plants and produced nearly 200,000 model US6 2.5-ton trucks, in both 4x6 and 6x6 drive configurations (GM and REO also made the truck). Roughly half went to Russia, where for a time, the Russian word for truck was "Studebaker." Many went to the British, though a large number were captured or destroyed by the Germans at Dunkirk. Studebaker also built roughly 64,000 Wright Cyclone R-1820 radial aircraft engines. All of these engines went into the B-17 Flying Fortress bomber.

And finally, Studebaker built an unusual vehicle called the M29 Weasel. It was a tracked troop carrier, slightly larger than a Jeep and able to cut through the toughest terrain—snow, ice, swamps. Some Weasels were even amphibious. Conceived by British chemist Geoffrey Pike, Studebaker used the straight-six engine from the Studebaker Champion to power the vehicle. Though weighing nearly four thousand pounds, the Weasel's outstanding feature was the minimal ground pressure it exerted—less than that of the human foot thanks to extra-wide tracks. Studebaker produced nearly fifteen thousand Weasels.

The automobile companies were forbidden to work on new car designs during the war. Raymond Loewy, however, had his own design firm and was free to work on any project. Studebaker made the ambitious decision to commission him to work on a complete restyling, to be ready in time for the post-war return to making cars. Unbeknownst to him, Studebaker executive Roy Cole had also contacted Virgil Exner on his team and asked him to also work on a new car design. When Loewy discovered this separate "skunk works" within his own shop, he fired Exner. The separate designs were combined and represented quite a dramatic departure from existing styling.

At war's end, the Studebaker 1942 models, with very minor changes, were carried over for a short time, from December 1945 to March 1946. Championing the brand new models with the slogan "first by far with a post-war car," the new line was introduced that April as 1947 cars. The sleek automobiles were rapidly dubbed the "coming or going" cars as the wraparound rear window and long rear deck on the Starlight coupe resembled the front of the car and begged the question, "which way was it going?" It seems that the long rear deck was initially in plan to develop a rear engine version but that was dropped. The four-door models also had limousine or "suicide" doors where both doors opened at the center, something normally found only in very expensive cars. All in all, it was jarringly different from the warmed-over, boxy, pre-war cars coming out of competitor plants. On the strength of the new models, Studebaker jumped all the way from 15th place in sales to seventh.

Not many auto companies made it out of the Depression, but those that did were heavily involved in war production. Packard survived the 1930s in good financial shape and retained its cachet as a quality brand. A 1940 visit by Rolls-Royce determined its main role for the war—building the Merlin V-12 aircraft engine. The engine, already famous for powering the British Spitfire, was being manufactured by Rolls-Royce and Ford of Britain. But with Germany threatening, Rolls-Royce wanted an American partner. The obvious choice was Ford, but as we have seen, Henry Ford nixed the contract in a fit of pique over losing the contract for his V-12 aluminum aircraft engine. Packard had built the Liberty aircraft engine during World War I, and the Merlin project ended up being a good fit. Though Rolls-Royce hand-built each engine, Packard applied its automotive know-how and turned out over fifty thousand of the complex power plants in assembly line fashion. Many of those engines went into the famous P-51 Mustang plane.

Packard emerged in fine shape in 1945 but was slow in moving to new designs. When the 1948 Cadillacs rolled out with sleekness and fins, Packard was caught flat-footed. The Big Three had the resources to redesign and retool frequently. Packard, as a small independent, did not. Feeling it needed to get bigger to compete, Packard bought Studebaker in 1953. This, however, compounded the company's problems rather than addressing them. Studebaker by this time was losing money, and the chosen fix—using Studebaker designs and components in Packard cars—was anathema to the typical high-end Packard buyer.

Nash, the former Rambler and Jeffrey operation that Charles Nash bought after he left Buick and General Motors, had a busy war. It was a major supplier of the Pratt and Whitney R-2800 Double Wasp engine that powered a number of key airplanes, including the Hellcat. It also manufactured Sikorsky helicopters, propellers, rocket motors, and trailers. Knowing that the post-war honeymoon for old cars would not last, Nash went small and reintroduced the Rambler brand in 1950 as a compact car.

Hudson had made aircraft engine components and was a major supplier for the B-29. Moving quickly and with limited resources, the company was able to roll out a redesigned, sleek, and exciting Hudson Hornet in 1948. Though Hudson went on to dominate NASCAR racing in the early 1950s, it remained an uphill battle for a small independent to survive. Hudson and Nash were later to merge to form American Motors.

Ransom Olds's signature car company, REO, made great cars in limited volume through the 1920s, with great names like the Flying Cloud and the Royale. But the company did not make it through the Depression. It stopped making cars in 1937 in favor of trucks. This did not please Ransom Olds, and he severed his relationship with his namesake company. During the war, REO produced twenty-two thousand trucks based on the Studebaker design.

The pent-up post-war demand for automobiles encouraged several others to jump into the fray, against all odds. One such individual was Henry J. Kaiser. He was justly famous for his production of Liberty ships during the war but had already had great success as a contractor building the Hoover, Grand Coulee, and Bonneville dams. But, like several thousand men before him, he wanted to have an automobile in his own name.

He met another individual who had the same objective, Joseph Frazer. Frazer was an automobile industry veteran, having done stints at Maxwell and Chrysler before coming on board as president of Willys-Overland in 1939. He left the company in 1944 and acquired a small automobile company of high-end, aerodynamically designed cars called Graham-Paige. The company did not make it to the war, stopping production of cars in 1940. But Frazer was able to keep the factory going by producing LVT tracked landing crafts.

The two men, together as Kaiser-Frazer Corporation, decided to go big. They leased the Willow Run bomber facility from the War Production Board (Ford was not interested) and proceeded to turn out not one but two new automobile brands—the Kaiser and the Frazer. They raised $50 million to get started (in hindsight it was woefully too little cash to effectively challenge the Big Three). Before they parted ways, they produced about 700,000 cars at Willow Run from 1947 to 1953. Kaiser was not sufficiently happy with one eponymous automobile so he added a second, the Henry J, in 1950.[86] This car was supposed to address the low-priced segment but did not gain much traction. Kaiser then took out a page from the automotive playbook that said "if you can't beat them, join them" and purchased Willys-Overland in 1954. Seeing that his name was missing, he changed the company name to Kaiser-Jeep. Though the Kaiser, Henry J, and Frazer did not last, Henry Kaiser was eventually able to prove another automotive truism: anyone who owned Jeep was in good shape.

Another run at the post-war automobile boom came from an unlikely source, one with significantly less money than either Kaiser or Frazer. He was Preston Tucker, and he relied on his considerable salesmanship talents to start a new car company from scratch. With very limited funds, Tucker engaged a stylist who had worked on the Cord, Auburn, and Duesenberg luxury automobiles. The completed design was called the Tucker Torpedo. Tucker was then able to convince a roster of prominent auto executives to help him take the design to production. He signed a lease in July 1946 for the Chrysler Chicago plant that had been building the Wright R-3350 engines for the B-29 bomber.

To stimulate interest, Tucker produced several prototypes and toured the country. Renamed the Tucker 48, the car was a sensation, with swooping lines that created a buzz wherever it went. It also resulted in a significant backlog of orders. It was innovative in both design and function, with many features that would become standard in cars years later, including the padded dash, safety cage for passengers, disc brakes, and pop-out windshield. Tucker even staged a rollover much as Walter Chrysler had done with his Airflow model to demonstrate the car's safety and build quality. Finally, the front end featured a bullet nose that predated Studebaker's famous bullet series. However, his "bullet" was actually a working third headlight that would turn as you made a turn.

Back in Chicago, Tucker faced the realities of actually producing automobiles in volume. He needed additional funds for both the factory lease and continued car development. He issued stock in the company, which brought in roughly $26 million. This was not nearly enough. He tapped the long waiting lists of customers for new Tucker cars with an accessory program. If you purchased an additional option for your future Tucker automobile, you would move up in the waiting list. Whether by design or by error, these funds were plowed into development rather than held in escrow for each customer.

Tucker and his team had built fifty-one Tucker cars when disaster struck. The Security and Exchange Commission had been on active alert after the government had loaned the Kaiser-Frazer group $200 million and then felt the money had been misused. With all of the money coming in through creative financing and no cars coming out, the SEC accused Tucker of conspiracy to defraud, claiming he never intended to actually go into production. A lengthy trial ended in acquittal, but by that time the damage was done.[87] The exciting Tucker automobile was not to be. The Chicago plant ended up producing Dodges, not Tuckers.

In April 1942, the US Department of Agriculture took some Jeeps to a farm in Auburn, Alabama. Given the performance of the Jeep in US Army trials, the USDA was interested in seeing how they would perform in farm tasks. The military Jeep was tested pulling a turn plow, disk harrow, grain drill, corn planter, and hay mower. The results were promising, and the department issued a favorable report.

Willys-Overland took note and did not wait for the war to end before acting on the report. Starting in 1944, the company placed ads extolling the use of Jeeps on the farm. Once the war was over, Willys-Overland went to work on formally adapting the Jeep for farm work. The first civilian Jeep was modified, with a larger clutch, lower gear ratios, and lower hitch in back. In 1949 Willys-Overland sent the modified Jeep CJ-3A to the Nebraska Tractor Test Lab for evaluation. There, it predictably suffered in comparison with purpose-built tractors. Still seeing farm applications, Willys announced two special Jeep versions—the Farm Jeep and the Farm Tractor. The Farm Jeep was a stock Jeep CJ-3A with a factory-installed hydraulic lift, drawbar, propeller shaft guards, heavy duty springs, and variable-speed belt-driven governor. The Farm Tractor had all of the above but was shorn of all components that were required to take the vehicle on the road. Both versions significantly inflated the price over a stock Jeep.

Though he was certainly intrigued by these farm models, John Shaffer bought a regular Jeep in April 1951 for $1,224. It was a utility vehicle to use all over the farm in place of general tasks, where the Case tractor was overkill. This Jeep had a rough life on the farm. After several years of abuse, the gas pedal was replaced with a string of bailing wire that was routed through the firewall to the carburetor. The brakes went out, and instead of replacing them, John and his boys simply drove the vehicle into a fence post to stop. As the battery deteriorated, the old Model T starting ploy was put to use. The Jeep was parked on a hill, and you simply rolled it down and let out the clutch. Other than those minor adaptations, the Jeep worked fine.

17

Fins, Fins, and More Fins

P AUL SHAFFER WAS discharged from the Army just before Christmas 1945 and headed back to Williamsfield, staying at Lucile's parents' house in town. He secured a job with Caterpillar. The position would only serve to build up additional cash as he planned to go on to graduate school. Much as it was before the war, getting to and from work at Caterpillar in Peoria was again a challenge. Both the 1938 and 1939 Chrysler Royals were long gone, and cars of any kind were scarce. It was back to the pre-war Route 150 routine. Lucile would drop him off at the main junction south of Laura, and he would hitchhike into Peoria. On occasion he would stay overnight with Verne at her house in town. This was clearly not a sustainable arrangement.

Despite all the training and experience gained in his war service, Paul felt that he needed an MBA to jumpstart his career. That decision was helped by the GI Bill, which Roosevelt had signed in June 1944. It provided "reentry" assistance to returning servicemen, including education reimbursement and low-interest home loans.[88] Paul had discussed graduate study with his Ultra colleague Frank Richardson, who encouraged him to apply to Stanford, his alma mater. Paul did not get into Stanford (a recurring theme with the Shaffers) but had also applied to the business school at the University of California at Berkeley. He was accepted with the caveat that he maintain a B average. Now, a car was a must.

When the war was over, John really wanted a new car, his first new car. He offered the Studebaker to Paul, who readily accepted. John toured the local dealerships and found a Chevrolet 210 Stylemaster for sale at the W. F. Harding dealership in Brimfield. The Stylemaster was technically new, fresh off the assembly line. But it was still the 1942 model with slight cosmetic changes, such as a new grille and chrome trim. Demand was still at a fever pitch, and most new cars had long waiting lists. In addition, returning veterans were given top priority. For John, though it wasn't a Chrysler, it was a new car. For Paul, he was now the owner of a Studebaker, a company with quite a storied history.

Studebaker was a well-known name out west and on the farm. Many of the wagons used for the western migration were Studebaker wagons. It all started in South Bend, Indiana, with the five Studebaker brothers. Coming from a family that were primarily blacksmiths and wagon makers, one of the brothers, John M. Studebaker, built his own wagon and drove it in 1853 to California for the gold rush. He did not have much success in panning for gold, so he started building wheelbarrows to sell to the miners. Back in South Bend, two of his brothers, Henry and Clement, wanted to ramp up a wagon-and-buggy manufacturing operation. They convinced him to return, along with the $7,000 that he had made in his one-wheel venture.

The H & C Studebaker Company had got going in 1852. Besides wagons that plied the Santa Fe and Oregon trails, the company built thousands of wagons for the Union Army during the Civil War. And it expanded into a broad range of buggies, including sulkies, broughams, clarances, phaetons, runabouts, victorias, and tandems. In the Midwest, the company's forte was the sturdy Studebaker farm wagon. J. M. bought out Henry's share of the business in 1858 and the enterprise became the Studebaker Brothers Manufacturing Company.

By the turn of the century, the brothers knew that the future was not in wagons, though they had over 3,000 workers building 100,000 horse-drawn vehicles each year. Clement died in 1901 and J. M.'s son-in-law, Fred Fish, pressed the company to produce a horseless carriage. Their first bet, in 1902, was an electric car. It had a top speed of 13 mph and a range of forty miles. Thomas Edison was involved in the batteries for the car and ended up buying one. The ascendancy of electric cars was very brief and they were quickly eclipsed by a deluge of gasoline cars. The Studebaker brothers produced about 2,000 electric cars before they got the message and rolled out a gas car in 1904 in a partnership with the Garford Company. Garford built the chassis and shipped it to South Bend for the coachwork. It was marketed through Studebaker wagon dealers as the Studebaker-Garford.

Success for Studebaker was slow in coming until they partnered with E-M- F, a company headed by Barney Everitt (a former carriage supplier to Olds and Ford), William Metzger (formerly of Cadillac and a principal in the ALAM cartel), and Walter Flanders (the Ford manufacturing alumnus). Studebaker moved up to number three in sales, behind Ford and Buick. Garford, now without a dealer channel, struggled until 1913 when they were bought out by John North Willys. In 1911, Studebaker used Goldman Sachs to manage an IPO that combined Studebaker Brothers and E-M-F into the Studebaker Corporation. Studebaker, which already had a presence in Detroit with a factory on Jefferson Avenue, moved into the Piquette Avenue factory that had been vacated by Henry Ford.

The Studebaker Brothers era ended in 1915 when Albert Erskine took over the reins of the company. It was Erskine who inadvertently helped Walter Chrysler get going by letting the key engineering team of Zeder, Skelton, and Breer go after they completed the design of the 1918 Studebakers. Yet in the early years, he kept moving Studebaker forward. By 1920, all Studebakers were six cylinders, featuring the Light Six, Big Six, and Special trio. The company reached an early high-water mark in 1923 with revenues of $166 million and income of $18 million, selling 145,000 cars. The company had slipped one notch as Bill Knudsen's Chevrolet had taken over the number-three spot, but things were still in good shape when Dan McCoy bought his Studebaker Brougham in 1925.

Erskine then embarked on a strategy, which though completely sound, would through a series of missteps and back luck end up bankrupting the company. His template was General Motors, United States Motors, and Chrysler, which all sought to create a family of brands that spanned the automobile market, unlike Ford's single-minded focus. First, he decided that Studebaker, a strong midrange marque, needed a low-cost model to compete with Ford and the entry segment. As he was fascinated by all things European and in fact wanted to market the car in Europe, he had designer Ray Dietrich give the car all sorts of Continental touches. It wasn't until 1927 that the car finally appeared, produced at the Piquette plant. Though the car was nicknamed the Little Aristocrat, the Studebaker board decided to call it the Erskine. The car's debut in London, Paris, and New York was favorable but the timing couldn't have been worse. Henry Ford had announced the change from the Model T to the Model A, a thoroughly modern car that sold for about half the price of an Erskine. Erskine's car lasted another four years, mainly by upgrades to move it up in the brand space, before it was dropped.

In 1928, Erskine effected a merger with Pierce-Arrow, an investment that cost $2 million. His strategy called for a luxury brand above the Studebaker marque, and Pierce-Arrow certainly fit the bill. But once again, bad luck intervened. The Great Depression hit the following year, forcing all automobile makers to deal with an over 70 percent contraction in demand in just three years. The challenge for brands such as Pierce-Arrow was even worse.

It was in the face of this existential challenge that Erskine did the unthinkable—he paid his shareholders. Over the first four years of the Depression, Studebaker had a total net income of $4.3 million yet paid out $31 million in dividends. Erskine's view of the corporation was diametrically opposite to that of Henry Ford's. For Erskine, his primary job was to reward shareholders. He even took it a step further, rewarding the shareholders regardless of business results. Henry Ford would first invest in new plants, then in customers with lower prices, before even thinking about shareholders. And, the idea to first reward shareholders during the worst years of the Depression when cash should be conserved and investments made to stay competitive was just not sound.

On top of this, Erksine made a third major mistake. He took another crack at competing with Ford and Chevrolet in the low-price field, once again sound strategy but plagued by poor execution and bad luck. This time it was with a new car called the Rockne. It was, of course, named after the famed Notre Dame coach, who happened to be a good friend of Erksine and a sales executive for the Company. The Rockne automobile sported a new, lightweight six-cylinder engine in order to compete with the Ford Model A. Knute Rockne had been killed in a plane crash shortly before development was complete and the car was christened the "Rockne" as a memorial. Once again, Erskine's timing with Ford could not have been worse. Ford announced the follow-up to the Model A, the Ford V-8, at nearly the same time as the Rockne's debut. The Ford was significantly cheaper, faster, and had two more cylinders than the Rockne. And of course, it was a Ford. The Rockne was gone within the year.

By 1933, Studebaker was in receivership and Erksine had been ousted. Sadly, Albert Erskine took it hard and took his own life. Two of his executives—Harold Vance and Paul Hoffman—picked up the reins at Studebaker. They formed a very effective duo, and, quite miraculously, they proceeded to lead a turnaround at the company. They guided Studebaker to a small profit by 1936 and moved the company up to number eight in sales by 1938. That same year, they engaged Raymond Loewy as a designer. Starting out as a window designer in New York for Macys, Saks, and Wannamaker, he made his name with famous designs for Pennsylvania Railroad's stream-lined diesel locomotive, the Greyhound Scenicruiser bus, the Lucky Strike cigarette package, and the Coca-Cola fountain dispenser.[89] In 1939, Studebaker made its third attempt at competing in the low-price market dominated by Ford, Chevrolet, and Plymouth. With the Loewy-designed Studebaker Champion, the company finally had a winner in its hands. Production numbers doubled. Plant capacity was upgraded to 250,000 cars per year. The year 1941 was Studebaker's best year since the onset of the Depression. Raymond Loewy, supervising a team that included Virgil Exner, designed new looks for the entire line, from Champion to Commander to the top-of-the-line President. Turning the corner into 1942, the future looked very bright.

Though Paul was the third owner of the 1942 Commander Skyway, he ended up with a very nice car. The car sported two-tone paint, a one-piece windshield, and plenty of chrome. Running boards were noticeably missing, a thing of the past. It was a two-door sedan powered by an inline six-cylinder engine putting out 94 horsepower. The transmission was a three-speed manual with the shifter on the steering column.

With his acceptance into the MBA program at Berkeley, it was time to pack up and head for California. Paul first made a trip to Sears in Galesburg to buy a trailer for the trip. In August 1946, the Studebaker and trailer were loaded up and headed down Route 66 with Paul, Lucile, and young Jane. Arriving in Oakland, they settled in the married students' complex. This was the former Kaiser Shipyard housing project, built during the war to accommodate the many thousands of workers building Liberty ships.[90] Rent was $30 per month for a "furnished" two-bedroom apartment. The GI Bill covered most of Paul's college expenses. Lucile taught at a nearby nursery school. Paul was a teacher's assistant with office hours for several different professors and courses.

▷ ▷ ▷

In June 1945, tired of teaching and armed with a degree in chemistry, Detta Lou started working as a chemist for the USDA Agricultural Research Service at the Northern Research Lab in Peoria. This was one of four regional labs created by the Agricultural Adjustment Act of 1938. The Agricultural Research Service was the same organization that Paul would go to work for in 1948.

The Northern Research Lab specialized in finding additional uses for farm products. One area of focus was soybeans. This is an area that Henry Ford had spent considerable time and money working on. He was interested in using soybean-based compounds in his automobiles, potentially as a fiber for his Model T seats.[91] Though unsuccessful with the upholstery, he continued to invest in soybean research, and by 1935, upwards of a bushel of soybeans went into every Ford car. Soybeans were used in the paint, control knobs, door handles, and timing gears.

Detta Lou was assigned to work on penicillin. Her lab had played a historic role in the emergence of penicillin as the first antibiotic wonder drug. The fungus *Penicillium notatum* had been famously discovered by accident in 1928 by Alexander Fleming. Though he immediately realized its medical implications, he was also painfully aware of the difficulty in producing penicillin in quantity. Two other British scientists were able to make some progress in this effort when World War II intervened. Made aware of the Peoria lab's work in developing farm-based nutrient solutions to stimulate cultures, the British team (Howard Florey and Norman Heatley) made the trip to Peoria in 1941 to enlist the lab's help. Once on board with the challenge, the lab focused in three areas: (1) finding a sufficient starter mold to work with, (2) adding a nutrient mix to spur the mold's multiplication, and (3) devising an industrial process that could be turned over to the drug companies.

One of the scientists at the lab, Mary Hunt, started canvasing the local food stores in search of rotten fruit or vegetables that might contain the *Penicillium* fungus. She struck it rich at the Illinois Fruit and Vegetable Company at 533 Main Street in Peoria, where she came upon a cantaloupe covered with a golden mold. It turned out to be a different strain of the fungus (*Penicillium chrysogeum*), and as luck would have it, it was a strain that would yield twenty times the penicillin that Fleming's strain had yielded.

With the starter mold, the lab worked on the second task: combining the fungus with nutrients to accelerate growth. The lab was already familiar with corn steep liquor, a by-product of the corn milling process. It turned out that the new strain responded dramatically to this nutrient solution. The lab also added an aeration step to the process—using a vat-like washing machine—to further speed up the penicillin creation and prevent any contamination. Once the new strain and process were released to the drug companies, a sufficient supply numbering in the billions of doses was manufactured in advance of D-Day 1944. The golden mold on that Peoria cantaloupe was the ancestral source for all of that supply. This was the team that Detta Lou joined in mid-1945.

Now working in Peoria, Detta Lou lived with Verne in town. That summer, she met Jim Winter at the Illinois State Fair in Champaign. Winter had just been discharged from the Army, where he had served on a bomb demolition team. He was a farmer in Sibley, Illinois, about seventy-five miles east of Peoria, the town where Detta Lou had taught high-school home economics and chemistry. They were married in early 1947, and Detta Lou moved from Peoria to Jim's farm.

Working at the lab in Peoria, Detta Lou would occasionally spend nights at Verne's house to avoid the long drive home. It was there in September that she collapsed, suddenly struck with a brain aneurism. In critical condition, she was moved to the Mennonite Hospital in Bloomington, where she died. She had been married to Jim for just six months. Detta was only twenty-six and had a whole life and bright career ahead of her. She was buried next to her father and brother in Elmwood. For Verne, the pain of losing her daughter was unbearable.

≻ ≻ ≻

After a couple of years by the bay in Berkeley, Paul graduated in July 1948. He had been within one course of graduating with his class, so he stayed for the summer term. Once he had the newly minted MBA degree in hand, he packed up the Studebaker and trailer and the family drove back to Williamsfield.

Late that year, he received an offer from the State of California. This was probably a result of some lobbying by his good friend Frank Richardson. Once more, the family packed up the Studebaker and trailer and drove back to California. Working for an analytical section in the state government, his first assignment was to determine fair compensation for state employees who drove their car on state business.

Paul had just completed the study when he received an attractive offer from the USDA in Washington, DC. This meant packing up the Studebaker and trailer once again and heading east. He was hired by a new group within the USDA's Agricultural Research Service to conduct efficiency studies. Using some of the same methods that Henry Ford and his team applied to automotive manufacturing, the mission of the new group was to find new ways to increase the efficiency of the nation's food distribution system. This would be done by using time-and-motion studies. Paul would go into food warehouses and supermarkets armed only with a clipboard and stopwatch. He would break down each step in a given work process, record the times, and then tabulate the results. The workup of the raw time-and-motion data was done on a Friden calculator, which was an impressive machine but still a few steps down from the Ultra computing "bombe" that had fed him Nazi intercepts.[92]

The final step would be to analyze the results and recommend changes that would reduce steps or motion and thus increase efficiency. This would be somewhat analogous to watching the Ford magneto assembly line and recommending changes, but armed with a stopwatch and the Friden machine. The recommended changes might be a more efficient workflow in the distribution warehouse or a redesign in how grocery checkout stands were configured. Similar to the revised layout of the assembly line, a recommended checkout redesign would aim to eliminate wasted motion and avoid any tiring motion by the clerk. Once a study was complete, it was published in USDA research books and Paul would make the rounds at industry conventions to present the latest findings.[93]

As the junior member of the USDA research staff, Paul was tasked with many different field assignments. This took the intrepid Studebaker and its tag-along Sears trailer to Charleston, West Virginia; Louisville, Kentucky; Chicago; and Pittsburgh. The USDA pay was good, and the field studies came with per diem allowances. That made it very easy for Paul to trade in the 1942 Studebaker on a new Studebaker. He chose the famous "coming or going" model, a Studebaker Starlight. It was a 1949 model that was only slightly changed from the debut "first by far with a post-war car" 1947 model.

After numerous moves and field studies, it was time to work up and publish the results. That meant a move to USDA headquarters in Washington, DC. A two-year stint there ended in January 1951 with a transfer to Atlanta and more field studies.

While Lucile and family returned temporarily to Williamsfield, Paul loaded up the trailer and headed down to Atlanta. Near Piedmont, North Carolina, a recovering addict who had recently been released from a rehab center entered the divided highway going in the wrong direction and collided head-on with Paul. He suffered a broken knee and fractured ribs, thanks to the lack of seat belts or a padded dash. He was taken by ambulance to a hospital near the Pinehurst golf course, where the patella of his right knee was removed. The 1949 Studebaker Starlight was taken to a nearby junk yard, a total loss.

Once discharged, Paul flew to Atlanta, and Lucile and the family joined by train. A new car was an immediate priority. Once again, the current leader in automobile styling was Studebaker, making it an easy choice. Paul bought a 1951 Studebaker Commander from a dealer in north Atlanta. This was the famous bullet-nose Studebaker. The front grille featured a chrome bullet nose in the center with pods on either side holding the headlights. If you envisioned the headlights as aircraft engines and added wings on the side, you might come up with something akin to the P-38 fighter plane. This was another styling tour de force by Raymond Loewy's design company, with Bob Bourke taking the lead. Bob had been toying with a bullet nose since 1941, though the concept did not start with Studebaker. As we have seen, it had been used on the 1948 Tucker, where the "bullet" was the third headlight, and on the 1949 Ford.

The rear deck wraparound windows and the suicide doors of the "coming and going" 1947 Studebaker remained. The starter had an interesting twist—it was a button under the clutch pedal. You pushed the clutch pedal all the way down and the car roared to life.

Studebaker reached its peak years for sales and employment with the 1950 and 1951 bullet-nose models. The company sold 343,164 cars in 1950 and 268,564 cars in 1951, numbers that were the highest in its history. The following year was the company's centennial, marking a hundred years of producing transportation. It was likely the only one of the nearly five thousand wagon makers that was still standing. It had produced a total of seven million vehicles, including all the wagons to conquer the West and the trucks to defeat the Axis.

The company had unquestionably earned the right to celebrate. In February 1952, a parade was held at Notre Dame in South Bend. Led by John C. Studebaker's (the father of the five brothers) original Conestoga wagon, it was followed by many of the wagons and carriages of the early days, the automobiles that started with the Edison-designed electric, the 2½-ton trucks and Weasels produced during World War II, and the latest post-war models. That May, the parade was repeated at the "Brickyard" before the start of the Indianapolis 500. The official pace car for the race was a light-blue Starliner Commander convertible.

Studebaker appeared to be in a good position. It had survived the Depression, shined in World War II, and its stylish 1947 Studebaker had stunned the industry. The company had followed it up in 1950 with the iconic bullet-nose Studebaker, cementing an early design lead coming into the 1950s. Though sales declined from the peak in 1950 in part due to production restrictions enacted during the Korean War, the mood in South Bend during the centennial was upbeat. The company was clearly the strongest of the independents struggling against the oligopoly of the Big Three.

But even as the wagons and automobiles were paraded in South Bend, there was trouble brewing. As the experience of the Depression had shown, small independents could not make any mistakes and still survive. It would seem even clearer that Studebaker could not make the same mistakes that nearly drove it out of business under Albert Erskine. Surely, the current executives Harold Vance and Paul Hoffman, who had lived through those trying times, would know how to avoid such pitfalls in the future.

Yet, that was exactly what was brewing. The centerpiece of the Erskine debacle was the flawed sense of shareholder primacy that put dividends over all else, particularly ongoing investment in the business. The year 1951 was a pretty good one financially, with over $500 million in revenue and $12 million in net profit. It should have been concerning that the profit margin was only 2.5 percent (General Motors' margin was nearly 20 percent), and that margin was less than half what it had been in 1949. However, it was past concerning that Studebaker elected to hand out 56 percent of that slim profit in dividends to shareholders. This was the backdrop to a number of other mistakes involving high costs, underinvested factories, missed opportunities, and leadership failures. These were all amplified when favorable market conditions turned against the company. Against the Big Three, there was no margin for error—and unfortunately, Studebaker made many errors.

For openers, Studebaker's labor costs were the highest in the industry and were coupled with the lowest productivity. Studebaker had avoided strikes by agreeing to union terms, resulting in labor costs that were 20 percent higher than its Big Three competitors. One would think that the higher pay would at least ensure higher productivity, but that was not the case. One would also think that higher pay would ensure higher quality, but this was also not the case. As an independent automaker, right out of the chute it cost significantly more to produce a Studebaker Champion than a Plymouth. This was a complete failure on the part of management to communicate to the rank and file the dire straits the company was in and the absolute need to get competitive. It did not help that Hoffman had left in 1948 and Vance was less effective as a solo executive.

The money spent on dividends and labor left little to invest in new automobile designs and upgraded factories. The early 1950s saw a race for bigger cars and higher performance. A V-8 engine became the cost of admittance to the race. Studebaker developed its own V-8 engine. The company also invested in a new automatic transmission and new truck line. The scarcity of investment funds contributed to a design fiasco for the 1953 model year. A new Studebaker had been planned for 1953 to replace the bullet-nose line. In fact, the plan called for the new models to participate in that year's centennial celebration. Robert Bourke, working as part of the Raymond Loewy design group, produced the Starliner coupe, a stunning design that looked to eclipse even its stylish 1947 and 1950 predecessors. Yet, it was a two-door coupe with styling that had to be reflected in the entire line. Escalating costs and impending deadlines caused the coupe's striking design cues to be clumsily grafted onto the larger four-door sedan, creating a singularly unattractive automobile. In addition, the components of the coupes and the sedan were needlessly different. In essence, they represented two separate lines, and this created turmoil, delays, and defects in manufacturing.

The problematic emergence of the 1953 models also occurred at the worst possible time for Studebaker. Military business associated with the Korean War accounted for nearly 50 percent of total sales in 1951, helping across the board with revenue, profit, and plant utilization. With the 1953 armistice, that business evaporated.

In addition, by then the lofty post-war demand had cooled. The easy years were over, where just about anything would sell and there was plenty of demand for all the carmakers to prosper. It was at this juncture that Henry Ford II decided to launch what was in essence a price war. He wanted to expand his share of the US market and gain ground over GM. Studebaker and the other independents were forced to follow suit. Vehicle sales for Studebaker plummeted to half of the 1950 peak while the company's already thin margins came under brutal assault. Net profit dwindled to $3 million. For the three years ending in 1953, Studebaker earned $29 million but paid out $21 million in dividends.

During this critical year for the company, an interesting opportunity surfaced—or, more accurately, resurfaced. Volkswagen had approached Studebaker in 1947 with an offer to become its US distributor. Riding high at the time, Studebaker turned the offer down, as did every other US auto manufacturer. In 1953 with Volkswagen starting to gain some traction in America, the German automaker came calling again. Studebaker rebuffed Volkswagen a second time.

In hindsight, it would seem clear that this could have been a valuable lifeline. The year had pretty much delivered a knock-out blow to Studebaker as well as the other independents. Though General Motors was under active antitrust investigation, any immediate help would not be forthcoming. For Studebaker, it was now down to desperation options. Though there was some discussion about assembling the remaining independents (Studebaker, Nash, Hudson, Packard, Kaiser, and Willys) into a single competitive force, that merger did not happen. Instead, Studebaker and Packard elected to merge while separately Nash and Hudson combined to form American Motors.

▷ ▷ ▷

Paul and family had spent a brief time in Atlanta before a transfer to Miami provided a break from constant relocations. The family grew as Bill (your author) arrived in 1950 and John was born in 1955. The respite in South Florida ended in 1955 with Paul's transfer to Minneapolis to conduct studies at Super Valu and Red Owl. It was a good time for a new car. The Studebaker Starlight was getting a little cramped. Having three Studebakers over a period of ten years should have given Studebaker the inside track for the next car.

But, the mistakes at Studebaker kept coming. The merger with Packard in 1954 had attempted to keep both brands alive, but both struggled, even with Hoffman returning to head the operation. In 1956, the company signed a management agreement with Curtiss-Wright, which agreed to manage Studebaker at cost with an option to buy. Though the new arrangement did not stem the bleeding, it did add another marque to the Studebaker showroom. Through Curtiss-Wright, Studebaker became the US distributor for Mercedes Benz, an unusual combination that lasted until 1965. Still, Studebaker declined precipitously from peak sales in 1950 of 321,000 cars that had put it in the number-eight position. By 1956, Studebaker sold only 69,000 cars and dropped to number thirteen. The brand was now below both the Nash and DeSoto brands.

Paul was considering an Oldsmobile for his next car. In contrast to
Studebaker, Olds had been on a tear since the end of the war. The division
had risen to number eight in 1951, number six in 1952, and to number five
in 1954, where it settled in behind Chevrolet, Ford, Plymouth, and Buick.

When we last discussed Oldsmobile, both Ransom Olds and his little
Curved Dash automobile had been kicked out by Billy Durant. The company had been number one from 1903 to 1905 but plummeted out of the
top ten with Durant's changes. Olds made a brief appearance at number
eight in 1918 and then slipped far down the list until the Depression.

Alfred P. Sloan had taken the reins of GM from Durant and went
through a period of experimentation with his division structure. This
would continue to be a constant constraint for any GM division wanting
to break out of its assigned role. The initial GM lineup that Sloan inherited
had Cadillac, Buick, Oldsmobile, Oakland, and Chevrolet, in that order.
In the 1920s, Sloan perceived some interbrand gaps as too wide and so
attempted to fill the gaps with what were called "companion cars." He originally hired Harley Earl to design the first companion car, the LaSalle, to
fit in the space between Cadillac and Buick. In the perceived gap between
Buick and Oldsmobile, two different companion cars were tried: the Marquette and the Viking. Both were launched in 1930 and died soon thereafter. The gap between Oakland and Chevrolet was filled in 1926 with a
companion car called Pontiac. However, in a twist, the companion entry
survived and killed off its progenitor, the Oakland. Sloan had it mostly
sorted out by the end of the Depression with the revised lineup of Cadillac,
Buick, Olds, Pontiac, and Chevrolet. The LaSalle was in the mix until 1940.
Oldsmobile, after fending off cars above and below its designated slot, rose
to number six in 1934.

Sloan and head of engineering Charles Kettering allowed the individual divisions some latitude in doing their own research and development.
With Oldsmobile on firmer footing in the 1930s, it aimed to elevate Sloan's
development profile in a big way. For starters, it took on an innovation
simply begging for a solution: the automatic transmission.

Once the hand-crank starter had been largely eliminated from automobiles, there remained an even larger source of dissatisfaction with the
operation of an automobile—the never-ending chore of manual shifting.
The 1938 Chrysler Royale made one small improvement with the automatic
shift into overdrive, but the bulk of the work remained with the driver.
The search for a solution progressed slowly, from a seemingly intractable

problem to a partial and compromised design to a luxury option and, finally, to a satisfactory solution that became an absolute requirement.

Oldsmobile built a team to develop an automatic transmission. This was not a simple engineering problem. It required emulation of the clutch mechanism synchronized with the speed of the car. The Olds team initially designed a semi-automatic "safety" transmission, a compromise that retained the clutch and, thus, driver involvement. It debuted as an option on 1937 Oldsmobiles but was gone by 1939.

The Olds team went back to work, focusing on eliminating the clutch. Their solution was a series of planetary gears combined with hydraulics that actuated the shift based on road speed. The new transmission was dubbed "Hydra-Matic" and first appeared on Oldsmobiles in 1940. The division was given a one-year exclusive on the innovation, but in 1941 only the Cadillac division elected to adopt the Hydra-Matic. The war interrupted, and the Hydra-Matic transmission was used extensively. It was matched with the twin Cadillac V-8 engines in the Sherman tank and found its way into a total of some twenty-five thousand vehicles by war's end.

Post-war, the automatic transmission quickly became a requirement, not an option. Pontiac opted for the Hydra-Matic in 1948. Lincoln bought the GM transmission in 1949, followed by Nash, Hudson, and Frazer. Buick and Chevrolet finally relented and implemented variants of the Hydra-Matic.

The Olds team was not content with the Hydra-Matic success, though. They accepted the additional challenge of developing a higher compression engine, a continued focus for Charles Kettering. In the 1940s, he led GM's work on improved engines to take advantage of high octane gas. His thinking was that high octane and high compression would result in more horsepower per engine size and thus facilitate smaller, more efficient power plants. Of course, just the opposite occurred. The more powerful engines were used to propel the land yachts of the 1950s.

The most important project was a new overhead valve V-8 for Oldsmobile. Kettering experimented with an engine of 12.5 to 1 compression and 94 octane gas. It resulted in 25 percent more horsepower and 40 percent better mileage than existing V-8s. Kettering retired from GM in 1947, but Oldsmobile engineers continued the work. Once the new engine was complete, the team wanted to call it the "Kettering," but Alfred Sloan did not agree. He did, however, like the name "Rocket V-8". The first production version of the Rocket was installed in the 1949 Oldsmobile, a newly designed Olds that sported small fins in back, P-38 style air scoops in the front, and a new hood ornament—a rocket ship.

The relatively light 1949 Oldsmobile combined with the powerful Rocket V-8 engine resulted in a very fast car. It dominated the NASCAR circuit from 1949 to 1951 (before it was eclipsed by the Hudson Hornet). Besides the high racing profile, it certainly did not hurt to have a song named after your new engine. "Rocket 88" by Ike Turner's Kings of Rhythm was number one on the rhythm-and-blues charts in 1951.[94] For Oldsmobile, it harkened to the early days of the Curved Dash Olds, when "In My Merry Oldsmobile" was a nationwide hit song.

The Oldsmobile division sat at number seven or number eight in sales before the 1949 redesign. Sales surged over 40 percent with the new model, moving Olds up to sixth position (behind Chevy, Ford, Plymouth, Buick, and Pontiac). The surge continued, and Olds moved to number five in sales in 1955, ahead of Pontiac, with sales of 583,000 cars.

Given his ten-year relationship with Studebaker, Paul felt he had to do some due diligence before making a final decision on his new car. The Studebaker Commander four-door sedan was slightly improved in comparison to the disastrous 1953 model that tried to graft the coupe design on the sedan. It was a lighter car, powered by a 170 horsepower V-8 engine. Prior-year Studebaker sales were just over 100,000, but the trend line was certainly dramatically down. The Oldsmobile was on a hot streak. It was powered by the Rocket V-8 engine, generating 230 horsepower. The Holiday 88 hardtop was a long, sleek car available in twenty-six two-tone paint combinations. Prior-year Oldsmobile sales were nearly 600,000.

Unfortunately for the Studebaker Company, it was an easy choice. Paul traded in the Studebaker and purchased an Oldsmobile at a Miami Springs dealer. It was a four-door Series 88 Holiday hardtop, a beautiful blue-and-white two-tone car. The new Olds had the Hydra-Matic automatic transmission, finally eliminating the steering column manual shifting. In the summer of 1956, Paul and family headed north from Miami, bound for Minneapolis, with stops at Williamsfield and the farm. The route traveled over a few remnants of Carl Fisher's Dixie Highway. As usual, the Sears trailer tagged along behind the Oldsmobile.

John had purchased his Jeep in 1951 to work as a farm vehicle. He also bought another car that same year, a Chrysler New Yorker. The post-war demand had abated, and cars were now generally available. That meant it was out with the Chevy and back to Chryslers. The New Yorker was the top-of-the-line Chrysler, just below the Imperial. Whereas the Chrysler Royal sold for just over $1,000, the green New Yorker he selected went for $3,300.

The farm was doing well. Farm prices were up, and farm productivity was unfettered, in contrast to the struggle with wartime shortages. New equipment, hybrid seeds, and the latest methods combined to increase yields. John would eventually have two tractors, one light duty and one heavy, always Case. He would also purchase a combine for the harvest. The days of the contract thresherman were long gone.

In addition, there was no need to nurse a Chrysler year after year. John traded the 1951 New Yorker in on a 1953 New Yorker, presaging a steady diet of Chryslers in the years to come. In fact, some of the old Chryslers never made it off the farm. There was that steep gully in the back of the farm that ran down to French Creek. Many cast-off vehicles eventually found their way there.

Though John was sold on Chryslers, it proved to be a tougher sale for others as the K. T. Keller era of uninspired designs continued. Chrysler had moved ahead of Ford to number two during the Great Depression and was slightly ahead coming out of the war. Yet, by 1947 the company had slipped back to number three. New Chrysler designs finally arrived in 1949, but they continued to be the tall, boxy automobiles that Keller favored.

Competitors were not standing still. Studebaker had already laid down the styling mantle with the 1947 cars. In 1949, Ford and GM left pre-war designs behind with clean, streamlined models. Henry Ford II had the Chevrolet killer he had focused on since taking charge. Harley Earl at General Motors started the GM design renaissance at the top with a long, low 1949 Cadillac sporting modest tail fins.

Despite his stale design leadership, Keller did take one action in 1949 that would have long-term positive implications. He hired Virgil Exner to his styling department as a favor for Roy Cole, the head of engineering at Studebaker. Exner had started at GM under Harley Earl and had risen quickly to be the youngest divisional lead when named Pontiac styling chief, shortly after designing the 1937 and 1938 Pontiacs. Raymond Loewy hired him away from Earl at double the salary and set him to work on the Studebaker account. After the debut of the 1947 "coming and going" Studebakers, Exner and Loewy continued to clash. One had to go, and it turned out to be Exner. He had unsuccessfully sought work at Ford before Keller hired him.

Once on board at Chrysler, he was assigned to work on concept cars.[95] Though his cars were exciting, he must have been frustrated to be associated with Chrysler's dowdy product line after the stylish cars he had designed at Pontiac and Studebaker. And with Keller still in charge, it was unclear if or when he would get the chance to design Chryslers to compete with Ford, GM, and Studebaker.

Exner first had to establish himself as a styling force and then wait through several product cycles before his impact would see the light of day. Keller moved up to the Chrysler corporate board in 1950, and his influence on the product line diminished. A major redesign finally was in the works for 1955. The cars were dramatically better—lower, sleeker, more streamlined. They even had some fins, though just tacked on as part of the taillights. Quite a bit of money went into the 1955 cars; they were unveiled as the "Hundred Million Dollar Look." Exner was only partially responsible for the new line, but, like Raymond Loewy, he took full credit.

The 1955 cars also featured a major engineering innovation, the Hemi V-8 engine. Fitted in the Chrysler 300 model, it was the first 300 horsepower V-8. The car proceeded to take over the NASCAR circuit from the Hudson Hornet.

The new Chrysler cars were way overdue. With staid designs coupled with the price war that Henry Ford II started in 1953, Chrysler's market share had dipped precipitously. GM's share of sales increased above 50 percent despite active antitrust proceedings. Ford expanded its number-two lead, growing from the pre-war 20 percent share to 29 percent by the end of the 1950s.

The 1955 models were a start. But clearly, more was needed. Exner, newly installed as styling chief, was already on the case. He fully embraced the longer, lower, highly finned look that Earl's team was developing at GM. But he decided to go much further. Late in 1956, one of Harley Earl's designers was snooping around Chrysler headquarters at Highland Park. He spied some prototypes in the back lot that momentarily took his breath away. They were Exner's new designs, slated for the next model year. The prototypes had been subjected to the full Exner treatment—longer, lower, and swept back—with mountains of chrome and really big tail fins. The tail fins were much taller than anything GM had in the works.

The new Chryslers arrived in 1957, deemed the "Forward Look." All of the brands got the full treatment, including Plymouth. Exner's "Forward Look" design was later immortalized in the 1983 Stephen King book

Christine, about a jealous and vindictive 1958 red Plymouth Fury with a mind of its own. The subsequent movie production had to track down twenty-four red Furies for the shoot, no small task given that only five thousand were built in 1958.

After years in the doldrums, Chrysler surprisingly moved into a leadership position with the new styling. The "Forward Look" promised to halt Chrysler's decline in the market. But it was not to be. In the rush to get the cars to market, manufacturing quality suffered. That included producing cars that were prone to rust. Chrysler's reputation took a serious hit. The timing was also not good, as a recession in 1958 slowed auto sales. Chrysler market share plummeted to 11 percent in 1959. After the war, the Plymouth and Dodge brands were normally number three and number four on the sales charts. Chrysler and DeSoto, the upscale brands, were ranked in the 9–12 range. However, Dodge had slipped to eighth place by the end of the decade. DeSoto, hit especially hard by the recession, did not recover and was gone by 1962.

Exner was not the only designer pushing styling beyond normal bounds in the 1950s. "Land yacht" sized automobiles made possible by high performance V-8 engines had created a lot of territory to accessorize. All manner of chrome accents and various design baubles other than tail fins made their way onto the cars. Perhaps the most famous, or notorious, effects (depending on your point of view) were the two conical front bumper attachments that prominently graced Cadillacs and a number of other cars of the era. They were originally designed by Harley Earl to resemble World War II artillery shells. However, they came to be called "Dagmars" after two of the most notable physical characteristics of a 1950s TV personality named Dagmar.[96]

These styling excesses started to recede late in the decade. The high point for fins was probably the 1959 Cadillac Eldorado. Long-time designer Raymond Loewy, who had ended his stint for Studebaker with the Starlight, sounded the early death knell. He derided the Harley Earl style as just "the flashy, the gadgetry, the spectacular" that was simply "too big for most people, too expensive, too costly to maintain, and too gaudy."[97] Functional values such as utility, cost, safety, and efficiency were left on the design room floor.

It wasn't too long before the Paul Shaffer family outgrew the Olds, even as big as it was. Paul and Lucile's fourth child, Sara, arrived in 1959. Now, a family of six making frequent trips out West from Minneapolis needed something a bit more spacious. In the early 1960s, the answer was the station wagon. By the early part of that decade, station wagons had risen from just 3 percent of car volumes in 1950 to nearly 20 percent.

The term "station wagon" did not even surface until the 1920s. The first vehicles that looked like station wagons were called "depot hacks." The term derived from the hackney, a horse-drawn commercial vehicle, and depot, the place where many hackney cabs picked up their passengers. It is no surprise that the initial depot hacks were built of a Model T chassis with a "hack" body attached. The first major-production station wagon was the 1929 Ford Model A.

As we have seen, the bodies on early cars were predominantly made of wood. As steel replaced the body structure, wood trim was retained in the 1930s and 1940s as a styling enhancement and used quite often on station wagons, to the extent that many wagons in the 1940s and '50s were called "woodies." The use of real wood disappeared in the early 1950s, to be replaced with a wood-look composite like vinyl.

Paul traded in the Oldsmobile on a 1961 Ford Country Squire station wagon. It was longer and heavier than the Olds. It only remained in the driveway for four years before Paul upgraded to the Mercury Colony Park station wagon, which was even longer and heavier than the Country Squire. This would seem to be the last hurrah for station wagons, though they would reappear with the next generation.

1911 Moline Dreadnought, winner of the 1910 Glidden Tour, a four-cylinder, 35 horsepower touring car, one that Verne's father (John Henderson Reed) purchased. (Wikimedia Commons)

A very wealthy and successful Henry Ford with this slightly restyled (thanks to Edsel Ford) 1921 Model T. (Public domain)

First assembly line, magnetos for the Model T at Highland Park. Build time per magneto was reduced from 20 minutes to 5 minutes. (Public domain image)

1910 Detroit Electric Victoria, a very simple electric compared to the typical, elaborate opera coach models. It was 1 of 1,500 built that year. (Courtesy of B. R. Howard Automobile and Carriage Conservation)

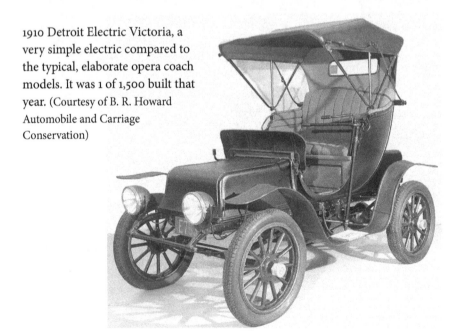

Model T (circa 1914, with gas headlights) tackling a road under construction. (Public domain image)

1927 Ford Model A, a completely modern replacement for the Model T with Lincoln styling influence designed by Edsel Ford. (Wikimedia Commons)

Will, standing, with left to right,
John, Paul, and Benjamin Franklin, "BF."
(Author's family collection)

1904 Buick Model B, with Walter Marr at the wheel and Tom Buick seated.
Powered by the Buick valve-in-head two-cylinder, 15 horsepower engine.
(Public domain image)

1922 Buick Model M45 touring car, quite the step up from the Model T, with six-cylinder, 60 horsepower engine. (Courtesy of New York Public Library)

1925 Chrysler, John (standing at right) and Detta Lou (sitting at lower left) joined by local friends. (Author's family collection)

The 1860s Shaffer farmhouse and outbuildings, circa 1900. (Author's family collection)

Detta Lou with draft horses Bill and Bob, circa 1934. (Author's family collection)

1934 Chrysler Airflow, a revolutionary car, but unfortunately years ahead of its time. (Walter Chrysler Museum, photograph by Greg Gjerdingen)

1938 Chrysler Royal parked in front of the Shaffer farmhouse. (Author's family collection)

US Army testing the Bantam Jeep at Fort Bragg, 1941. (Library of Congress, Prints and Photographs Division)

Willow Run B-24 Liberator factory, final assembly, 1943. (US National Archives and Records Administration)

Detroit Tank Arsenal, production lines for M4 Sherman tanks, circa 1942. (US Army)

M4 Sherman tanks disembarking at Omaha Beach, 1944. (US Army)

F6F Hellcat fighter plane. (US Navy, National Museum of Naval Aviation)

Hellcat flight platoon with the author's father-in-law, Charles Erwin, at the lower right. (Author's family collection)

Flight platoon at Melbourne Naval Air Station with Ensign William Shaffer standing, second from left. (Author's family collection)

Camouflage over the Lockheed factory complex, 1943. (Photograph courtesy of Lockheed Aircraft Company)

USS *Wolverine* stationed off Glenview Naval Air Station, 1945, part of the "Corn Belt Fleet." The carrier started life as Frank Kirby's SS *SeeandBee* steamship, built in 1911 and converted in 1942. (Public domain image)

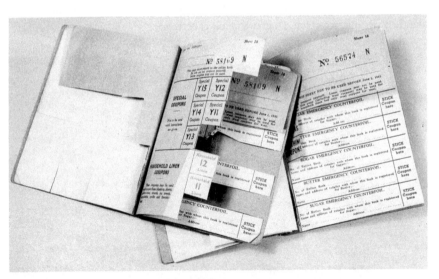

Home front ration book with coupons redeemed. (Public domain image)

The family in wartime. Paul and Bill (standing), Detta Lou, Verne, and John (sitting). (Author's family collection)

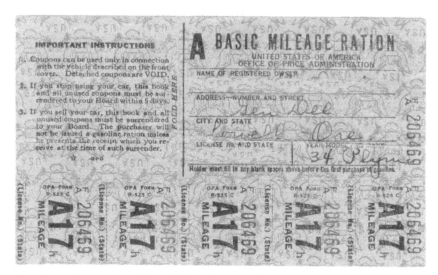

Gasoline ration coupons from Office of Price Administration, Level A user tied to this specific automobile, a 1934 Plymouth. (Public domain image)

1936 Volvo PV36 "Carioca," 1 of only 500 built, it debuted a year after the Chrysler Airflows. (Public domain image)

1942 Studebaker Commander with Sears trailer in tow. Young Jane standing. (Author's family collection)

1948 Tucker Torpedo, a styling sensation with bullet swivel headlight in front.
(Image courtesy of Rex Gray, Wikimedia Commons)

1976 AMC Pacer, the "first wide small car," also known as the "Flying Fishbowl."
(Author's family collection)

The third generation family with dual Mustangs, a 1965 on the left and 1970 on the right.

Henry Shaffer (1754-1849)					
James Shaffer (1786-1872)					
Benjamin Brooks "BB" Shaffer (1814-1891)					
	William Caldwell Shaffer				
	James Alexander Shaffer				
	Sarah Jane Shaffer				
	Benjamin Franklin "BF" Shaffer (1848-1924)				
Elizabeth Caldwell		Thomas B. Shaffer			
		Bertha A. Shaffer			
		Ada Elizabeth Shaffer			
Thomas Foster		William C. "Will" Shaffer			
	Sara Lydia Foster				
Sarah Blakeslee				John Shaffer	
				Paul Shaffer	
Joseph Spriggs Reed				Detta Lou Shaffer	
	John Henderson Reed			William C. "Billy" Shaffer	
Elizabeth Henderson					
		Verne Reed			
Daniel J. McCoy					
	Margaret McCoy				
Mary Jane Steward					
		Isidor Daub			
				Lucile Daub	
		Gertrude Wesner			

A subset of the Shaffer family tree, dating back seven generations to Henry Shaffer. The author would be off the page to the right.

18

The Third Generation

I T'S TIME TO shift gears again. The next generation was waiting in the wings, and a station wagon definitely would not do as a first car. Your author was part of this third generation of the Shaffer family taking the automobile journey. Whereas the first car of choice for Will's generation was overwhelmingly the Model T, the generation growing up in the 1960s had a first car in mind that had quite a bit in common with Will's automobile. It was the Volkswagen Beetle.

I was born in 1950 in Washington, DC (at a time when my father, Paul, was back in town to write up his field studies). The family moved with Paul's many assignments across the country, and I ended up in high school in Houston in 1967. This was a good time to have a car, and with some financial help, I purchased a 1965 VW Beetle. It also turned out that my significant other, who was also born in 1950 and similarly well-traveled, ended up with a VW as her first car.

The Volkswagen backstory is not an attractive one. Germany was beaten in the Great War (aka World War I), and the country, once a leader in automobiles, with companies like Daimler, Benz and Maybach, had lagged in the interwar years. In 1926 there were nearly twenty million cars in the United States and only 295,000 cars in all of Germany, or one car for every 242 Germans. Despite this, vast sums were being spent building the German autobahns. This effort was started under the Weimar Republic and continued after Adolf Hitler took over in 1933. Hitler had long been passionate about automobiles. Besides continued spending on the autobahns, he started pushing plans to increase car ownership in order to put those new highways to use. After he attended the Berlin auto show in 1934, he came away wanting to build an inexpensive "peoples' car." He found a ready confidant in Stuttgart auto designer Ferdinand Porsche.

Porsche was a fellow Austrian who had established a reputation as a top automobile designer, eventually hired as the chief technical engineer at Daimler. In 1926, when Daimler and Benz and Cie merged to form Daimler-Benz (with Mercedes Benz as the brand), he left. He was interested in designing smaller cars and relocated to Stuttgart to work as an automotive consultant. There, he started discussions with Hitler about his "Volkswagen" ("peoples' car"). He soon became a German citizen and subsequently a Nazi Party member.

Hitler wanted a lightweight, air-cooled car that could go 60 mph, get 40 miles per gallon, and sell for 1,000 Reich marks. At the time, this was equivalent to about $250—about $200 less than the least expensive Ford model. Hitler gave Porsche the go-ahead to design the car in 1934. Porsche worked on the design for several years, though all the work was not his own. Notably, he appropriated the basic look largely from the Tatra T97, a car designed by fellow Austrian Hans Ledwinka.[98] Porsche's concept had the same shape, same rear engine, and same air cooling as the T97. In fact, Hitler was familiar with the T97, having ridden in it and even having dined once with Ledwinka.

Notwithstanding the theft from Tatra and Ledwinka, the Porsche design created a ground-breaking automobile. None of the individual elements were especially new, but the combination of an all-steel body, torsion bar suspension, rear engine, and rear drive in a low-priced car was unique.

The completed design was called the Type 1, but, of course, it would eventually be deemed the "Beetle." It featured the familiar rounded shape with a four-cylinder air-cooled engine that generated 24 horsepower and propelled the car to a maximum speed of 70 mph. The car was first shown at the 1939 Berlin auto show. It was called the Kdf-Wagen, where "Kdf" represented the German "Kraft-durch-freude," or "Strength through Joy." Hitler set up a program for Germans to buy the car on the installment plan via a stamp book. By 1945, roughly 700,000 Germans would join the savings program, with some 336,000 actually completing it.[99] By 1939 there were a total of 337,000 orders waiting for a Kdf-Wagen.

In the meantime, Hitler had trouble finding a German car company willing to build the car. He had to turn to the German Labor Front, a Nazi organization that had replaced the independent trade unions and, not inci- dentally, had confiscated all of their funds. The labor front had the money but not the expertise. Hitler turned again to Porsche, who agreed to build a factory. Porsche had spent two months in the United States in 1936 and toured Henry Ford's Rouge River factory as well as the Packard, Lincoln, and GM plants, so he was somewhat schooled in automotive mass produc- tion. The new plant would be built at Wolfsburg in central Germany.

Even before the first cars came off the line, it was readily apparent that the car could not be produced for 1,000 Reich marks. This would have been a problem if the Nazi propaganda line that the factory would be producing 1.5 million "peoples' cars" annually had any basis in fact. But it didn't, and Hitler's war conveniently halted production.

By the time Hitler invaded Poland in September 1939, setting off World War II, only 630 cars had been produced. They were pre-production prototypes, and most went to Nazi Party officials. Porsche's factory was re-missioned to build war material. One of the first projects was a scout car version of the Kdf-Wagen called the Kubelwagen (meaning "bucket-seat car"), which became known as the German Jeep. Roughly 50,000 Kubel- wagens were produced before Porsche moved on to building Tiger tanks and V1 rockets. By then, he was using slave labor from the eastern front.

Not only was the production of the Kubelwagen a fraction of that of the Jeep (there were 660,000 Jeeps built during the war), but the vehicle it- self was significantly inferior. The Kubelwagen was an adaptation of a very light passenger vehicle, whereas the Jeep was really a four-wheel-drive light truck. The Jeep had double the payload and towing capacity of the Kubel- wagen, thanks in part to a rugged 60 horsepower engine, compared to the 25 horsepower engine in the Kubelwagen. Though Hitler had specified that his car should be capable of mounting a machine gun, the Kubelwagen was hard pressed to support much of anything.

The factory at Wolfsburg, located roughly ten miles west of the agreed- upon East German Zone, was heavily damaged by Allied bombing during the war. It was initially captured by the US Army, but the Americans were not interested in the site and moved on. The factory and surrounding town then fell into the hands of the British Army. A British officer, Major Ivan Hirst, a mechanical engineer with a tank maintenance battalion, took a closer look and realized it could quite easily be made operational. He orga- nized the remaining workers and supervised the assembly of a few cars for use by the British Army.

The factory was a candidate for war reparations and was offered to Allied automakers for free. A commission led by Britain's Lord Rootes looked at the Volkswagen automobile and concluded, "the vehicle does not meet the fundamental technical requirements of a motor-car." Ford did not want the plant to start building competitive cars but also had no interest in acquiring it.

The bitter-cold "hunger winter of 1946–1947" set in and changed the Allies' minds about war reparations and punishing the Germans. Under the Marshall Plan, it became policy to rebuild West Germany as a bulwark against encroaching Russia and communism. Major Hirst was challenged to restart the auto plant and produce a thousand cars a month. With help from Richard Berryman, a British RAF officer who worked for GM before the war, they succeeded in ramping up production. The cars they produced were no longer Kdf-Wagens. They were now Volkswagens, though for a period they were all painted in Army khaki.

Once the decision was made to open up for civilian production, the new hurdle was how to sell the cars coming off the line. Ben Pon, a car dealer from the Netherlands who had met Hitler before the war at the Berlin auto show, was interested in selling the cars. He started importing and selling Volkswagens in 1947. In January 1948, Hirst hired Heinz Heinrich Nordhoff to take over the plant operations. Nordhoff had worked for GM Opel before the war, but that organization had been unwilling to rehire him because of his Nazi Party association. Though Nordhoff was unimpressed with the car, he went to work centralizing the organization and preparing the factory for higher production.

That higher production became a critical necessity within months as the Nazi Reich mark was replaced by the Deutschemark in a switch that greatly increased the buying power of West Germans. The Volkswagen plant was flooded with orders, and by 1949, VW was Germany's leading car producer. This was not a problem for Nordhoff, as he brought an intense Fordism, including automation, to Wolfsburg production and was able to ramp up quickly, with the one millionth VW coming off the assembly line in 1955.

There were a total of two Volkswagens sold in the United States in 1949, both imported by Ben Pon. Without much of an organization, sales were in the hundreds for the next few years. Advertising was strictly word of mouth. Nordhoff's entreaty to Studebaker to sell VWs in its dealerships fell on deaf ears in South Bend.

In 1955 the Volkswagen of America organization was created to bring focus to the little car. Sales increased dramatically, to 90,000 in 1957. That same year, another small, European economy car rolled into the United States. It was the Renault Dauphine, and it quickly presented a challenge to Volkswagen.[100] Two years later, Studebaker debuted the Lark, the first relatively small US car. Cars like the Volkswagen and Dauphine had prospered as alternatives to the big, gas-guzzling American cars. The small-car market was just not of interest to the Big Three automakers. Yet, the success of the Lark quickly changed Detroit minds, and very soon the Chevy II, Dodge Dart, Plymouth Valiant, and Ford Falcon hit the showrooms.

Heinrich Nordhoff's first response was to veer from the Henry Ford playbook and actually enhance the car. A heater was added, better brakes were installed, and new paint colors were made available. The horsepower was increased from 40 to 57, though this was done in part because German autobahn speed limits had been increased above the top speed of the car. Nordhoff graced the cover of *Time* magazine in February 1954.

But he had his sights set far higher. Nordhoff installed Carl Hahn as head of US operations. One of Hahn's first actions was to hire the advertising firm of Doyle, Dane, and Bernbach. Their campaign for the "Beetle" was to become legendary, even being rated the most effective ad campaign of the twentieth century by *Advertising Age*. The Volkswagen's Nazi past was not well-known in the United States at the time. Otherwise, the ads might have been less well received.

The VW ads were understated and wry, invoking a sprightly image. The "Think Small" tag line sought to turn a perceived negative about the car into a positive. Volkswagen owners were made to feel good about their simple, honest, plucky little automobile, in sharp contrast to ads for Detroit's big cars. The classic Volkswagen ad showed a very small VW at the top of an otherwise blank page with the caption at the bottom, "Think Small." Another ad had a Volkswagen with a flat tire above the caption, "Nobody's Perfect." And an ad that was relevant to the author (being tall) had the 7'1" Wilt Chamberlain trying to get into a VW with the caption, "They said it couldn't be done. It couldn't," along with the explanation that if you were 6'7" or shorter, you would fit fine.

The campaign worked. Sales of 140,000 in 1959 rose to 400,000 by 1968, a number representing nearly 40 percent of Volkswagen's worldwide sales. The number-one movie of 1969—Disney's *Herbie the Love Bug*—launched the image into overdrive. And the book *How to Keep Your VW Alive* sold two million copies. It turned out that Volkswagen did not need Studebaker's dealer network. It just needed a good advertising company.

Back in Germany, Volkswagen had become the dominant German car producer. By 1963, fully one-third of German cars were Volkswagens. Nordhoff was very much in control, earning the nickname "King" Nordhoff.

The combination of the Studebaker Lark, the Volkswagen, and the Renault got the Big Three going on small cars, perhaps just defensively. McNamara and Ford threw together a conventional small car, much like the approach of Studebaker, with the Ford Falcon. GM's Chevrolet designers, by contrast, took a more radical approach. They decided to go one better than Volkswagen, designing a car with an air-cooled rear engine and rear drive layout, just like the VW. And yet, because it was supposed to be faster and sportier than the VW, they wedged a six-cylinder air-cooled engine into the rear compartment. This heavier engine further worsened the car's weight balance front to rear and made it difficult, if not dangerous, to steer. Cars like the VW and Porsche 911 with rear engines compensated for their weight by installing an anti-roll bar in the front. But in part because of the high costs in developing the air-cooled power plant (shades of GM's air-cooled copper engine fiasco in the 1920s) and the incremental cost of the anti-roll bar, Chevrolet decided to leave it off. Ralph Nader's book *Unsafe at Any Speed*, published in November 1965, pointed out the folly of this move. Though Nader gets the blame for the Corvair's demise, it was really the car that appeared in April 1964—the Ford Mustang—that sealed the Corvair's fate. Corvair limped along until 1969.

In February 1972, the Volkswagen passed the sales record of the Ford Model T as it moved past fifteen million cars. It was perhaps fitting that the VW took over the Model T's title of best-selling car, as there are numerous parallels between the two. For starters, they were both envisioned to be "universal" or "peoples'" cars. They were both rugged, high quality, very affordable cars that were easy and inexpensive to maintain. They both enjoyed huge aftermarket support. Both utilized "Fordism" mass production techniques to drive down the cost and increase factory efficiency. Nordhoff eventually had a new Volkswagen coming off the line in less than a minute. Both the Model T and the Volkswagen enjoyed high standing in their times and culture. And finally, both were blinded by success and late in adapting to changing markets. Volkswagen made 78,000 engineering changes over the course of the car's production run, but this was not nearly enough.

My Volkswagen was a 1964 model with domed hubcaps and the all-chrome bumpers that easily gave away the year. The car weighed in at 1,675 pounds and was powered by a diminutive four-cylinder, 72 cubic inch, 40 horsepower air-cooled engine that was shoehorned in back. The "frunk" up front contained the spare tire, gas tank, and very limited storage. There was a definite emphasis on the Spartan. For example, there was no electric motor for the windshield washer fluid. Instead, the spare tire was overinflated and connected to the washer tank, providing pressurization (a separate valve was added in 1962, but you still had to manually put in the pressure). The entire dash consisted of a speedometer, odometer, fuel gauge, wiper and headlight buttons, and, if you splurged, a radio.

I should have been happy that I had a fuel gauge. The Volkswagens built before 1961 did not come with one. You didn't have to stick a wood ruler into the gas tank as with the Model T, but the fuel setup was no less unusual. There was a small black lever on the floorboard above the accelerator pedal. This controlled access to a reserve level of gasoline (1.1. gallons) at the bottom of the fuel tank. When the engine started to sputter, you would reach down and move the lever to the right. This would open up access to the reserve amount left in the tank, and the engine would come to life again. Once you refueled, you had to remember to return the reserve lever to its normal upright position.

The VW was a great first car, as driving it was a breeze. It had a standard H-format gear shift on the floor, providing smooth shifting. You could easily shift into the upper gears without the clutch simply by syncing the motor speed. For reverse, you pushed down on the shifter and moved it down and to the left. Performance was not the Beetle's forte. Before the engine was upgraded from 25 to 40 horsepower, the top speed was 72 mph. The car would lumber from 0 to 60, taking about thirty seconds. If you were merging onto an expressway, you tended to rock back and forth, hoping that would somehow propel the car faster. You did get good mileage, though, at 32 miles per gallon.

Cynthia's Volkswagen was the same year as mine, but not nearly so nice. I was introduced to it when she drove up for our first date. It was a three-tone job, and not by design. It was mostly beige, with a mismatched light-blue hood and a black rear deck. She paid $500 for the car in 1972. She had learned to drive in the family's Ford Falcon with a three-speed stick on the steering column, so driving the VW was not a big stretch. The car was not much to look at, but, of course, I was not looking at the car.

One final parallel exists between the Volkswagen and the Model T. Both cars changed so little over the years that they spawned a game in divining the model year. As we have seen, the 1914 and 1915 Model Ts were completely identical except for one major change: going from gas to electric headlights. The little vent at the top of the headlight told you that it was a 1914 model.

Likewise, slight changes in the Volkswagen were the keys to guessing the model year. The elaborate, multipiece chrome bumper immediately told you the car was produced prior to 1968. That year VW moved to a simpler bumper with a black rubber stripe in the middle. A small round taillight was likely a 1961 model, whereas an oval taillight with a rectangular license plate light was a 1963 model. Most of the changes were of this order. They basic shape and styling remained the same.

19

Mustang

T HOUGH THE VOLKSWAGEN BEETLE was my first car, it would not be long before I was ready for a second car, preferably one with slightly more horsepower. I traded the VW in for a 1968 Ford Mustang, the first of five Mustangs that we would eventually own. For our family, it had been a long dry spell without Fords.

The Mustang was the greatest car success story of the 1960s. It was developed under the direction of Lee Iacocca, a car guy who had worked his way up the ladder to run the Ford Motor division. He had made his mark as a regional sales director for Ford with the "56 for 56" program, a program where you made fifty-six payments for a Ford car in 1956. He had a bag of potato chips placed upside down on each car, making the point that this was a great deal when the chips were down. It was a great success during a down year for US autos. From there, Iacocca moved up fast with former Whiz Kid Robert McNamara promoting him to Ford Division general manager in 1960. McNamara himself had recently made his mark, shepherding the Ford Falcon to production, and was promoted to president of the Ford Company (though it was very short-lived as he soon joined the Kennedy administration as secretary of defense).

Iacocca's vision for the Mustang could not have been more unlike the Falcon. He was looking for a sporty car with bucket seats and a floor shift, weighing in at no more than 2,500 pounds, that would sell for less than $2,500. Crucially, it would seat four and come with a wide range of options in order to appeal to more than just sports car buyers. Iacocca set up a design competition between several departments at Ford. Five prototypes were produced, and the 1962 concept prototype rose to top. Crucially,

Henry Ford II made the call and gave the go-ahead for the program. Ironi-cally, the Mustang would be built on the Ford Falcon chassis because of low cost and short development window constraints set by Henry. It was first dubbed the "Special Falcon" before the code name "Cougar" (the name was recycled for the Mercury version) was used right up to production. Named after the famed P-51 World War II fighter plane, the Mustang was unveiled at the 1964 New York World's Fair as a 1964 ½ model.

Mustang sales were reminiscent of the Ford Model A right out of the chute. There were fifteen orders for every available car. Iacocca initially committed one full Ford plant with a capacity of 250,000 cars per year. Then, he committed a second plant, bringing capacity to 400,000 cars. And, just before the announcement, he committed a third plant. Ford sold 100,000 Mustangs in the first four months and 420,000 in the first year. Over the first twenty-four months, a million Mustangs were sold. The first-year profit for Ford was over $1 billion. Mustang sales peaked in 1966, with over 600,000 sold that year. Over the first ten years, three million Mus-tangs hit the road.

For Lee Iacocca, the father of the Mustang, it turned out to be a mixed bag. He was lauded as an automotive genius and appeared on the covers of both *Time* and *Newsweek*. Unfortunately for Iacocca, the genius tag did not last long. Though there was some controversy over who was responsible for the Mustang, there was none with regard to the Ford Pinto. This was Lee Iacocca's car. The idea for a "mini" Mustang began in 1967. Iacocca rushed development, completing the program in twenty-five months (against an industry average of forty-three months). The car debuted in 1971 and was very successful, with 3.1 million sales over a nine-year run. The good news ended with a series of high-profile fires in rear-end collisions, resulting in a number of deaths. Subsequent lawsuits unveiled Ford's callousness in weighing the costs to improve the fuel tank placement against additional accidents and lives. The negative publicity led to two reviews by the Na-tional Highway Safety Administration. The second review resulted in the largest recall in US history—1.5 million cars. Ford could have fought the recall but risked further damage to its brand. It stopped Pinto production in 1980. Later analysis determined that the Pinto was actually average or above average in its crash-worthiness and vehicle deaths. The stories of the Mustang and the Pinto bring to mind the adage, "Success has many fathers while failure is an orphan."

Racing continued to be a key marketing focus for the automakers, and Ford was no exception. Henry Ford II was supportive of Ford racing in the

United States, with a focus on the NASCAR and GT circuits. A former driver and now automotive designer named Carroll Shelby used Ford engines in developing the Cobra, one of the most successful cars in GT racing. Shelby also took stock Mustangs and redesigned them for racing. Lee Iacocca engaged him to produce the Mustang GT500, a street-legal performance car.

Henry Ford II was a jet setter and frequently visited Europe. There the pinnacle of automobile racing was the twenty-four hours of Le Mans. Iacocca pressed him to consider racing Fords in Europe. Since Ferrari was dominant at Le Mans, it seemed to Henry II that the quickest approach was to simply buy Ferrari. He approached Enzo Ferrari with an offer to buy the company (at the time, Ferrari was hand-building five hundred cars a year while Ford was producing 3.2 million). Ferrari agreed, and the deal was to be announced on July 4, 1963. At the eleventh hour, Ferrari backed out over terms relating to his continued racing as the Ferrari brand.

If you recall, once upon a time, Henry Ford interviewed for a job with Alexander Winton. He was brusquely rejected. He never forgot the affront and served up Winton with not just one whipping but two. It was the same with Henry Ford II. Enzo Ferrari had jilted him, and Henry was livid. He was reported to have said, "Okay then, we'll kick their ass."[101]

With Lee Iacocca running interference, Henry Ford II pushed hard on a crash program to build a Ford winner for Le Mans. At the 1965 race, none of the Fords even finished the race. Iacocca suggested that Ford turn to Carroll Shelby. Shelby had a storied career in racing, culminating in winning the Le Mans race in 1959. Shelby took Ford's 7.0 liter engine and built the Ford GT40 around it. Ferrari had won Le Mans the previous four years and again looked unstoppable. In 1966, the new Ford GT40 won the Daytona race, finishing 1-2-3, and then followed it up with a 1-2-3 finish at the 12 Hours of Sebring. Both winners were driven by Ken Miles. Henry Ford II had thirteen GT40 cars ready for Le Mans. The lead GT40, again driven by Ken Miles, built a huge lead and was positioned to win. It was suggested to Henry Ford II that they could instruct Miles to slow down and then have three Fords finish 1-2-3 side by side. Though Miles was denied the coveted trifecta, Henry loved the spectacle of three Fords crossing the finish line in tandem, far ahead of the Ferraris. And, Ford came back the following year and won again. As with his grandfather, Henry Ford II had taken Enzo Ferrari to the woodshed not once but twice.[102]

My first Mustang was a green 1968 model with a floor-mounted three-speed stick shift. Green was fine, as I took the car to Dartmouth College in New Hampshire, whose athletic teams happened to be known as the "Big

Green." The Mustang took me through college in style. Once I had graduated and started a job with IBM in Miami that required a lot of account
travel, the three-speed shifting was much less practical. I sold it and bought
a second Mustang, a beautiful canary yellow 1970 model with black interior, and thankfully an automatic transmission.

By 1974, Cynthia and I were married, and her multi-toned VW had finally run out of gas. We needed another car. A neighbor, a pilot for Eastern
Air Lines, happened to have an original 1965 Mustang for sale. We became
a two-car family with two Mustangs.

Moving forward to 1976, I made my lone grievous Mustang mistake. I
sold the beautiful 1970 Mustang and bought a 1973 Mustang Grande. This
was an obscenely large Mustang built around the Ford's big block 351HP
V-8 engine. It was Bunkie Knudsen's project. One positive note came out
of the short time with this one: I learned how to do a proper oil change.
Coming home to Miami from New England, I had changed the oil without
properly lubing the oil filter ring. An emergency stop in North Carolina
averted disaster. I proceeded to do hundreds of oil changes correctly.

Bunkie Knudsen's monstrous Mustang was gone by 1974, which coin-
cided with the introduction of the Mustang II. Sponsored by Lee Iacocca,
designed around a body designed by Ghia of Turin, and built on the Pinto
frame, it was long viewed as an "economy" Mustang designed as a response
to the oil shock of 1973. Some sources say the Mustang II started as a rebuke
to Knudsen's Mustang Grande. Regardless of its gestation, the Mustang II
remained an outlier, shunned by real Mustang enthusiasts. My mistake
Grande only lasted a year. I sold it, and by then having lost all automobile
sense, I purchased an AMC Pacer.

I am not sure if there is any kind of acceptable line of reasoning leading
from the Mustang to the Pacer. I was still calling on accounts in Miami
and had grown tired of the lack of comfort in the big Mustang Grande. At
6' 5", I was looking for something wider and taller. This was years before
the advent of SUVs. Well, along comes the Pacer, the "first wide small car."
The interior space in the Pacer was dramatically different, and in a good
way. Apparently, AMC designer Richard Teague had designed the car from
the inside out, and it certainly showed. It was, however, a different looking
car—short, wide, and tall, with mountains of glass. *Car and Driver* magazine would christen it the "Flying Fishbowl."

At the time, I wasn't quite up to speed on the concept of the American
Motors Company. The original idea was to combine all the independents

still standing in the 1950s into one company that could hold its own against the Big Three. Nash and Hudson merged to form AMC, but Packard decided to go in a different direction, acquiring the money-losing Studebaker. That would eventually sink them both. AMC soldiered on until a new executive took control in 1960. He was Roy Chapin Jr., and the name should ring a bell. Yes, he was the son of Roy Chapin, famous for driving the Curved Dash Olds to New York City, then rising to take the reins of Hudson Motors. Once at the AMC helm, Chapin Jr. met with Edgar Kaiser and negotiated the acquisition of Jeep. In the ensuing years, Jeep would continue to flourish, and Chapin was able to have some success with smaller cars, including the Nash Rambler and the Gremlin.

Chapin also started the Pacer project, and it was one that should have been a success for a company majoring in small cars. The concept was to produce a small car with a roomy interior. For Chapin, the key to the plan was the Wankel rotary engine. General Motors had one in development, and he reached an agreement with GM to supply the engine for the new car. In fact, the Pacer was designed around the engine, enabling a small engine compartment, sufficient power, and low weight for good economy. At the eleventh hour, GM canceled its rotary project, and AMC was left without a power plant for its new car. Its engineers decided to squeeze AMC's existing six-cylinder engine into the small engine compartment, creating a much heavier car with poor fuel economy and, as it turned out, numerous maintenance issues.

Despite this, the Pacer was an exciting new car and sold briskly after it was announced. There were 145,000 Pacers sold in 1975, its first year, and it continued to be popular the following year. Then it rapidly slumped, and AMC ceased production after only four years. It appears that most of the buyers that were intrigued by the car had bought it in the first couple of years, and that was it.

Still in Miami, I was slow to understand the effects of the amount of glass on the Pacer. The body surface was 37 percent glass, compared to 16 percent for the average car. It was one thing to have wraparound windows on the 1947 Studebaker. It was quite another to have the Pacer level of windows. In Miami, winter turned to summer and we quickly realized that the air conditioning would be fighting a losing battle with all that glass. We had the Pacer less than a year before we made the switch to Volvos.

Indeed, after two failed acquisitions with the oversized Mustang and the overweight Pacer, we decided to opt for Swedish common sense. The

fact that Volvo had just released its beautiful 1978 242GT sports car did
have some bearing on the move. The backstory on Volvo was nowhere
near as cataclysmic as that of Volkswagen. In 1924, Assar Gabrielson, sales
manager for the Swedish ball-bearing company SKF, teamed with engineer
Gustaf Larson to design an automobile. SKF was not initially interested
in funding the venture, so Gabrielson underwrote the first ten test cars
himself before obtaining the go-ahead from SKF. The cars were baptized
"Volvo," which is Latin for "I roll." The distinctive hood ornament on all
Volvos is the Swedish symbol for iron.

The early years of Volvo were not especially propitious. Given that this
was Sweden, Gabrielson and his team wisely switched from touring cars
to closed sedans. Still, fewer than three thousand cars were produced in
the first three years, and that low volume did not generate any profit. Financial problems mounted, and SKF finally decided to sell the company,
finding a willing buyer in none other than Charles Nash. Nash was riding
high after leaving Billy Durant and General Motors, having purchased the
Rambler-Jeffrey automobile company and starting Nash Motors. However,
just a day before Nash was to arrive by boat at Gothenburg to conclude the
sale, Gabrielson convinced SKF to call off the arrangement. Despite this
last-minute snub, Nash and Gabrielson became good friends.

The company still struggled, selling only fifty thousand cars over the
next fourteen years, until World War II intervened. One of the automobiles
built during this period was the 1935 Volvo PV36, known as the Carioca after a popular dance at the time. The Carioca debuted a year after the Chrysler Airflow and was eerily similar. It turns out there was a reason for that.
The Volvo designer, Ivar Ornberg, had been chief engineer and designer
for Hupp Motor Company, working with Raymond Loewy. He returned to
Sweden in 1933 to work for Volvo. The Carioca was very similar in design
to the 1934 Huppmobile, which in turn was a dead ringer for the Airflow.

Only five hundred Cariocas were built to test the market. That proved
to be a good decision as the Airflow streamline look was again perceived
to be ugly. The Carioca was replaced the following year with the PV52. It
retained part of the streamlining but went back to bulbous torpedo headlights to satisfy conventional tastes, again very similar to the Chrysler rebound strategy.

Sweden tried to maintain neutrality during World War II, enabling Gabrielson and his team to develop a smaller Volvo, the PV444. This four-
cylinder, 51 horsepower model lasted with few changes until 1965. Volvo

did not start selling cars in the United States until 1955. It was not until 1958 that Volvo produced a station wagon version of the car.

By the time Cynthia and I adopted Volvos, safety was the company's mantra. Volvo was a leader in three-point seat belts, impact cages, disc brakes, and telescoping steering wheels. It wasn't too long after the 242GT that we purchased the first of several Volvo station wagons. Though the energy crisis, minivans, and SUVs had cratered the mainstream market for station wagons, Volvo soldiered on. We would stick with them for the next thirty-five years.[103]

Into the twenty-first century, it seemed that pony cars had more than run their course. Ford kept producing them, but they had lost the style and cachet that had once led them to prominence. Then the company, now run by Henry Ford II's nephew, William Clay Ford Jr., decided to go retro. The result was the 2005 fifth-generation Mustang, which drew direct inspiration from the 1970 Mustang. This was the first Mustang with its own chassis, not one borrowed from a Falcon or Pinto. It was introduced in late 2004, and by March 2005, one of every two sports cars sold in the United States was a Mustang. As the Big Three were still alive and kicking, it came as no surprise that the other two had to respond with their own retro sports cars. The following year saw new Chevy Camaros and Dodge Challengers. The new Mustang would eventually drive total Mustang sales over ten million, short of the Model T and the VW but well ahead of the competition.

The chief engineer on the new Mustang was Hau Thai-Tang. He had escaped from Vietnam at the fall of Saigon in 1975, at age nine. As a kid in Vietnam, he had seen classic Mustangs on USO tours in the city. They were a revelation when compared to his family's car, a homely two-cylinder Citroen. He had worked on Ford's IndyCar racing program before rising to design chief and leading the rebirth project.

As the yellow 1970 Mustang had been my favorite, it was hard to resist the new classic. Being male and fifty-five years old, I was probably in the sweet spot of Ford's target market. And resist, I did not. I pre-ordered one of the first new Mustangs and didn't hold back, opting for a bright red convertible with a five-speed, short throw stick. It was one of the first 2005 convertibles, and when it arrived, the dealer had set it up in a special display room so that others might be wowed and order a similar one. He looked somewhat crestfallen when I drove it away. The car had its own theme song—"Born to Be Wild" by Steppenwolf—which, of course, starts out with "get your motor running." And, when you did get the motor running, Hau and his team had tuned the exhaust so that it sounded just like the muscular 1970 Mustangs.

Though it was a fabulous automobile, it was less than practical in wintry Colorado. My older son was a senior in high school during this time, and nothing could be finer than putting the top down and driving it to baseball practice. I purchased the car in 2005 and sold it three years later. Both sons were supremely crushed when the new owner drove the car away.[104]

20

Going Electric

IN THE VERY early years of the automobile, electric cars comprised 40 percent of the market. Electric taxicabs in several cities were on the rise. Henry Ford had purchased three Detroit Electrics for his wife Clara, the first one bought just a few weeks after the debut of his Model T. His friend Thomas Edison also owned a series of Detroit Electric cars, as had Henry Joy of Packard, Child Wills of Ford, and Frank Duryea. Yet, those early electrics had many limitations, including minimal range, low top speed, long charging times, and the lack of a supporting infrastructure. For a time, the limitations of the competing options (steam and gasoline) were viewed as equal or greater, and electrics continued to sell.

Edison had been working on enhanced batteries. While he had encouraged Henry Ford to keep working on his gasoline automobiles when they met in 1897, he thought his nickel-iron batteries could power an improved electric car several years later. He engaged his friend Henry about using his new batteries in a car. In 1914, both Ford and Edison confirmed that work was being done on such a car. Ford produced a prototype based on the Model T frame.

Though Ford wanted to use Edison's batteries, they were not easily adaptable for powering a car, as they were too expensive and performed poorly in cold weather. Switching to standard lead-acid batteries would have added significant weight, too heavy for the Model T frame, and would not have represented any improvement over existing electric cars. He shelved the program and moved its lead engineer, Eugene Farkas, to his tractor project. The low cost of the Model T and the emergence of the electric starter to replace the hand crank spelled the end for electrics. They ceased being a factor in automobiles by 1920.

It was a growing concern about auto emissions and global warming that sparked a renewed interest in electric cars in the late twentieth century. In 1990 the California Air Resource Board (CARB) issued a zero emissions mandate in response to deteriorating air conditions in Southern California. That mandate specified that 2 percent of automobiles sold in California had to be zero emission by 1998, with the target rising to 5 percent in 2001 and 10 percent by 2010.

This sparked an initial rush by the major auto manufacturers to produce a zero emission vehicle (ZEV) while at the same time they pursued court action to delay or eliminate the mandate. General Motors did produce a ZEV car by 1996, the EV1. It was only available via a lease arrangement, and production was limited to slightly more than a thousand cars. The batteries for the EV1 alone cost $40,000, and the total cost of each car was north of $250,000. It technically addressed the mandate but was clearly not sustainable. The first EV1 models used lead-acid batteries and achieved 80–100 miles on a charge. In 1999 GM replaced the lead-acid batteries with a new battery technology—nickel-metal hydride—which increased the range to 100–140 miles. But, the new batteries were even more expensive.

In the meantime, the auto companies were able to force CARB to backtrack on the zero emission mandate by slyly touting the soon-to-be-available fuel cell technology (which has still gone nowhere as of 2020) and resetting the compliance timeline. Once the mandate pressure was eliminated, GM quietly repossessed each leased EV1, trucked them to Arizona, and had them crushed.

While not a pretty story, the problem remained that the underlying constraint for a successful electric car had not changed since the efforts of Henry Ford and Thomas Edison. The early EV1 models used lead-acid batteries, and all the inherent constraints of lead-acid were the same. Real progress had to wait for battery technology to go through several innovations.

In the meantime, real meaningful electric progress came in the form of hybrid electric vehicles, where the primary motive power, a gasoline engine, was aided by an electric battery. The Toyota Prius, which debuted in 1997, was the most successful implementation of this approach. It reduced total emissions by dramatically increasing mileage. The Prius used nickel-metal hydride batteries, which were more than adequate in a role of assisting a gas engine. However, they could not effectively take over and solely propel a vehicle.

The automobile industry at the start of the twenty-first century was mature, worldwide, and seemingly immune to new entrants. The colorful pioneers were decidedly in the rear view mirror. And yet, with the sheer amount of carbon dioxide that automobiles had been pouring into the atmosphere for a century, the existential danger of global warming and climate change has become real and imminent. Into this milieu and against all odds, another pioneer, disrupter, and colorful individual appeared and might actually succeed where so many others had failed, even turning the entire automotive world upside down.

That would be Elon Musk and his Tesla electric car company. Much like Henry Ford, Musk started with a grand vision, that of addressing climate change and ending the age of petroleum by creating a sustainable ecosystem of solar panels, batteries, and electric cars. He would not have to start from scratch, however. Early on, he founded the start-up Tesla, named of course after the famous electrical engineer and inventor, Nikola Tesla. Tesla the company was started in 2003 by two engineers, Martin Eberhard and Mark Tarpenning, who began work on a low-slung electric roadster. It was powered by 6,800 small lithium ion cells matched to a drivetrain from AC Propulsion, the same company that had supplied the drivetrain on GM's EV1.

Tesla was not making much headway when it came to the attention of Musk. He had made a fortune as one of the founders of the payments giant PayPal and was ready to move forward on his vision. He bought into the company in 2004, investing $75 million. He soon fired the two founders and started working with chief engineer J. B. Straubel on a viable, marketable roadster. Several years away from even having the initial roadster for sale, he kicked off a follow-on program called WhiteStar (destined to become the Tesla Model S sedan). The following year Musk took his ambition one step further, publicly stating his grand strategy. In his own words, "the master plan is (1) build a sports car [the Tesla Roadster]; (2) use that money to build an affordable car [the Model S]; (3) use that money to build an even more affordable car [the Model 3] and while doing above, also provide zero emission electric power generation options [the Solar City company]."

The Tesla Roadster finally was unveiled in 2008. It featured electric motors driven by lithium ion battery cells, generating 248 horsepower and propelling the car from 0 to 60 mph in 3.7 seconds. Top speed was 125 mph, and the range was over two hundred miles per charge. Prices ranged from $100,000 to $130,000. The car was certainly impressive. It cut against the prevailing grain of making electric cars that were slow and boring. For Musk, it was making the car that was the challenge. The initial Tesla Roadsters were virtually handmade at separate work centers, recalling how the early Model Ts were made at the Piquette factory.

Tesla had spent nearly $140 million producing the Roadster but would need significantly more capital to move to the next stage of Musk's very public stated vision, the "affordable car." In 2008 and 2009, Musk secured nearly a billion dollars in new funding, including a $465 million loan from the Department of Energy, $50 million investments from Daimler and Toyota, and $225 million from an initial public offering of Tesla stock.

Tesla used part of that haul to purchase the 5.3 million square foot NUMMI factory in Fremont, California. NUMMI (New United Motor Manufacturing, Inc.) was a joint investment by Toyota and General Motors, who had invested upwards of $1 billion in the assembly plant. Tesla was able to buy it for $42 million from Toyota while at the same time securing a $50 million investment from the automaker. The deal compares very favorably with Kaiser and Frazer getting Ford's Willow Run factory for next to nothing at the end of World War II.

The new car would be called the Model S. Unlike Henry Ford's straightforward scheme of starting with Model A and working his way down to the Model T, the ever media savvy Musk decided to name his first four models "S", "E", "X", and "Y" in order to emphasize that electric cars were not stodgy but supremely high performance. Unfortunately, none other than the Ford Motor Company had a trademark on the Model "E", putting a temporary damper on his plan. Musk had an answer for this, but it would have to wait.

The Model S project got underway in 2005. Musk set up the project team at SpaceX headquarters. Oh, I forgot to mention that he had started a rocket company at the same time. Here, his modest stated mission was to replace the work of NASA and Boeing in developing manned spacecraft that would eventually take colonists to Mars.

But, still on the ground at SpaceX, Musk hired Franz Von Holzhausen, a designer who had worked on the New Beetle, to design the new car. Unlike the Roadster, it would be s a very conventional four-door sedan. They actually bought a Mercedes CLS class sedan, tore it apart, and used it as a model for the S design. The new car would feature the then unheard range of three hundred miles per charge with off-the-chart performance numbers—a 140 mph top speed and a 0–60 time of 2.3 seconds.

Even more groundbreaking was the electronic foundation of the car. The Model S was essentially a large computer with four wheels, a battery pack, electric motors, and seating for four. Most of the componentry was electrically driven and computer controlled. This enabled Tesla to simply download fixes, changes, and enhancements to a customer's car over the air. The pinnacle of the electronics was "Autopilot," the software and hardware implementation that could eventually lead to full self-driving operation.

Another major investment accompanied the Model S. This was a vast network of chargers across the country, which addressed head-on a major concern with electric cars: range anxiety. While gasoline cars had a mature supporting infrastructure of 168,000 filing stations, there was virtually nothing for electric cars. And Tesla took it a step further. The electricity at Tesla charging stations was free for Model S customers for the life of the car.

One final detail had to be resolved—how to sell the Tesla. The quality of the car and the mystique of Tesla tended to sell the cars by publicity and word of mouth. Tesla did not need to do any advertising, nor did it really need dealer salesmen. However, brick-and-mortar locations were needed to provide service. Tesla's solution stole a page from Norval Hawkins's Model T sales strategy: sell through company branches. There was, though, a slight problem with this approach. In a situation that harkened to the monopolistic American Licensed Automobile Manufacturers (ALAM) that Henry Ford faced, Tesla was unable to open showrooms in a number of states that had dealer franchise laws that prevented an auto manufacturer from selling directly to customers. Not to be deterred, Tesla augmented its branch strategy by selling online and delivering the cars direct to the customer or to its service centers.

The Model S was unveiled in 2009 at a glitzy press show event but did not arrive until 2012, a delay that would become a common theme with Tesla. The Model S was *Motor Trend*'s Car of the Year in 2012. It received the highest rating ever achieved in *Consumer Reports* testing (99 out of 100). More importantly, the Model S was about 60 percent efficient in turning energy into propulsion (whereas gas cars are about 10-20 percent efficient). This translated into an equivalency rating of about 100 mph.

Despite all of these positives, this was a very precarious time for Tesla. The company had never made a profit and continued to burn cash at an alarming rate. Now a public company, it was highly covered by the financial press, and the coverage was mostly negative. Typical reports forecast slow sales and plummeting resale values for the Model S. In a move not unlike Henry Ford's response to the threat to his customers from the Selden patent, Musk pledged a resale value guarantee. And in a response to the slow sales, he appointed many of his employees as temporary salesmen. They proceeded to sell 4,900 cars in the final quarter of 2012 and generated Tesla's first quarterly profit on revenues of $562 million. Musk then paid off the $465 million Department of Energy loan, plus interest.

Absolutely critical to the success of Tesla's grand strategy was cutting-edge lithium ion batteries with high energy density, produced at an affordable cost, and available in the numbers to support the Tesla volumes Musk envisioned. The key benchmark was to produce lithium ion cells at a cost below $100 per kilowatt hour. This was pretty much the same problem that Henry Ford and Thomas Edison sought to solve a century earlier. For Tesla, hitting that benchmark would put the cost of the 75 kilowatt-hour battery pack at $7,500, which could make the target price of $35,000 for the "even more affordable" car much more achievable.

To make this happen, Musk partnered with Panasonic in creating a massive battery facility. It was to be called the Gigafactory, as its objective was to produce gigawatts of total battery power. The factory is located north of Reno, Nevada, with the mission to manufacture the individual lithium ion cells (each about the size of an AA battery) as well as populating the cells into a car-ready package, each composed of thousands of those cells. Tesla and Panasonic split the cost of the factory, estimated to be about $5 billion. The factory opened in 2016 and by late 2018 was able to produce the batteries for the five thousand cars that Tesla was building each week. When fully ramped up, the factory was producing close to 40 percent of total global production of these types of batteries.

The Reno plant had to be renamed Gigafactory 1 as Tesla expanded the concept. Gigafactory 2 was located in Buffalo, New York, and focused on solar roof panels for the Tesla subsidiary Solar City. Gigafactory 3 was built in Shanghai, China, and started producing battery cells for Tesla cars in late 2019. As this is written, Gigafactory 4 is under construction near Berlin.

According to Elon Musk's grand plan, the next step was to use the profits of the "affordable" car (the Model S) on an "even more affordable" car.

However, Musk took a detour to build the Model X, a mid-size SUV built on the Model S chassis. It featured an aluminum body and falcon-wing passenger doors, neither of which contributed to a smooth manufacturing ramp-up, and represented a bit of overreach on Tesla's part. First deliveries were a year late and more importantly, the issues surrounding the car took precious cycles from the critical "even more affordable" car.

Though not remotely profitable, Tesla's experience with Model S and Model X production at NUMMI and batteries at the Gigafactory certainly helped. Yet, it was mainly the Tesla mystique that continued to propel the company forward. Tesla had clearly demonstrated that electric cars could be both efficient and, shall we say, "SEXY." It was time for the Model E to complete the quadruplet, but Ford still had other ideas. Elon Musk decided to simply reverse the "E" and call the new affordable car the Model 3.

The Model 3 was similar in design to the Model S but smaller and lighter. It featured a range up to 310 miles based on a battery pack that contained 4,416 individual lithium ion cells. Top speed was 140 mph, and 0–60 time was 3.4 seconds, both comparable to the Model S. Though *Consumer Reports* originally recommended the car, it reversed that recommendation after testing the brakes and finding that the Model 3 stopping distance was worse than the big, hulking Ford F-150 pickup. This posed no problem for Tesla. Elon Musk's engineers analyzed the braking system and issued an over-the-air fix that reduced the stopping distance by twenty feet. *Consumer Reports* reinstated the "Recommended" rating.

I came back to Ford once again and took the electric plunge in 2012. The car was a Ford C-Max Energi, a plug-in hybrid electric vehicle (PHEV). The Energi was based on Ford's C platform that was popular in Europe, and, most importantly, the car was tall. It was powered by a 7.6 kWh lithium ion battery pack along with a backup four-cylinder gas engine. Range was 20–30 miles per charge. When the battery was depleted, the gas engine would kick in. The C-Max is used for local trips and thus runs almost exclusively in electric mode. Having been driving more than thirty-five thousand miles, it has averaged over 300 miles per gallon of gas. Though Ford appears behind in the race to produce fully electric cars, it has had hybrids for many years and cross-licensed hybrid functionality with Toyota. However, much like the very low-profile electric project that Henry Ford and Thomas Edison worked on, the current Ford Motor Company has been singularly circumspect about its early electrics like the C-Max, something that Elon Musk would never be accused of.

The Tesla Model 3 was planned to be formally announced on March 31, 2016, at which time first-day orders would be taken. That day was a bitter cold, snowy day in Colorado. Tesla did have a physical showroom in the Mountain West, located in a mall in south Denver. I made the trek from Boulder and joined a long line outside the mall, waiting for the Tesla store to open. Putting up a $1,000 deposit, I was just one of 180,000 first-day orders. Total orders rose to 425,000 within a couple of weeks, about the same number of pre-orders that the Ford Model A received in its first two weeks in 1927 (though Henry Ford required a 50 percent deposit).

All of the Tesla orders were made without any cars available to see or test drive. It would be over two years before any of the showrooms even had a car on display. Tesla was only able to produce about two thousand Model 3s by the end of 2017. That was twenty-one months after first-day orders. Musk's stated production target of five thousand Model 3 cars per week was not achieved for over two years. This could be chalked up to growing pains with Fordism, or rather, the Musk version of Fordism automobile mass production. Like most of Musk's goals, the manner of car manufacturing was ambitious. He wanted a near-automated factory and spent freely on the latest robots to populate the assembly line at Tesla's Fremont plant. He eventually had to back off on total automation and insert more people into the line.

As for my order, I was finally able to sit in a Model 3 two years after that snowy drive to Denver. Unfortunately, the relatively low-slung car was unable to handle my 6' 5" frame (let alone accommodate Wilt Chamberlain). I canceled the order and continued to drive the Ford C-Max. I was aware, however, that Elon Musk had some interesting new vehicles on the horizon.

The even more "affordable" Model 3 was a great success story, the best-selling electric car in the world. Yet, it was a small sedan, and the automobile world had moved on to SUVs and crossovers. It was time for the final car in Tesla's "S3XY" lineup, the Model Y. It was announced in early 2019, built on the same platform as the Model 3 and sharing many of the same components, but significantly taller. The car also incorporated the latest batteries from the Gigafactory, providing a range in excess of three hundred miles at an even lower cost.

Given that the car addressed the biggest and most attractive segment of the car market, the Model Y was virtually assured of success. Another huge backlog of orders was the inevitable result. To navigate to market, the

Model Y would have to compete with several other automotive projects that Musk had set in motion. There would be a new updated Tesla Roadster, this one a supercar with 0–60 time of 1.9 seconds and optional rocket jets. Tesla also announced that it would enter the long-haul truck market with an electric semi-truck. And finally, Tesla would be entering the highly profitable pickup truck market, competing head to head with the iconic Ford F-150.

As of April 2020, Tesla has sold roughly one million cars. That number broke down to about 2,500 original Roadsters, 460,000 Model S and X cars, and 525,000 Model 3 and Y cars. With US annual car sales at seventeen million, those numbers are pretty insignificant. But, Tesla was far and away the leader in the segments that it was competing in and was growing rapidly, with gigafactories and auto plants coming online in Europe and China.

Elon Musk once commented on the Model S naming, his first mainstream car, "We went through a bunch of iterations and the Model S sounded the best. And it was like a vague nod to Ford being the Model T in that electric cars preceded the Model T, and in a way we're coming full circle and the thing that preceded the Model T is now going into production in the twenty-first century, hence the Model S." Elon Musk owns a Ford Model T and certainly would entertain any comparison with Henry Ford.

The Tesla story is just beginning, and its accomplishments are to date nowhere near the impact that Ford had on the country and the world. That Tesla appears to be on its way to being the first successful new automobile company since Walter Chrysler in 1924 does gives some weight to a comparison. First, both were engineers. Musk got the automobile bug with the Roadster, then became intimately involved in the design of the Model S. In fact, his constant quest for perfection in that first "conventional" car led to a cash-flow crisis that necessitated bringing in a new CFO to create some financial order (not unlike Ford and James Couzens).

Second, both Ford and Musk were driven by a single, virtually unchanging vision—Ford with his universal car and Musk with a sustainable electric future. Third, both attracted capital and broad awareness with racing. Musk did not have a Barney Oldfield, but publishing the results on the track were enough to dispel the stodgy image of electric cars. Both Ford and Musk struggled with funding, with Ford blowing through two companies before making money almost immediately with his third attempt. Tesla has had the opposite experience, attracting all kinds of funds but still struggling to make a profit after fifteen years.

Third, both men were highly disruptive to the automotive industry. Ford fought the ALAM cartel, eschewed model changes, raised hourly wages, invested earning in his business rather than paying shareholders, and went his own way in so many other areas. Musk is challenging the foundational gasoline model and the franchise structure.

Production was a steep learning curve for Musk and Tesla. "Muskism" might be called Fordism on steroids. It is a given that Henry Ford would be impressed with the robots and automation at the Fremont facility. He would have been less impressed with the temporary tent factory in the parking lot.

Both Ford and Musk were one-man operators, though Musk carries it so much further. He works so many roles at Tesla—CEO, part-time architect, production manager, public relations director, and much more. Then, there are his other companies—SpaceX, Solar City, and the Boring Company. Like Ford, Musk is not particularly big on delegation.

Finally, it must be said that both men had/have prickly and controversial personalities. Ford was so sure of the rightness of his upbringing that he was blind to the prejudices that came along with that upbringing. Musk has used the scale and adulation of his success to convey a similar kind of rightness, and he is not reticent about getting involved in controversy outside his core mission and strengths.

At the end of the day, both Henry Ford and Elon Musk wanted to build an affordable car. Ford's focus on affordability became an obsession, leading to single-minded focus on price and virtually no enhancements for nearly twenty years. Musk and Tesla are just about Ford's opposite. Though the outward appearance of the Model S has not changed appreciably since its introduction in 2012, Tesla cars are under constant change. Even a 2012 Model S is still being enhanced via downloaded updates.

Tesla's success to date has forced existing automakers to at least hedge their bets and start to prepare for an all-electric future. They are investing heavily while moving forward slowly and warily. Though customer demand for electrics is still anemic, the case for electric vehicles has never been stronger. The range issue has been substantially solved, although more work is needed on the charging infrastructures. Battery costs are decreasing while battery capacity is up. Electric cars have far fewer operating parts, making them more reliable, cheaper to run, and higher in resale value. Finally, electric automobiles are far more efficient in converting power supplied to actual locomotion. And, there is one other, fundamental factor. There are currently about two billion cars on the planet, most powered by the internal combustion engine. That is nearly two billion tiny, individual power plants spewing carbon into the atmosphere. Electrics will take their power from the grid, and as the grid becomes less polluting with wind, solar, nuclear, and other sources, the electric car can immediately take advantage.

There are also growing mandates for electric cars. It is no surprise that Musk has a Gigafactory in China, the world's number-one automobile market, and one where incentives and mandates have resulted in a 30 percent market share for electrics. But China is not yet the world leader. That would be Norway, where roughly 60 percent of all new cars are electric. The percentage could be even higher in Norway, but there are waiting lists for electric cars, including Teslas. Despite being awash in North Sea petroleum, Norway aims to actually end the sale of gasoline cars by 2025. The country's record to date has been achieved by a wide range of incentives, including tax rebates, free tolls, free parking, and the availability of a widespread charging infrastructure.

One other hurdle remains for electric cars. As they are silent, there is a growing push for some kind of manufactured noise to alert pedestrians. A cottage industry is already working on this. Perhaps, the guttural sound of the Mustang GT could be the answer.

21

Epilogue

IT HAS BEEN a long and at times painful journey through the automotive age. Before moving on to the next chapter in the journey, we'll bring our story up to the present day.

In 1951, John Shaffer had a modern brick home built on the rise across French Creek from the farm. Verne moved into the new homestead while John, Georgia, and their three kids remained in the old farmhouse. That same year marked the 45th anniversary of Will's graduating class at Williamsfield High. Verne was joined by former principal R. C. Woolsey and a host of others for the annual meeting. Six members of the class had died, including Will and Floyd Wesner so many years before.

Verne had kept busy with the French Grove association, meetings with fellow Gold Star mothers, and occasional trips to see relatives in California. She was still driving in her sixties, in a Chrysler of course, even heading all the way to Miami to visit Paul and his family.

In 1959, she had just passed age seventy and was not in great health. She had a winter trip planned to California that February. John and Georgia advised her that it was not a good idea but she went just the same and spent two months in Glendale. She was ailing when she returned and checked into the Methodist Hospital in Peoria. She died a day later of a heart attack. Verne had endured much tragedy in her life and had kept the family together through the loss of Will, Bill, and Detta Lou, the Great Depression, and World War II. She never remarried but remained a pillar of the family and the French Creek community.

John continued to farm. Year after year, he rotated fields with mostly corn and soybeans while leaving the steep hill running down to French Creek as pasture for a small number of cattle. The Poland China hogs and their white houses were long gone. After the war and with farm technology raising yields, another golden era of agriculture ensued. Local farmland prices rose to $10,000 an acre. Though there was never a thought of selling the farm, its increased value made it much easier to buy equipment.

Illinois had instituted a program to recognize farms that had remained in one family. Your farm had to have been continuously farmed for one hundred years, hence the Centennial Farm designation. John and Georgia secured their Centennial Farm marker in 1990 when the farm had been in the family for 118 years, starting in 1872. The adjacent Reed family holdings also qualified, having been purchased in 1876. Yet, it was the Tuckers who had the bragging rights. The Tucker farm, the one that included the orchard where the Reed School was built, had been settled in 1840. It turned out that Peoria County had the most Centennial Farms in the state.

John was still farming in his seventies, though for the last several years he had help from another local farmer. He apparently had heart problems much like Verne, and it finally got to him in 1995 at age eighty. He had been farming for sixty-two years, ever since being thrown into the role unprepared in 1933.

Georgia managed the estate sale, and much like Verne's estate sale, it amply demonstrated the success of the farm. The auctioneer sold a large Case tractor, a small Case tractor (yes, it was always Case for John), a John Deere combine, a Ford pickup, several farm wagons, and an extensive inventory of farm implements (disk, harrow, planter, plow, cultivator, mower, hay rake, manure spreader, and auger). All the implements were powered units, unlike the horse-drawn equipment that Will had used. The Jeep had finally died for good and was rusting in the gully at the back of the farm.

With John's passing, Georgia had the old farmhouse razed and buried. Nearly 150 years old, in the end the bad memories outweighed the good. The kids—Eleanor, Reed, and Tom—had scattered to the four winds, so she rented the farm to a local farmer. She had the channel running down to French Creek dammed up for a lake and then stocked with fish. Georgia passed away in 2010 at age ninety-five. The farm continues in the family.

Paul left the USDA in 1967 for private consulting, doing similar types of efficiency studies. One irony of his work is that it helped make supermarket chains grow larger, with more efficient stores. The chain stores put more pressure on the small grocery stores in the farm towns like Elmwood and Williamsfield.

Lucile had been in poor health for several years and died of complications from cancer at age fifty. She and Paul had been married thirty years. Paul took on an extended consultant engagement at the Price Chopper chain in Schenectady, New York. This led to meeting Alice Swanson and embarking on another thirty-year marriage. In 1998 he attended the 60th reunion of the Knox Class of 1938. He finally retired to Delray Beach, Florida—and by the way, drove a Mustang throughout his eighties. He died in 2013 at age ninety-six after a long and full life. This was just three years before the Chicago Cubs won the World Series. He would have enjoyed that, a fitting end to a lifetime love affair with the Cubs that started as a youngster listening to the radio outside Waible Electric in Elmwood during the Depression.

The last we saw of Big Joe, he had moved with his second wife, Ella, and daughters Vesper and Hortense to the farm he purchased in Milestone, Saskatchewan in 1908. In the early twentieth century, Milestone was very much like Williamsfield, a pioneer town on the main rail line. He would be there permanently, becoming a naturalized Canadian citizen in 1912. He died in 1928 and is buried in the nearby hamlet of Creelman. There is no mention of any pyrotechnics ever happening in the area.

Dr. Vesper Shaffer continued in her general practice in Chicago. With her electric car replacing the horse and buggy, she was able to move farther west, to a simple Victorian house at 2258 North Central Park Avenue. Never married, she died in 1930 at age sixty-six. An overflowing crowd attended her Chicago funeral, many of whom were former patients. A second service was held at the Methodist Episcopal Church in Williamsfield. She was buried next to her father James and mother Louisa in French Grove.

There is no William C. Shaffer IV. Neither of our two boys got the automotive bug, a regrettable failing of their father. Though they could do an oil change in a pinch, neither has ever owned a car. Living in New York and Chicago, they represent a millennial challenge for the automobile industry. Their "wheels" are mass transit, Uber, car share, and an occasional car rental. Pushed for a car sometime in the future, they would opt for an electric.

▷ ▷ ▷

The settling of the Midwest created small towns nearly every five miles in all directions. The stage lines and principally the railroads sorted out which towns would prosper and which would fade away. The coming of the automobile changed this calculus. Mid-size towns like Galesburg and Peoria with their larger stores were now easily accessible, even commutable. Farms were consolidated and sometimes sold to large agribusinesses, reducing both the local population and the services that the towns had previously met. The wide variety of shops in the farm towns gradually declined to the bare essentials.

For Williamsfield, the golden age is long gone but the town is still hanging on. Its current population is close to six hundred but is purely residential. The Depression was tough on the town and its residents. The Bank of Williamsfield closed in 1931 before FDR stepped in to save the banks. The town reinvented itself as a commuter and retiree center. A new elementary and high school was built in the 1960s, with a nice public library a block away. For a time, there was a quick mart, but even that is gone. Two churches remain—Methodist and Catholic. There is a small Chevy dealership and feed operation north of town.

The railroad, the engine that drove early success, no longer stops. At first, the town became a flag stop, and then there was no stopping—the trains just barreled through. Catching the Santa Fe from Williamsfield meant going to the station at Chillicothe or Galesburg. Diesel engines replaced steam engines after World War II, meaning the need for water replenishment at Williamsfield was no longer needed. The train depot building did not survive.

Elmwood had always been more prosperous than its neighboring towns. Even as late as 1956, it still had five grocery stores, three hardware stores, two drugstores, three car dealers, a furniture store, feed store, lumber yard, a couple of barber shops, no less than five gas stations, and several restaurants. This was for a town of perhaps two thousand residents. Those days are gone, but the town is still vibrant—and still has the same population. The Palace Theatre still screens the latest blockbusters. The Elmwood Municipal Band still plays in Central Park. There is a new high school and country club at the outskirts of town. Verne's Depression-era house at the corner of Butternut and Magnolia still exists and is in great shape.

Brimfield finally got its transportation link after years of chasing rail lines and streetcars: Interstate 74 was completed just south of town. The Chicago, Burlington, and Quincy spur line is gone, and that is for the best. There is no need to remember that intersection for this family. Brimfield's population hovers around a thousand, with several good-size employers.

Douglas was one of those towns that did not even make the transition into the twentieth century. BF certainly saw the writing on the wall when he decamped early for Williamsfield. The tracks are gone, and several houses and a field agricultural station are all that is left. That is more than can be said of French Grove. Even at its height in the late nineteenth century, French Grove was only a church, general store, and post office. Today, all that is left is the cemetery.

➤ ➤ ➤

The horse was the foundation of nineteenth-century farming. And, it was the most immediate victim of mechanization across cities, towns, and farms, replaced with automobiles, trucks, and tractors. From a peak of twenty-six million horses in 1925, the horse population dwindled to roughly three million in 1960. The USDA had tracked horse numbers as part of the census every ten years. It stopped counting draft horses in 1960 as the numbers had nearly gone to zero. And then, there was a resurgence in horse numbers in the 1970s and 1980s, with some estimates having the overall total as high as nine million. Draft horses participated in that resurgence, aided in no small part by Budweiser and their showy Clydesdales. Draft horses were thought to comprise about 5 percent of the total number, with Percherons about 70 percent of the figure.[105]

➤ ➤ ➤

Over two thousand automobile makes went into production in the early days of the US automobile industry. After the bicycle craze faded, it was clear that automobiles were the next big thing, or rather the next big thing on an entirely different scale. After the pioneers like the Duryeas and Alexander Winton and Ransom Olds had established the concept, virtually anyone could jump in and produce an automobile. Many makes were just assembled cars, using components that were bought from suppliers. The barriers to entry were low enough that it was easy to get in on the game.

But, as we have seen time and time again, even with the exalted automobile pioneers, you needed to quickly reach a level of production that was profitable, and that number kept increasing as the industry heated up. It turned out that so many things had to go right: the right car, the right price, effective marketing, cash to expand, and the know-how to ramp up production. In the very early days, you even had to select the right power source—steam, electric, or gas. Most of the early automobile brands did not put all of these elements together soon enough, resulting in cars that were going out the door at a loss. Receivership, bankruptcy, or liquidation were quite often the only remaining options.

The result was that few of the two thousand lasted more than a year or two. At the same time, the brands that had put the elements together—Ford, General Motors, and Chrysler—quickly grew so large that they changed the game, and the path to success grew narrower year after year, and then essentially closed. The Big Three had end-to-end product lines, vertical integration, and the volume to drive prices down and keep competitors out. The genius of someone like Walter Chrysler is that he succeeded so late in the game. Thus, besides the Big Three and a handful of independents, most automobile companies failed to make it past the early decades of the twentieth century. Of the select few that made it to the start of the Great Depression, only the Big Three and six independents existed at its end.[106]

William Durant was aware right from the beginning that you needed to get big and get big fast. Perhaps it had been Colonel Pope that had laid this groundwork with his bicycle trust. It is interesting that getting big is still the watchword today. In the early days, the so-called brass era of automobiles, the United States produced about 90 percent of all the cars in the world. By 1950, the country was still building nearly 80 percent of the 10.5 million cars produced that year. As I write this in 2020, the worldwide car market has already passed production of a hundred million cars annually while the US share has shrunk to seventeen million, or just a 17 percent share. The Chinese market alone is roughly double the size of the US market. In this echo of Billy Durant, the twenty-first century mantra is to get bigger or perish. By the year 2000, just six car companies controlled 80 percent of worldwide production (GM, Ford, Daimler Chrysler, Volkswagen, Renault, and Toyota). And, this was before China really got going.

In the United States, the Big Three did not age well. In the 1950s the US auto market was neatly apportioned between these leaders, with shares of roughly 46 percent for GM, 44 percent for Ford and Chrysler, and the remaining 10 percent split among the independents. The Big Three, and especially GM, were highly motivated to maintain this system. There was a tacit collusion to maintain market share, and this was enforced mainly through pricing power. At the beginning of each model year, General Motors would roll out its preliminary prices. Ford and Chrysler would peg their prices at GM's level. This resulted in Big Three volumes that left about 10 percent for the independents to fight over.

This arrangement was briefly broken in 1953 when Henry Ford II started a price war by posting much lower prices than GM, creating a gap. GM and Chrysler matched the lower prices in order to maintain share. The total volume of car sales shot up 45 percent, GM's share surged to 50.4 percent, and the Big Three took in about 95 percent of total US sales. The independents were severely squeezed as they did not have the economies of scale to match the prices and still turn a profit. This result left GM exposed to antitrust action. More importantly, the profits of the Big Three suffered. With the next model year, it was back to the tried-and-true scheme of setting prices, and the profits for the Big Three returned.

This system stifled innovation. It required comparable models to be roughly equivalent, with price the key factor. This meant everyone was to move in lockstep with any changes. When Vigil Exner surprised GM and Ford with much bigger fins in 1957, they rushed to match it. Or when Studebaker came out with a whole new category of automobile—the compact Lark in 1959—it was only a year or two before everyone else was on board.

Though Studebaker and Nash were a mere hindrance and quickly taken care of, the shift from the 1950s land yachts to smaller cars soon became a tidal wave, with foreign makes, particularly the Japanese, jumping into the fray. The Big Three proved to be less adept at making smaller cars, in part because their bureaucracy and production model required the much higher profit margins that large cars provided. This held the seeds of destruction for them, though it would take place in slow motion over many years.

In January 1956, the Ford Motor Company went public, something that Henry Ford I would never have even considered. Yet, Henry Ford II realized that he needed far more cash to remain competitive with GM and Chrysler. The public offering was structured with two classes of shares, with the Ford family owning only 2 percent of the total shares but retaining 40 percent of the voting rights. This arrangement provided Henry Ford II with both needed cash and continued control.

A down side of the additional cash was a new-found capability to address what was long perceived as a gap between the Ford and Mercury brands. GM's mid-brands (Pontiac, Buick, and Olds) outsold Mercury four to one. Chrysler's mid-brands (Dodge, DeSoto, and Chrysler) outsold Mercury three to one. Even before the public offering went final, Henry

Ford II gave the go-ahead to work on a new division. This would turn into a $250 million investment with eighteen different models planned right from the start. The new division would have its own dealers, and 1,100 promptly signed up. An extensive pre-debut marketing campaign was geared up. Nothing was to be left to chance. The new brand was called, of course, the Edsel.

It was released in late 1957 at the start of a recession, about the same time that the target midrange segment shrunk from 40 percent of the market to just 25 percent, making way for smaller cars like the Lark and the Rambler American. Then, there were quality problems in production. And, there was a sense that the Edsel was simply a warmed-over Ford or Mercury. But most of all, the Edsel was seen as an ugly automobile, particularly the grille, which resembled a horse collar or even a toilet seat. If this all sounds familiar, it should. The Edsel became the biggest automotive fiasco since the Chrysler Airflow, and for many of the same reasons. The brand lasted just two years. Robert McNamara, who had predicted its early demise, proved several years later that the perceived gap between Ford and Mercury simply required a new model, the Ford Fairlane.

Henry Ford II rued the day he had agreed to the project and lamented that the car's name had besmirched his sainted father. But the company took the Edsel's failure in stride. McNamara shepherded the Ford Fairlane into production and then followed that with the Ford Falcon and Mercury Comet in response to the Lark and Rambler small-car challenges.[107] When McNamara left to work for the Kennedy administration, he was replaced with Lee Iacocca, who continued to drive Ford's ascendency.

Besides the Mustang and Pinto, Iacocca had overseen the development of the Ford Maverick and the very successful Lincoln Continental Mark III.[108] He had risen rapidly to president of the Ford division. Still, the Mustang adoration of Iacocca never set too well with Henry Ford II, an echo of past Ford executives who grabbed too much glory at the expense of his grandfather. Iacocca was passed over for the presidency of the Ford Motor Company in 1969 in favor of Bill Knudsen's son, Bunkie Knudsen. Bunkie had risen quickly as a GM executive before being hired by Ford, but he lasted all of two years before he was pushed out the door in 1970.[109] That's when Henry Ford II reluctantly turned to Iacocca. Lee delivered strong results, culminating in 1978 when he guided the company to a $1.8 billion profit. Nevertheless, later in that year, Henry Ford II summarily fired Iacocca, famously saying, "I just didn't like him."

Henry Ford II retired in 1982 but called the shots until his death in 1987. A series of CEOs (Philip Caldwell, Don Petersen, Red Poling, and Jac Nasser) were tasked with fighting back against the growing encroachment of foreign makes, to mixed results. The high point was 1986 when Ford outdid GM in profit ($3.3 billion to $2.95 billion) for the first time since 1924. Bill Ford, Edsel's grandson, took over the reins in 1999, at a time when Ford's share had deteriorated from a high point of nearly 26 percent in 1993 to 22 percent. He then presided over an even greater decline, losing nearly $14 billion and riding a market-share tumble to 17 percent before he hired Alan Mulally to run the company. Ford lost $12.7 billion in 2006 alone, prompting Ford to secure a $23.5 billion loan package by mortgaging the Ford headquarters, factories, and even the famous blue oval logo.

Alan Mulally started at Ford in September 2006. He had been a very successful executive at Boeing, rising to lead its commercial airplane division and manage the development of Boeing's best-selling aircraft, the 777. In 2005 he was passed over for the CEO position at Boeing. This made him all the more receptive when Bill Ford came calling. Knowing that Ford was on track for one of its worse years ever and that Bill Ford had already taken desperate measures to build cash, Mulally clearly understood the scope of the challenge he faced. He may have even expected one immediate challenge, a charge that he was not a car guy. His response, "An automobile has about 10,000 moving parts, right? An airplane has four million, and it has to stay up in the air." That was one challenge quickly handled.

After enduring losses in 2007 and 2008, Mulally engineered a complete turnaround at Ford. He cut the Ford brands down to two—Ford and Lincoln—while dropping Mercury and selling Volvo, Jaguar, Land Rover, Aston Martin, and the Ford investment in Mazda. He reduced the number of Ford automotive products worldwide from ninety-seven to twenty. He promoted the "One Ford" mantra, with the focus on developing world cars that shared technology. He attacked the Ford bureaucracy, substituting a lean management system that improved decisions and reduced the time to bring new cars to market. And, he clearly communicated Ford's dire situation to the United Auto Workers union (UAW), resulting in a reduction of average labor costs from $76 per hour to $55 per hour. These actions put Ford on a much firmer footing heading into the 2008 Great Recession. As the healthiest US car company, Ford did not seek nor require a bailout in 2009. During Mulally's very successful eight-year run at Ford, the company racked up a total of $38 billion in net profits. Bill Ford would have certainly liked Mulally to have stayed on past 2014.

Ford announced in 2018 that it would stop making cars and instead focus on pickups, SUVs, and cross-overs. What would Henry Ford have to say about Ford not making cars? He probably would have agreed, as the change was nothing more serious than touring cars going out of fashion in the 1920s and being replaced by closed-body cars. Now, it was the traditional sedans that were being phased out. Ford did announce one exception to this new strategy—the Mustang. With well over ten million sold, the Mustang was getting close to Model T and Beetle numbers territory. And wonder of wonders, the new Mustang was poised to go fully electric. Ford finally used the Model "E" as in Mustang Mach-E, which is positioned in 2020 to directly take on Tesla.

▷ ▷ ▷

When we last visited Chrysler, its market share was steady at 12–14 percent. Virgil "Excess" Exner was unbound with fins and the company had taken over styling leadership. And, John was still buying Chrysler New Yorkers. But the rollout of the 1957 models was botched, and all the Chrysler brands suffered, with production of the DeSoto ceasing in 1961.

The following year, the mechanics of the Big Three "collusion" was comically illustrated, but to disastrous effect for Chrysler. At a party in the car executive enclave of Grosse Pointe, new Chrysler president William Newberg overheard Chevrolet general manager Ed Cole say that they were working on a new small Chevy for 1962. He was talking about the Chevy II compact, designed to replace the slow-selling Corvair. However, Newberg wrongly interpreted that Chevrolet was downsizing its full-size cars. He instituted a crash program to downsize the full-size Dodge and Plymouth models that had won Virgil Exner so much acclaim. Exner had already completed the full-size designs for 1962 and was ordered, despite his protestations, to chop them down into smaller cars. Newberry also greenlighted a bizarre grille for the cars that was reminiscent of the strange "horse collar" grille on the Edsel. Exner called the cars "plucked chickens" and categorically disowned them.

Sales for the new Dodge and Plymouth models tanked while the new Chevy II, now unveiled as an additional compact and not a replacement for full-size Chevrolets, did well. By this time, Newberry had already been fired, not for his monumental blunder but for profiting from supplier contracts. However, the remaining Chrysler executives were still looking for someone to take the fall for the disaster and it turned out to be Virgil

Exner, who was fired. Adding insult to injury, Exner's original full-size designs, essentially restored for 1963, did very well. The episode shined a light on just how insular and inbred the Big Three had become.

If mistakenly going too small in 1962 was a disaster, then not going small in the 1970s was even more of a calamity. Chrysler struggled to survive in the era of the oil embargoes and onslaught of smaller foreign cars. By 1978, chairman John Riccardo was staring at huge losses and a sagging product line, not to mention 100,000 unsold cars sitting in a lot (shades of the thousands of Maxwells that Walter Chrysler had to unload in 1921). Riccardo decided to bring in someone with a pretty good track record of automotive success: Lee Iacocca.

As Iacocca settled into his new job at Chrysler, the company's market share plunged to a nadir of only 9 percent. On the brink of bankruptcy, Iacocca worked to secure a $1.2 billion loan from the US government. A turnaround was slow in coming. Iacocca was forced to sell Chrysler's very profitable and rightly famous tank division to generate more cash. The new mid-size K cars debuted and performed reasonably well. But, more importantly, the K platform provided the basis for a car that Iacocca had envisioned while back at Ford—the minivan. It was an immediate winner. Chrysler had a significant head start on this brand new car category and was never seriously challenged by GM or Ford.

Chrysler's sales doubled between 1980 and 1985. The government loan was paid back. And, signaling a shift to offense, Iacocca purchased American Motors in 1987, a move that was clearly aimed at acquiring Jeep. He also engaged his old racing buddy, Carroll Shelby, to design a high-performance car for Chrysler. It was the Dodge Viper, not so subtly keeping the snake motif that had been used on the Cobra when Iacocca was at Ford. Iacocca retired in 1992, having taking Chrysler back from the brink to a nearly 14 percent market share.

By 1998 it was clear that smaller car companies needed to get bigger in order to survive and thrive on the world stage. Chrysler was acquired by Daimler-Benz in what was billed as a merger of equals. It was not and did not last. The Germans did not want to see vaunted German technology on Chrysler cars, and Chrysler felt Daimler-Benz lacked basic cost controls. The year 2001 marked the final year for Plymouth, which had grown to become a redundant clone of Dodge. By 2007 Chrysler's market share was trending down once again, and Daimler decided to sell its interest to Cerberus, a private equity firm.

The Great Recession hit the following year, shrinking Chrysler's market share to 9 percent and putting the company on the brink of bankruptcy. As part of the US government's actions to save the auto industry, Chrysler received $12 billion in loans in exchange for an arrangement that steered ownership to Fiat and the United Auto Workers union.

Fiat Chrysler Automobiles (FCA), under the dynamic leadership of Sergio Marchionne, charted a path to becoming a major world automobile power. The new loans were paid back, and by 2014 the combined company had rebounded with its four US divisions (Dodge, Chrysler, Jeep, and Ram) and the three European divisions (Fiat, Alfa Romeo, and Maserati). Dodge basically produced just performance cars, and Chrysler built minivans and the 300 sedan. It was Jeep and Ram trucks that were the real stars. Jeep especially continued to shine. Its worldwide annual production was approaching two million, and it was now ranked as the number-fifteen car brand in the world.

The US market share for Fiat Chrysler climbed back to 13 percent, compared with 18 percent for General Motors and 15 percent for both Ford and Toyota. Though Marchionne died in 2018, his vision of a global company continued. FCA merged with PSA (Peugeot, Citroen, Opel, and Vauxhall) in 2020, creating the fourth-largest automobile company in the world. It appears that the name "Chrysler" will reach the end of the road as the new company plans to go forward in 2021 as "Stellantis".

➤ ➤ ➤

The idea that General Motors would go bankrupt seems more than a bit far-fetched. At the height of its power, in 1954, it was responsible for 54 percent of the automobiles sold in the United States and represented an astounding 10 percent of the total US economy. Yet, GM did in fact file for bankruptcy in 2009.

Though the Great Recession of 2008 served the final blow, the genesis of GM's destruction lay in its very bigness and its resultant inability to respond to the challenges of competition. Initially, smaller cars like the Beetle, Lark, and Nash were like fleas on the back of an elephant. But, then the Japanese arrived followed by the energy crises of the 1970s. The old Big Three game was completely changed.

The year 1981 marked the first annual loss at GM in over sixty years. It was also the year that Roger Smith took over the helm.[110] Coming from an accounting background, he understood what needed to be done. The company had a bloated bureaucracy, chronically underutilized plants, high union costs, enormous pension obligations, an uncompetitive product line, and mostly older customers. Unfortunately, he failed across the board in addressing these deep-seated problems. Paradoxically, one of his first actions actually increased the GM bureaucracy. He combined the brand divisions into two super groups—Chevrolet, Pontiac, and Canada in one, and Buick, Olds, and Cadillac in the other. This diluted the ownership and authority of division general managers, violating a core principle of Alfred Sloan's organizational approach. At the same time, Smith seemed to conclude that the existing divisions were not capable of developing a successful small car, so he created a completely new and separate division: Saturn. This was perhaps a good idea at the start, but he proceeded to dump $5 billion on the project that took seven years before the first Saturn came off the line.

During that period, the US government had imposed voluntary limits on the imports of Japanese cars. However, for some reason, Smith supported lifting them, in spite of Ford and Chrysler opposition. The elimination of the limits occurred in 1985, with predictable results. Though challenged by the Japanese incursion, he also believed their methods could be applied to GM. In 1984 he entered into a joint venture with Toyota to reactivate a dormant GM plant in Fremont, California, and jointly produce cars. GM could learn Toyota's lean manufacturing methods, and Toyota would get experience with its first plant in the United States. This was the New United Motor Manufacturing, Inc., or NUMMI, venture.[111] Also in the vein of increasing efficiency and reducing costs, Smith spent big in acquiring two large high-tech companies—EDS and Hughes, both of which increased bureaucracy rather than efficiency.

One element of the Japanese approach to car manufacturing at the time was the increasing use of automation. Smith decided that this would address a multitude of problems at GM. He spent roughly $80 billion in the 1980s on robots for plant automation. Unfortunately, the technology was not yet mature enough for widespread use. In addition, there was severe pushback, even sabotage, from union workers in the plants where automation was deployed. Much like Studebaker's failure to bring union costs in line with the company's dire prospects, GM continued to accede to UAW demands in order to avoid costly strikes. One contract the company signed included the notorious jobs bank provision that kept paying furloughed employees. The issue of labor cost became critical in 1982 when Honda's Marysville, Ohio, plant went into production, rolling out Accords built by nonunion employees that were steeped in efficient Japanese manufacturing processes. It wasn't very long before GM's cost per car was $1,500–$2,000 higher than Japanese brands.

While the Saturn investment was plodding along, there was also pressure to develop a more competitive midrange car. GM had endured a scandal in 1977 where Chevrolet engines were installed in Oldsmobiles without telling customers. The customers naturally expected a "Rocket V-8" Olds engine. Despite this experience, Smith and GM decided to go full bore on the cross-sharing of components across divisions. Smith instituted a $7 billion program to provide all GM divisions with a common midrange vehicle. The program, called GM-10, took seven years to fruition and resulted in the massive loss of brand identity, as a midrange Cadillac looked just like a midrange Buick or Oldsmobile. The GM-10 development project also added about $2,000 to the cost of each car.

At the time, Ford was making significant investments overseas, and GM jumped into the game with investments in Subaru, Saab, Suzuki, Isuzu, and Fiat. None were especially fruitful, but the Fiat venture was probably the most ill-advised. GM paid $2 billion to secure a share of Fiat and then had to pay an additional $2 billion later to get out of the investment.

During Roger Smith's time leading GM, its share plummeted from 46 percent to 35 percent. Most of the problems he identified going in remained when he stepped down in 1990. A series of follow-up CEOs failed to stem the decline. Revenues over the period of 1995 to 2007 were in excess of $4 trillion, yet the total profit was only $13.5 billion, a rate far less than 1 percent. This was not the same General Motors that earned fat 20 percent margins in the 1950s.

In 2004 the once-proud and pioneering Oldsmobile division was phased out. Though it sold over a million cars as recently as 1986, it had become a weak clone of Chevrolet. The division tried to remake itself with the "not your father's Oldsmobile" campaign. This served only to alienate their older customers while doing nothing to bring in younger ones. The elimination of Oldsmobile cost GM $1 billion as it was required by franchise laws to compensate the cast-off dealers.

By 2008 GM's market share sagged to just 22 percent, though it was still producing 2.9 million cars a year. GM finally succumbed during the Great Recession of 2008, and the corporation itself was partially to blame. Its financing arm, GMAC, was heavily invested in subprime mortgages, and as one of the top ten "banks" in the United States, required its own bailout.

This was hard to believe until it actually happened. General Motors entered bankruptcy on June 1, 2009. In order to qualify for federal bailout funds, it had to agree to drop or sell most of its brands, including Hummer, Saab, Opel, Lotus, Daewoo, and Saturn. Opel and Saturn would have been quite useful in addressing the small-car market going forward. There was one other brand to be dropped, and this one was especially painful: Pontiac. Established in 1926 as one of Alfred Sloan's gap "companion" cars, it ended up replacing Oakland. Pontiac enjoyed a renaissance in the 1960s with John DeLorean as chief engineer and then general manager, rolling out such classics as the GTO, Firebird, Trans-Am, and Grand Prix.[112] It had lost its way in the 2000s, satisfied to rebadge Chevrolet models and sell them for less than Chevrolet (a violation of Sloan's rules).

The bankruptcy and subsequent reemergence of a new GM left just four divisions—Chevrolet, Buick, Cadillac, and GMC. The US government became the reluctant owner of 70 percent of the new company's shares. So it was that the unthinkable actually happened. Unlike Alfred Sloan's handling of GM during the Great Depression, GM had failed to address its basic problems while incurring an unbelievable litany of missteps.

➤ ➤ ➤

As we have seen, despite a strong post-war start, Studebaker continued to make and remake mistakes that, as a small independent, it could not afford to make. The merger with Packard did not turn out well. Both companies were struggling. Packard simply did not have the resources to compete with the Big Three upscale brands who could afford to retool each model year. The 1957 and 1958 Packards were nothing more than rebadged Studebakers. The once-proud brand, founded in 1899 by James Packard, who felt he could build a better car than the Winton, was retired in 1959.

In 1957 Studebaker accepted an offer from Mercedes-Benz to become its US distributor. This would have been a valuable lifeline for Studebaker's dealers. The final crucial mistake came with Studebaker's handling of the success of the Lark. Along with AMC's Nash, it had created a whole new car category. There would only be a limited window of opportunity to capitalize before the Big Three would surely respond. Lark sales of 160,000 cars in 1959 yielded a $28.5 million profit. Amazingly, Studebaker decided to use the money to diversify, buying up totally unrelated companies (an airline, a forklift manufacturer). The profit could have been invested in its core business. Perhaps, the current leaders felt it was a lost cause.

A new CEO, Sherwood Egbert, decided to make one last-gasp effort. He brought back Raymond Loewy in 1961 to design a sporty car that would appeal to younger buyers. Ray was given just forty days to complete the design. It was a dramatic design, with a fiberglass body like the Corvette, though it had mostly Lark components underneath. It was called the Avanti ("forward" in Italian). The Avanti was a four-seat sports car that beat the Ford Mustang to market by over a year.

The Avanti was produced in seven months and an early production model debuted at the 1962 New York auto show in April, where it received very positive press. There were problems, though. One major issue was its price. At over $4,000, it was more expensive than a Corvette Sting Ray and would be $2,000 more than the price set for the Ford Mustang a year down the road. Besides the price, production issues that were primarily related to the fiberglass body, delayed getting the car to market until late in the year. Studebaker sold fewer than four thousand Avantis in 1963 and just 809 in 1964 before it pulled the plug. However, the car did have a pretty good second life. A local Studebaker dealer bought the rights and came out with the Avanti II. It was a nice car. Even Raymond Loewy bought one.

➤ ➤ ➤

Though George Mason envisioned combining all of the remaining independents in 1954, he initially settled for combining Nash and Hudson and launching American Motors. He intended to add Studebaker and Packard, but he died before he could get it done. His successor, George Romney, had no interest in pursuing this plan. In 1957 Romney phased out Nash and Hudson and replaced them with the Rambler brand. It became a runaway success, rising to number three in US sales by the early 1960s. But the Rambler's success was short-lived. Roy Chapin Jr. took over AMC in 1967, dropped the Rambler brand, and focused on becoming a nimble number-four automaker that could move more quickly than its far larger competitors. In 1970 Chapin bought the Jeep brand from Kaiser. Though Jeep had no competitors in its unique segment, the Big Three were not interested.

AMC focused mainly on small cars (Gremlin, Hornet, Javelin, Pacer), with an occasional midsize offering (Matador) and a quasi-full-size car

(Ambassador). The company was adept at creating new models with the minimum of cost. After the Pacer debacle, AMC needed cash and secured an investment from Renault. Because a US defense contractor cannot be owned by a foreign company, AMC was forced to sell its very profitable AM General military division. Chrysler purchased AMC in 1987. The remaining AMC and Renault models were phased out, leaving only Jeep. The AMC factory in Kenosha, Wisconsin, stopped producing cars after ninety years.

▷ ▷ ▷

When we last checked in, Volkswagen was riding high. The company had sold 1.3 million Beetles in 1971 (525,000 in the United States) and then passed the Model T sales record of fifteen million cars the following year.[113] However, with rising incomes, there was a transition from small to midsize cars. VW dealers weren't asking for much—bigger engines, automatic transmissions, and more creature comforts. Volkswagen certainly did not repeat Henry Ford's mistake in failing to adapt a "universal" car to changing tastes. Like the Model T, a Beetle owner was unlikely to buy another Beetle. But initially, Volkswagen was slow to offer a choice. Volkswagen owners that wanted to trade up, traded out. In the 1970s, Volkswagen rolled out new models—the Golf, Passat, and Polo. It sold over a million Golfs (called Rabbit in the United States) in two years.

Meanwhile, US sales of the Beetle stopped in 1979, the end of a great run. Or, so it seemed. A new Beetle prototype had been shown at the Detroit auto show in 1994, and in 1998 the new Beetle debuted. It was the opposite of the original Beetle: water-cooled, front engine, front-wheel drive, heated seats, 122 horsepower, stereo sound, and airbags. Though the only real carryover was its shape, the new Beetle was an immediate hit. During its run from 1998 to 2019, Volkswagen sold 1.7 million Beetles, bumping up the overall Beetle record to 21.5 million.

During this time, Volkswagen had become a dominant car company. The sales of the Beetle were mostly a rounding error. What was not a rounding error were the liberties that the company's engineers took on diesel engine testing. Cheating on emission testing via software manipulation has already cost Volkswagen an estimated $33.6 billion, a number that is still rising. This is over and above the damage to the company's reputation. One interesting element in the scandal's settlement was a requirement to spend at least $2 billion to build a network of two thousand electric charging stations in the United States. Despite this major setback, the Volkswagen group has risen to become the largest auto company in the world, selling in excess of ten million cars annually, with brands that include Volkswagen, Audi, and Porsche.

One last comment. As we enter 2020, there is talk of yet another Beetle, this time an electric one.

▷ ▷ ▷

At this point, we take one last look at the man who started on this journey: Henry Ford. A good place to start would be his own assessment, one reported in a conversation he had with a young lad named John Dahlinger.[114] Ford was expounding on the value of one-room schoolhouses and McGuffey readers when the boy interrupted, "But sir, these are different times, this is the modern age." To which Henry responded, "Young man, I invented the modern age."

Many in isolated farming communities in the early twentieth century would agree with Henry Ford's assessment. Some will say that he "rode the wave" of the automobile rather than created it. Or, that his genius hastened the change in an especially dramatic way. Many views of the man are colored by the actions and prejudices of his later years. Had Henry Ford retired near the age of sixty and passed the baton to Edsel, much of the controversy surrounding his legacy might have been averted. He was successful because of the qualities he brought to the age of automobiles. He was an experienced machinist and inventor. He had an eye for outstanding people and the unwavering vision to lead them. Though he floundered early on with too much tinkering, he righted the ship and refocused on the simple idea of building the universal car at the lowest price possible. Along the way, he made good on his philosophy of making "the best quality of goods possible at the lowest cost possible, paying the highest wages possible." He delivered on low cost as he revolutionized mass production. He delivered on wages with the $5 day. Despite saying in so many words that "history is bunk" at his 1919 libel suit against the *Chicago Tribune*, Ford went on to enshrine history. He spent part of his vast resources building and stocking Greenfield Village and the Henry Ford Museum with artifacts of the nineteenth and early twentieth centuries. Those artifacts included that first Westinghouse steam engine he worked on in 1882. He had it tracked down by serial number and returned to Dearborn. In addition, he transported Thomas Edison's entire Menlo Park workshop to Greenfield Village.

Yet, Henry Ford did not retire at sixty. There seemed to be a progressive erosion of the very qualities that had made him so successful. His early tendency to perfectionism underwent a startling reversal once the Model T was completed. As if by light switch, he turned off engineering and innovation and focused on expanding production. As the company grew almost without bounds, he failed to adapt to a vastly different enterprise. Ford Motor was Henry Ford and Henry Ford alone. His only son Edsel was only nominally in charge. In sharp contrast to General Motors and Alfred Sloan, Ford did not see any value in controls, administration, and even engineering. He paid dearly by losing money throughout the Depression.

A dark side surfaced. He may have felt that with his great success, everyone was out to steal his money and especially his glory. He had 161 patents in his name, clearly well in excess of the number that he was directly responsible for. The talented people who were instrumental in his success were soon shown the door.[115] He did not show his son Edsel the door, but his intimidating treatment of his only son was far worse and likely contributed to Edsel's early death. He hired Harry Bennett and a whole department of thugs to control his workers and stamp out any budding union movement.

Henry Ford had developed various life views based on his upbringing. Those morphed into dangerous prejudices, and once he was world famous, they came out into the open. He was distrustful of bankers, Wall Street, the DuPonts, and communists. He became virulently anti-Semitic and used the Ford house publication to excoriate Jews. He admired Adolf Hitler, even accepting the Nazi Party's highest award for foreigners in 1938. With Edsel's premature death in 1943, he briefly resumed control of the company until he was forced out and his grandson took over in 1945. Henry Ford died two years later.

We are now on the cusp of another journey, one that may prove to be no less traumatic than the one we just profiled. What will prove to the equivalent of that Winton automobile driving into 1899 Williamsfield? Will it be a self-driving car? Will electrics reign supreme, vanquishing the mighty Otto engine? With two billion automobiles and counting, how many more can the Earth withstand? Can we finally take up the challenge of global warming? What will the fourth generation, the millennials, do? Will either of our boys ever buy an automobile? Will there be yet another Volkswagen Beetle?

Stay tuned.

Acknowledgments

Central Illinois Towns

A good part of this book takes place 175 miles southwest of Chicago in prime "Corn Belt" farm country, in a frontier area called French Grove. Though the settlement of French Grove did not survive, the farms and families did, and they were supported by the neighboring towns of Williamsfield, Brimfield, and Elmwood. I appreciate the support provided by the libraries in all three of these communities. Williamsfield has a nice, modern library adjacent to a new high school. In addition, the town has a vibrant Facebook community dedicated to the history of the town. A special shout-out to Sheila Johnson and Erma Nodeen for their local knowledge.

The Morrison and Mary Wiley Library in Elmwood is another great resource for local history. The same goes for the Brimfield Public Library, but as I mention in the Bibliography, it also has a great resource in its online, digital database of the entire publishing run of the *Brimfield News.*

French Grove sits midway between Peoria and Galesburg, and both of those towns helped in this project. I visited Bradley University in Peoria and was assisted by special collections archivist Elizabeth Bloodworth. Traveling in the opposite direction, I am indebted to Knox College and the Galesburg Public Library. I'd like to thank Sharon Clayton at Knox for access to the college's archival materials. She also directed me to the Galesburg library, where I found nearly all of the back issues of the *Williamsfield Times* on microfilm. Somewhat farther afield, I found additional historical materials at the University of Illinois in Champaign-Urbana, guided ably by their archivist, Krista Gray.

Automobile Museums

What is a book on automotive history without visits to automobile museums? That's right, not much. Since Henry Ford plays a central role in the story, my visit to the Ford Piquette Avenue Plant museum in Detroit, Michigan, was especially valuable. A private grassroots group has done an outstanding job in saving and restoring Ford's second manufacturing facility. Special thanks to docent Tom

Genova for his excellent tour and outstanding on-going guidance. That included review of the relevant sections of this book by Tom and his fellow experts Don LaCombe and Jack Seavitt. Their input is much appreciated.

Of course, at Piquette you are only twelve miles from the Ford "mother ship," the Henry Ford Museum. It provides a beautiful museum experience, with a vast collection of automobiles (in all makes) as well as the various farm equipment that was Henry's second passion. The museum staff is very supportive, including the offer to dissemble a Model T and then put it back together.

A bit farther west, I visited the Studebaker Museum in South Bend, Indiana. Though the company shut down in town in 1963, it lives on in a state-of-the-art museum facility. And, I'll add a special thanks to Andrew Beckman for reviewing the Studebaker sections of the book.

Much farther west in Sylmar, California, I spent a good deal of time at the Nethercutt Museum. It contains an excellent collection of early automobiles plus a backroom automotive research library staffed by experts. Several of its experts are Model T owners who liberally added to my knowledge of the "universal" car. Also located in California is the Horseless Carriage Foundation, which maintains an excellent digital repository of the early automotive trade periodicals.

Somewhat late in my research, I discovered another automotive museum right under my nose, just ten miles north in Longmont, Colorado. The Dougherty Museum is an outstanding local resource that focuses on early automobiles and farm equipment. A decidedly low-profile affair, the museum is only open for a brief time in the summer, but if your timing is right, the payback is great. As my story veers from strictly early automobiles to some of the early automotive machines that transformed the farm, getting face-to-face with all manner of farm equipment was very valuable. And, that was not the end of it. The museum conducts a large open house in the middle of the summer, where many of the machines are wheeled into the broad fields surrounding the main building and cranked to life. It's one thing to write about thirty-ton steam traction engines driving enormous "Rube Goldberg" threshing machines. It's quite another to experience them in action. The deafening noise, clatter, and heat generated by an Avery steam tractor propelling a Yellow Fellow thresher is quite something to behold.

Notes

1. Having to hold the clutch pedal down to stay in low gear was a common Model T complaint, not that it got any traction with Henry Ford. The transmission functioned just the same for the entire Model T run.

2. One source shows that Heinrich's father was Johann Jacob Shaffer (born 1712) in Biedershausen, Sudwestpfalz, Rheinland, and his mother was Irma Bettenberg. Other records show Johann's wife as Anna Elisabetha Stegner (1712–1767). One record indicates that Johann died on January 7, 1741, which is before Heinrich was born.

3. Heinrich served an indentureship as a tanner, with conflicting records indicating it was either in Baltimore or New Jersey.

4. His second wife, Mary, remained at the farm, dying in 1854 at age eighty-six. Both are buried in the Wyatt cemetery.

5. Frink and Walker (John Frink and Martin Walker) was the dominant stagecoach line in the Midwest during that period between the start of the western migration and the coming of the railroads, starting in the 1840s. The line's roughly two thousand miles of routes covered Illinois, Michigan, Wisconsin, Iowa, Indiana, and Missouri. The roads were desperately bad, and stagecoaches' ascendancy ended quickly with the coming of the railroads.

6. While the damage was serious, it did not compare to the fire that swept through town in September of that year. It started in the livery barn, which happened to be where the village stored its brand new fire engine. Twenty buildings and two complete town blocks were destroyed, resulting in losses in excess of $10,000. Most of the town structures were rebuilt, albeit in wood. In September 1920, yet another fire engulfed Williamsfield, wiping out most of the business section of town. Of course, Williamsfield's woes were not unique. Brimfield experienced a business district fire in 1886 that resulted in the loss of $50,000.

7. A. J. "Archibald" Morton (February 1, 1855, to July 1, 1898) was born in Kilbirnie, Ayrshire, Scotland. He practiced in Williamsfield 1889–1894, then in Elmwood until 1898, when he died at age forty-three. His son, David Morton, became a doctor and would also figure in the Shaffer sagas.

8. The "Gold Cure" was developed by Dr. Leslie Keeley, a doctor working in Dwight, Illinois, about a hundred miles east. It was the most famous of the dependency cures that surfaced in the late nineteenth century. The "cure" involved injecting a solution called "bichloride of gold" into the patient four times daily. This tended to make the individual placid and content. It was certainly no cure but did keep the patient away from his or her dependency temporarily. Dr. Keeley

claimed over 400,000 addicts took his "cure," with a 95 percent cure rate. A 1907 lawsuit revealed that the "gold" elixir was composed of strychnine, atropine, boric acid, and water. Dr. Morton may have initially believed in the treatment's efficacy but dropped the program after several years.

9. The impressive National Institute building was, like most of the town's buildings, completely constructed of wood. Fires were a common occurrence, and a fire in 1903 destroyed the institute and, with it, a dramatic part of the town history.

10. Hiram Percy Maxim, an early automotive pioneer who worked for Colonel Albert Pope, observed years later on the influence of the bicycle, "It has been the habit to give the gasoline engine all the credit for bringing the automobile—in my opinion this is the wrong explanation. We could have built steam vehicles in 1880, or indeed in 1870, but we did not. We waited until 1895. The reason why we did not build road vehicles before this, in my opinion, was because the bicycle had not yet come in numbers and had not directed men's minds to the possibilities of independent long-distance travel over the ordinary highway. We thought the railroad was good enough. The bicycle created a new demand which it was beyond the ability of the railroad to supply. Then it came about that the bicycles could not satisfy the demand which had been created."

11. Marcus had many engineering pursuits and was not interested in fame or fortune nor in producing horseless carriages. However, Marcus was Jewish, and most of his records and reputation were destroyed by the Nazis in order to decree that Daimler and Benz were the true inventors of the automobile. Interestingly, a *London Times* reporter (John Nixon) helped this effort by writing *The Invention of the Automobile*, with the main sources being a race driver for Daimler-Benz and the Daimler-Benz company itself. There was not a single mention of Marcus in the book.

12. The de Rochas situation, where someone patents a concept but does not actually build it, would be repeated to much more damaging effect on the American automobile industry by one George Selden.

13. Also on the list of licensees of De Dion–Bouton were American start-ups Packard, Peerless, and Pierce-Arrow, what would become the three P's of US luxury automobiles.

14. One of those thirty-four departments was men's shoes. OT hired Jack Reagan in 1915 to run the department. Jack and his wife had a son named Ronald, who Jack christened "Dutch" due to his schoolboy haircut. Ronald Reagan attended grade school at Silas Willard School in Galesburg. In 1918, Jack was fired for drinking and the family moved to Monmouth. The "Big Store" lasted until 1978 when it closed. The building was lost to a fire in 2006 and is now an empty lot downtown. Ronald went on to bigger things and on the way married Nancy Davis. Her stepfather was Dr. Loyal Davis, a prominent neurosurgeon who grew up in Galesburg and went to Knox College.

15. Elwood Haynes spent years arguing that he was responsible for the first automobile in the United States, though he drove his first automobile a full year after Frank Duryea hit the streets in Springfield. In 1920 he even went so far as to secure

an official endorsement that he had invented the first US car from the National Vigilance Committee of the Associated Advertising Clubs of the World. This was a short-lived group that was formed to fight fraudulent advertising claims. Haynes apparently did enough of this type of campaigning to secure some favorable press mention in his obituary. The *Indianapolis Star* called him "the father of the automobile." The *Minneapolis Star* was slightly less effusive, calling Haynes "the inventor of the first American automobile." Haynes seemed to completely forget the contribution of Edgar and Elmer Apperson. The brothers were recognized by the Press Club of Indiana for "building the first practically commercially successful American automobile." This wording was carefully crafted not to clash with the Duryeas yet took some shine from Elwood Haynes. Haynes traveled to the New York City auto show in 1925 and was stricken with influenza, from which he did not recover.

16. Alfred P. Sloan Sr. was a machinist by trade. The son attended Brooklyn Polytechnic Institute, and then graduated from MIT in three years.

17. In 1894 Harry Knox was a recent engineering graduate who happened to be the next-door neighbor of Frank Duryea in Springfield. Duryea encouraged him to build his own automobile, and by the time of the first New York City auto show, he had done just that. The Knox debuted in 1900 as a three-wheel runabout. The Knox was one of the few air-cooled automobiles at the time, prompting the tagline, "the car that never drinks." He left in 1904 amid disagreements with his financial backers, who quite predictably wanted to build far more expensive cars.

18. Ransom Olds was not there. He was busy working on his first REO car, which he would debut at the 1905 show.

19. The Mayburys were from the same town in Ireland as the Fords and now were neighbors in Dearborn. Thomas's son William, a future mayor of Detroit, would play a prominent role in Henry's life.

20. Henry's schoolhouse friend was Edsel Ruddiman, the source of the name of Henry's only son and, much later, the much maligned automobile.

21. The early car pioneers were quite incestuous. Charles King had been an engineer for the Michigan Car Company before working for Ransom Olds. He worked alongside Jonathan Maxwell, and in 1902, the two Olds alumnae went on to develop their own automobile, the Northern. As was the case repeated many times over, Maxwell decided to leave Northern in 1904 to build his own eponymous car—the Maxwell. He secured funding from the Briscoe brothers, who had just bailed out of their investment with David Dunbar Buick. King himself would leave Northern when the operation was acquired by EMF. EMF would develop the Flanders car, named after Walter Flanders, who had a significant role in Henry Ford's march to the Model T. One definitely needs a score card to keep track of all of these comings and goings.

22. In 1904 Henry Ford located the car and bought it back for $65. It now resides in the Henry Ford Museum.

23. Leland was already a force in Detroit. He learned the machining craft back east with Colt and Brown and Sharpe. He traveled to Detroit in 1890 and, partnering

with Robert Faulconer, set up a machine shop to develop bicycle components. He graduated to automotive parts and became the engine and transmission supplier to Ransom Olds. At the time, he had developed a more powerful engine, which Olds had rejected. Among the graduates from his shop was Horace Dodge.

24. Ironically, Oldfield soon started racing for Alexander Winton, who supplied the cars. After a fallout with Winton in 1904, he signed with Peerless and raced the 100 horsepower Green Dragon. By 1910, he had bought a Benz and was racing the Blitzen Benz. He set the land speed record of 131 mph at Ormond Beach in the Benz car. Cooper was already gone, having been killed in an automobile accident in New York City in 1906, at age thirty. Years later, Oldfield and Henry Ford met at the Indianapolis Speedway. Ford reportedly told Oldfield, "We started together at the bottom and we owe each other a lot. It could be said that you made me and I made you." As for Alexander Winton, he became interested in diesel engines and less focused on his automobile company. After World War I, the company introduced six-cylinder cars at the low end but with the traditional Winton high prices. Sales nosedived. Ever unpredictable, Winton abruptly announced the liquidation of his company in 1924. He died in 1932, after his $5 million fortune had dwindled to $50,000.

25. Malcolmson set up FMC with a thousand shares. Besides his own investment, he secured contributions from lawyers John Anderson and Horace Rackham, Albert Strelow, Vernon Fry, Charles Bennett of Daisy Rifles, and Charles Woodall. He also added John Gray, a successful banker who happened to be his uncle. In addition to a salary, Couzens was able to make a small $2,500 investment in the company, which would eventually turn into $30 million.

26. Horace Dodge was the engineering side of the Dodge brothers duo. He worked at Flowers Brothers and Leland and Faulconer before setting up his own machine shop with brother John to make bicycle parts. They soon switched to automotive parts and became the principal supplier to Ransom Olds before the switch to Ford.

27. Other tongue-in-cheek admonitions included, "The speed limit on country roads this year will be secret, and the penalty for violation will be $10." Or, "Automobiles running on country roads at night must send up a red rocket every mile and then wait ten minutes for the road the clear. They may then proceed carefully, blowing their horn and shooting Roman candles." These were profiled in the *Brimfield News* (November 16, 1911), as first reported in the *Appleton City Journal*.

28. Henry Leland's first Cadillac was just a Cadillac. It was subsequently designated the Model A. He followed it in 1904 with the Model B, which changed the buggy design to a more conventional look with the engine compartment up front. The Model C came out mid-1905 and was a Model B with a detachable tonneau (the tonneau was a second seat row behind the front seats).

29. The class of 1904 had just six graduates, including Ona and Ada Shaffer. Ona was the daughter of Frank Shaffer, who owned the town general store. At the commencement, Ada recited an essay on "Sunshine" and Ona recited an essay called "The Greatness of Generals."

30. Robert Cushman Woolsey (1881–1960) was principal at WHS at just twenty-three. He went on to Knox College (1909) and then obtained his law degree from Harvard. At WHS, he was assisted by Ina Bohannan in the intermediate classes and Inez Oberholtzer in the primary grades. He married Inez in 1915. Later, he was a lawyer in Galesburg.

31. At the commencement in May 1906, Will (still known as "Willie") sang the solo "Goodnight, Beloved, Goodnight," then a popular song. Gertrude Wesner, Floyd's sister, recited the essay "The Value of a Reputation." Gertrude subsequently married Isidor Daub, a World War I veteran, and they became the author's maternal grandparents. Isidor was the night stationmaster of the Williamsfield train depot. The story goes that he applied for the job a day after another man—Bill Hahn. Since Hahn thus had seniority, he got the day shift and Isidor got the night shift, where he remained his entire working life with the Santa Fe.

32. James Shaffer Jr. (1884–1972) had recently graduated from Lombard College, where he was a standout football player with a powerhouse team that beat Washington University, Knox, and Monmouth.

33. The technique was developed by German doctors in Freiburg at the turn of the century. Designed to ease the pain and trauma of childbirth, it consisted of morphine to address the pain and scopolamine (allegedly used as a truth serum at times) to keep the patient conscious and responding to the doctor's commands. Dr. Bertha Van Hoosen, a colleague of Dr. Shaffer, was an outspoken advocate. Backlash at the predominantly male medical establishment's disdain for the procedure led to women's rallies in 1914–1915. Use of the treatment gradually eroded over time, replaced by new anesthesia methods.

34. The *Brimfield News* description of Verne: "The bride only lived in Elmwood a year but during that time has endeared herself to those with whom she associates. She is a cultured lady and all her friends extend hearty congratulations. The groom is a young man of sterling qualities and the fact that he has won one of Elmwood's finest young women makes him the object of congratulations."

35. Interesting enough, Will and Verne's family trees intersect several generations prior with the Caldwells, specifically Louisa Caldwell, who was born in Ireland. She was Verne's great-grandmother. James Caldwell (1724–1804) emigrated from Ulster, Northern Ireland, in 1740 at age sixteen with brothers John and David. They left in part to avoid blackmail by Highlanders in Northern Ireland. James married Elizabeth Alexander. The oldest of their fifteen children, John Caldwell, fought in the Revolutionary War and had experiences very similar to that of James and William Shaffer in the later War of 1812. John Caldwell helped construct Fort Henry in 1774, initially as a bulwark against the local Indian tribes. Their siege of the fort in 1777 was repulsed. In 1782 the Indian forces were back along with British soldiers for a second siege, again beaten back. John Caldwell was badly wounded in the leg on the west slope of Wheeling Hill when out scouting during one of the Indian attacks. This injury caused him to limp for the rest of his life.

36. Henry Ford's complete vision statement: "I will build a car for the great multitude. It will be large enough for the family, but small enough for the individual to

run and care for. It will be constructed of the best materials, by the best men to be hired, after the simplest designs that modern engineering can devise. But it will be so low in price that no man making a good salary will be unable to own one—and enjoy with his family the blessing of hours of pleasure in God's great open spaces." This ran in the Detroit papers shortly after the New York City auto show of 1906.

37. The Ford Model K, announced in 1906, replaced the Model B at the top of the line. It featured an inline six cylinder, forty horsepower engine (the only six cylinder engine that Ford produced until 1941). The car sold well and generated profits that kept the shareholders at bay and financed continuation expansion of the fledgling company. Henry Ford was happy to shunt most of the component production to the Dodge Brothers so that he could focus on core offerings like the Model N. Despite Henry's distaste for the luxury automobile, Couzens knew it was still good for the bottom line and had Norval Hawkins force Ford dealers to take deliveries of a certain number of Model K cars in order to get supply of the vastly more popular smaller models.

38. Henry Leland had learned his craft back East working for firearms manufacturers and well understood the value of interchangeable parts, built to exact tolerances. He decided to respond to the challenge made by the Royal Automobile Club of England to demonstrate interchangeable parts in automobiles. Three Cadillac Model K automobiles were selected at random. They were disassembled and the 2,100 parts were completely mixed up. Some additional parts from dealer stock were thrown in. The cars were then reassembled and upon completion, driven for 500 miles at high speed without incident. Cadillac was awarded the 1908 Dewar Trophy. Leland was back in 1912, winning another Dewar Trophy that year for the electric starter.

39. Harry Firestone was to become a major industrialist and camping partner of Henry Ford, along with Thomas Edison (they called themselves "the vagabonds"). Even though fast friends, Ford still sought to control the rubber for his tires, establishing a huge plantation in Brazil called Fordlandia. This was one Ford initiative that did not work out.

40. As with so many of Henry Ford's highly contributing lieutenants, Hawkins's relationship with Ford inevitably soured. He left in 1919 and went to General Motors in 1921. He had a large hand in driving Chevrolet's sales past Ford in the mid-1920s.

41. The Brayton engine was an internal-combustion engine developed by George Brayton in 1872, based on a concept by the Englishman John Barber. Termed the "Brayton cycle," it was a two-cycle engine that used a pilot flame to ignite a fuel/air mixture as it entered the cylinder, producing constant pressure on the piston, unlike the Otto cycle, where the power stroke was a violent explosion. Brayton did not want to risk explosion, so he used heavy petroleum. The resulting engine was very heavy, had low compression, and was much less efficient than the Otto cycle engine. With the exception of the 1905 Selden demo vehicle, no automobiles were ever built with the Brayton engine.

42. Exhibitors in 1911: Abbott-Detroit, Anderson Electric, Badger, Brush, Buick, Cadillac, Carter, Centaur, Chalmers, Cino, Coey, Colby, Cole, Courier,

Empire, Everitt, Federal, Flanders, Ford, Halladay, Hupp, Inter-State, Jeffery, Kissel, Krit, Lexington, Locomobile, Marmon, Marquette, Mercer, Moon, Nyberg, Ohio Electric, Otto Gas Engine, Olds, Overland, Elkhard, Moline, Packard, Parry, Pope-Hartford, Petrel, Reo, Regal, Ricketts, Speedwell, Stevens-Duryea, Selden, Simplex, Standard, Studebaker, Temple, Tennant, Thomas, United, and White.

43. So, Elon Musk of Tesla was not the first to build cars in a tent, as he famously did in 2018. It seems that he took a page out of John Willys's playbook.

44. Charles Nash had started out as a $1 a day upholstery stuffer of buggies for Durant-Dort and rose to be president of Buick under Billy Durant's General Motors group. After a falling out with Durant, he bought the Jeffery Company (formerly Rambler bicycles and Rambler automobiles) and renamed it Nash Motors. Years later, in the 1950s, the Rambler was resurrected as the Nash Rambler.

45. Though certainly no rebellion, the Tesla Model S had a similar effect, at least initially. An electric car needed no radiator, and thus had no grille.

46. The wide choice of electrics in 1911 on Chicago's Automobile Row included Anderson, Baker, Babcock, Broc, Brush, Columbia, Columbus, Chicago, Detroit, Flanders, Ohio Electric, Rauch and Lang, and Standard. This line-up was constantly changing as electric companies failed and new ones replaced them. All except Detroit Electric and Rauch and Lang were gone by 1920. Detroit Electric limped along on until 1939.

47. Automobile registrations for 1915 totaled 108,000 cars representing nearly 350 different brands. Fords constituted 40 percent of the total. The runner-up brand was Buick, with just 7 percent.

48. Todd Henderson, "Everything Old Is New Again: Lessons from Dodge v. Ford Motor Company," (Coase-Sandor Working Paper Series in Law and Economics, 2007). Repeatedly queried about the purpose of a corporation, Henry responded that his company was, "organized to do as much good as we can, everywhere, for everybody concerned. And incidentally, to make money." When asked how all this good was even possible, he responded, "We don't seem to keep the profits down."

49. GM under Sloan was very profit-focused and slow to implement "nonprofit" innovations like safety glass. The ethyl lead gasoline additive generated significant profits, and GM continually downplayed its dangers until decades of damage were done. Kettering invented another compound that had a similar noxious history. Searching for a replacement for highly toxic gases like ammonia that were used as a refrigerant, he developed Freon in 1928. Again, many decades passed before the real damage became evident (the destruction of the Earth's ozone layer). Most of Kettering's inventions and innovations were not like leaded gasoline or Freon, but were entirely positive contributions. Once he retired from GM, he partnered with Albert Sloan to found the Sloan-Kettering Cancer Institute.

50. Richard Tedlow, "The Struggle for Dominance in the Automobile Market," 1988.

51. Dr. David Morton was tall, with brown hair and brown eyes. He had grown up in Williamsfield, attending school there with Will's siblings Thomas and Bertha.

His father was, of course, Dr. A. J. Morton of the Gold Cure fame. After the Wil-
liamsfield facility shut down, A. J. moved the family to Elmwood. David went to
Elmwood High School (Class of 1899) and then on to Illinois Chicago Medical
School. He started practicing in Elmwood in 1904.

52. Interestingly, Dort was a classmate of Henry Ford at the Scotch School.

53. William "Big Bill" Little had worked for Locomobile before becoming plant
manager working for David Buick and Billy Durant. He followed Durant after his
1910 ouster from GM. Durant had purchased James Whiting's Flint Wagon Works
to manufacture the new Little and Chevrolet automobiles. The Little car may have
been an inside joke as William Little was a huge man and the namesake car was
tiny and fragile. The Little lasted only until 1913, when the newly revised Chevrolets replaced both it and Louis Chevrolet's expensive car.

54. The auction at the farm was held on February 25, 1923. Auctioneers Co-
chran and McMullen presided with M. A. Bundy and J. A. Maher as clerks and
H. E. Reed as the lunch man.

55. Briscoe's US Motors included Sampson, Brush Runabout, Columbia, and
Stoddard-Dayton.

56. The discovery of King Tutankhamun's tomb in 1922 yielded 5,000 artifacts
in many new colors, increasing the palette for automobile stylists like Oliver Clark.
Even Henry Ford added a few colors in the last years of the Model T.

57. By contrast, the Durant Motors Flint (built from that early ZSB design),
generated 69 horsepower from 268 cubic inches; the Stutz, 66 horsepower from
268 cubic inches; the Packard, 54 horsepower out of 268 cubic inches; and the
Buick, 65 horsepower with 255 cubic inches. The Chrysler, with its powerful engine, was the first American car to contest at Le Mans.

58. Verne passed on some of the other color schemes. The roadster was offered
in two-tone Copra Drab and Rosa Chicle with a Flamingo Carmine stripe in the
middle. The Royal Coupe featured Algerian Blue and Bambalina hues with Fawn
Gray striping. The top-of-the-line Imperial had body tones of Baghdad Green and
Topango Green with a Gold Bronze stripe in the middle.

59. Without proper crop rotation, you lose nitrogen, decrease productivity,
and encourage pests. Corn depletes nitrogen quickly. Clover, alfalfa, soybeans, and
other legumes store (fix) nitrogen in their roots. Soybeans became the primary
choice in the Midwest. It replaced oats as tractors replaced horses, had similar soil
needs as corn, helped control the corn borer, and emerged as a cash crop.

60. Bill and Bob were part of the total horse numbers that declined from
twenty-six million in 1915 to fourteen million by 1940.

61. To demonstrate the superiority of rubber tires, racer Barney Oldfield was
once again enlisted. He would race tractors with pneumatic tires against the old
steel-wheel models. This had to be a real spectacle.

62. Another automobile pioneer would meet the same fate. In 1925, a year after
his automobile company went bankrupt, Elwood Haynes traveled to New York
City for the auto show and to receive an award as a pioneer of the automobile
industry. Other pioneers receiving the recognition were Jonathan Maxwell, Edgar

Apperson, Charles King, Alexander Winton, Ransom Olds, and Charles Duryea (but not Frank). Haynes contracted influenza and died on his way back to Kokomo, Indiana.

63. Walter Chrysler personally financed the Chrysler Building in New York City. It was an Art Deco structure with distinctive diamond crowns at the top and decorated with gargoyles in the shape of Plymouth hood ornaments and Chrysler radiator caps. Walter had an expansive office on the top floor, adorned in part by the wooden tool kit that he used years previously in repairing steam locomotives. The structure held the title of world's tallest building for eleven months, at which time the Empire State Building took over the title. The building was the Chrysler headquarters until the 1950s.

64. Bel Geddes was applying his futuristic streamline designs to everything at the time. This prompted a cartoon in the *New Yorker* where a group of businessmen discussed designs and agreed that their "new biscuit must be styled by Norman Bel Geddes."

65. At the time, the fate of the beautiful Cord automobiles was still up in the air. Yet, there were manufacturing problems in getting Cords built, and the price was high for Depression times, even for a luxury car. The company was gone by 1937.

66. For some reason, Studebaker felt the need to respond and pushed its own car off a 100-foot cliff.

67. Verne and Detta Lou took the Santa Fe train from Galesburg to Chicago for the fair and would have been able to visit the large Chrysler expo building and see the Oldfield racing team in action as well as the new Airflow cars.

68. The $3 billion was just a start. Knudsen and his board would award over $225 billion in armament contracts during the war, or well over $3 trillion in today's dollars.

69. Georgia even talked John into performing at one of the school's community sessions in March 1942. As one-room schools faded during the 1940s, Georgia moved on to teach in Williamsfield and Brimfield.

70. At the outset of the war, a farmer had to have at least eight animal/crop units to qualify. There was an unusual measurement system for those eight units. For livestock, one unit would be tabulated for each milk cow, each group of nine hogs, for seventy-five hens, 125 chickens, or eight sheep. It would assume that the farmer would raise the feed for the livestock as well. For cash crops, there was one unit for each fifteen acres of wheat, as an example. In early 1944 there was a push to draft an additional one million men in order to reach 11.3 million men in uniform. The farm deferment unit bar was increased to sixteen units.

71. Ford continued to sell the GAA engine after the war, mainly for tractor pulls and funny cars.

72. His unit was Company D, 18th Battalion, 8th Armored Division, called the "Thundering Herd." The division had approximately ten thousand men, with eighty tanks across six tank companies. With the HQ and Service companies, there were four actual battalions, each with about seventeen tanks. It was formed at Fort Knox in 1942 and transferred to Camp Polk in February 1943.

73. The *Mariposa* made over thirty troop sailings from January 1942 to the end of the war. Its speed enabled it to sail solo.

74. The hotel is now a Marriott, and I don't think they are serving at peak fourteen thousand meals a day.

75. Paul never discussed Ultra, even when it was declassified. Ultra was a secret until 1974, when F. W. Winterbotham (chief of operations at Bletchley Park) wrote a memoir that disclosed the project. Until then it was a classified secret beyond "top secret." It was in its own special category, naturally called "Ultra."

76. Paul and his Ultra team stayed with a French family (the Pfeffers) in Phalsbourg, above their drugstore in the town, both during the advance and when they were pulled back. In 1979, years after Lucile had died, Paul contacted Yvonne Pfeffer, still living in Phalsbourg but now a widow. He invited Yvonne to come to Miami, and she agreed. They spent a week together reminiscing, though nothing long-term became of it.

77. The 8th Armored Division completed training and was ordered to Europe in October 1944. It shipped to England, then to the Continent at Rouen in December 1944. When Strasbourg was threatened in January 1945, the division raced 350 miles across northern France to Pont-A-Mousson, just a hundred miles from the front, standing ready to engage. Yet, General Devers and the Sixth Army Group repulsed the German advance.

78. Years later, Paul wrote a story for his grandkids called "Christmas Eve at Bridge B-661," which described the heroics of a tank crew manning a Sherman called "Demon" that helped stop the German advance threatening Strasbourg.

79. A "short snorter" is a banknote inscribed by people traveling together on an aircraft. During World War II short snorters were signed by flight crews and conveyed good luck to soldiers crossing the Atlantic by air.

80. The Capitol Limited ran from New York City to DC and on to Chicago. It was the B&O line's deluxe train, utilizing the latest streamlined locomotives and cars. The train would leave Union Station in DC at 5:30 p.m., make ten stops along the way, and arrive at Grand Central Station in Chicago at 8:00 a.m. the next day.

81. Frank Kirby, one of the first employers of young Henry Ford, had designed and produced over 125 vessels during his career, including huge steam sidewheelers with berthage rivaling the Queen Mary. The *USS Wolverine* started out as the SS SeeandBee, built in 1913 and converted in 1942. The *USS Sable* started life as the SS Greater Buffalo and was converted in 1943.

82. Verne went to Glendale in 1946 in part to see Charlotte, but Charlotte had no real interest in keeping ties. Interestingly enough, Charlotte ended up marrying another Navy Hellcat pilot (Howard Vernon Thompson) on June 29, 1947, in Los Angeles. He died in 1994 and Charlotte died in 2003.

83. Despite delegating to local officials for administration, the OPM was not fooling around. The application for a ration book required each name and address, for sure, but also asked for height, weight, hair and eye color, and family relationships. For War Ration Book #1, one also had to declare the amount of coffee and sugar (both brown and white) on hand, along with an oath that all the information was true under penalty of $10,000 fine and/or two years' imprisonment.

84. Ford was out with the first post-war automobile, though it was a rehashed 1942 model. The pressure built for a new Ford. An initial design by E. T. Gregorie was not accepted. Ford designer George Walker needed to come up with another design. He enlisted former Studebaker designer Richard Caleal, who had been recently let go by Studebaker), enticing him with a job if he could come up with a winning design in three weeks. Caleal recruited several Studebaker design colleagues, including Bob Bourke and Holden Koto, to help. They came up with the slab-sided, bullet nose design that became the 1949 Ford. It was a design that was similar to one that had been done at Studebaker but had been set aside in favor of the 1947 "coming and going" style. Thus, the question remains whether the highly successful 1949 Ford really started out life as a Studebaker.

85. Exner had originally been hired by Harley Earl of General Motors and had become, at age twenty-four, the youngest design chief when he headed up the Pontiac team.

86. Frazer may also have felt underappreciated in the naming department. He claimed he coined the name "Jeep" by slurring the Ford's "GP" designation. This is likely not true, but as president of Willys-Overland, he did in fact move aggressively to trademark the name, to Ford's considerable consternation. And, earlier in his career, working for Walter Chrysler, he suggested the name "Plymouth" for the company's new low-priced car, this based on farmers being very familiar with "Plymouth binder twine."

87. Though no consolation to Preston Tucker, the US Attorney who pressed the case against Tucker was himself convicted of conspiracy and bribery. He went to jail, the first federal appellate judge in US history to go to jail.

88. Part of the impetus for this bill was the experience after World War I, where veterans were paid little for their service but given bonus certificates (hence the term "Bonus Army") that could not be redeemed until years later. It was a far cry from previous wars, where veterans were often provided extensive compensation in the form of land. The unpaid bonuses sparked demonstrations and riots in Washington and was a factor in Hoover losing the 1932 election. FDR was not interested in revisiting this calamity.

89. The 1939 Studebaker was not the first automobile that Loewy designed. He had designed the 1932 and 1934 Hupmobiles. The 1934 Hupmobile, called the Aerodynamic, was announced the same day as the Chrysler Airflow and the two shared very similar streamline bodies. Unfortunately, the Hupp Company was already struggling, and a rapacious investor (Archie Andrews) succeeded in destroying what was left. Hupp did not make it to the war. In the final tally, Andrews was responsible for killing four automobile companies—Hupp, Moon, Kissel, and New Era.

90. Though an automobile was in his future, Henry Kaiser made his name during World War II building ships. He received major contracts for Liberty ships and proceeded to develop fast construction methods for their production, with an average of forty-five days from laying the keel to launching the vessel. In a shipyard competition, one of Kaiser's crews set the record for build time, just five days end to end. His shipyards launched 1,490 ships, mostly Liberty cargo ships. The influx of workers to build those ships at the four Richmond shipyards necessitated a huge

public housing effort, with twenty-four thousand units erected in a short time. With those units just five miles from the Berkeley campus, they were adopted for student housing after the war.

91. Using soybeans for seats actually came to pass in 2018 when the seat cushions for the Ford Mustang were produced in part with soybean extract.

92. The Friden was an electromechanical beast. The size of a large typewriter, it predated transistors and calculated by brute force. Adding numbers was somewhat tame, but multiplication and division turned the machine loose for upwards of a minute noisily crunching the answer, with the massive platen running crazily back and forth. Perhaps, the audio book version of this story could add the deafening calculating noise of the beast. For Paul's research, the Friden was tabulating the raw stopwatch figures, a process that was rendered far more sedate when Excel spreadsheets became available.

93. Examples of studies conducted by Paul include "Handling Groceries from Warehouse to Store," "The Check-Out Operation," "Using Slip Sheets in Trailers," "Handling Frozen Foods," and "Comparative Methods of Packaging Potatoes and Onions."

94. Some fifty years later, the Rock and Roll Hall of Fame would declare "Rocket 88" as the first rock and roll song.

95. Exner leaned on the Italian company Carrozzeria Ghia for some of his concept bodies. His low-slung K-310 coupe concept was a direct influence on the VW Karmann Ghia. The Chrysler Norseman concept car was completed by Ghia in Turin and shipped to be Chrysler's featured automobile at the 1957 auto show. Unfortunately, Ghia shipped the car on the SS *Andrea Doria*. It now lies in 160 feet of water off Nantucket Island.

96. The British got into the act with twin rubber bumper protrusions on the MG and Triumph cars. They were added to conform to new US regulations on crash-worthiness but quickly were deemed "Sabinas" after a particularly buxom British actress. Rubber tips that were added later were predictably called "pasties." This was certainly a high point in automotive design.

97. Raymond Loewy, "Jukebox on Wheels," *The Atlantic*, April 1955.

98. Just prior to the start of World War II, Tatra sued Porsche for infringement. The suit was rendered stillborn when Hitler invaded and occupied Czechoslovakia in 1938. In 1961 Volkswagen admitted that the design was lifted from Hans Ledwinka and Tatra Motors, and finally paid damages.

99. The installment monies collected were confiscated by the Russians. A suit brought on behalf of savings plan holders languished for ten years. In 1962 Volkswagen agreed to provide plan holders a fraction of their investment and only toward a purchase of a new VW.

100. The Dauphine challenge was short-lived as the atrocious quality of the Renault effectively blacklisted the French company from the United States and helped sink its latter import in a venture with American Motors—the Renault LeCar. In addition, the 0–60 time of the Dauphine at thirty-six seconds certainly did not help its cause.

101. Basem Wasef and Stirling Moss, "Legendary Race Cars," *Motorworks*, 2009.

102. Ford was determined to honor the 50th anniversary of its win at Le Mans by returning to the race in 2016 with a new GT racing car. Henry Ford II might have been slightly disappointed with the race, as the Fords did not 1-2-3. They finished 1-3-4, letting a Ferrari sneak in for second place.

103. In the new car world where getting big was a virtual requirement, Volvo became a threatened species. It suffered through a failed merger with Renault in 1993 and then was purchased by Ford in 1999. This provided critical access to Ford technology and resources over the next twenty years. Ford was forced to sell Volvo to Geely in 2010 to raise cash to survive the Great Recession.

104. They may have a chance to own their own Mustang someday. Ford announced in 2018 that it would be phasing out production of sedans and compacts, essentially all cars except SUVs. The one exception would be the Mustang, which is viewed as the "soul of the company."

105. Emily R. Kilby, "The Demographics of the US Horse Population," 2007.

106. The Big Three, with GM (Chevrolet, Pontiac, Olds, Buick, Cadillac), Ford (Ford, Lincoln, Mercury), Chrysler (Plymouth, Dodge, Desoto, and Chrysler), and the independents (Hudson, Packard, Studebaker, Nash, Crosley, Willys).

107. The Comet had originally been slated for the Edsel division. In hindsight, it would have been a lifeline for those star-crossed Edsel dealers. It could have also bought precious time to repair or salvage the Edsel brand. But the Comet was moved to Mercury, and the entire Edsel division was scrapped.

108. The 1969 Lincoln Continental Mark III was a luxury version of the Thunderbird. Iacocca shepherded the program, including adding the stand-up grille and rear tire bustle, homages to Edsel Ford's Lincolns. The Lincoln division, which reportedly had not made a profit in its entire history, went on a tear. Volumes ramped up from a baseline of 10,000–40,000 per year to nearly 200,000 by 1978.

109. Bunkie was never accepted by Ford executives, who had favored Lee Iacocca. They remembered the famous comment made by Henry Ford in a 1919 lawsuit where he essentially said, "History is bunk." The Ford team turned that around to "Bunkie is history."

110. Roger Smith is probably best known for his portrayal in Michael Moore's 1989 documentary *Roger and Me*, a scathing indictment of the impact of Smith's job cuts on Flint, Michigan. The home of Billy Durant and birthplace of General Motors was devastated by the closing of the sprawling Buick complex, with the loss of thirty thousand jobs. The factory was razed in 2002.

111. GM pulled out of the facility in 2009 due to its bankruptcy. Toyota pulled out a year later as it had by now many other US factories. In 2010 Tesla acquired the plant.

112. DeLorean rose fast, becoming general manager of Pontiac in 1965 and head of all GM car and truck divisions in 1972. He appeared ordained to be the next GM president. However, DeLorean always had a debonair, jet-setting image that clashed with staid GM and served to derail that final step. He left or was

fired in 1973. Ever the performance car guy, he started the DeLorean Motor Company (DMC) with $245 million in aid from Northern Ireland. That was not nearly enough money to start a car company in 1975. Famously, DeLorean was caught in a sting operation trying to secure more money and save DMC from bankruptcy. Yet, the problem was not money. The DeLorean GT car was slow, expensive, and arrived in a tough economic market in 1981. Only nine thousand of the stainless-steel, gull-winged sports cars were ever produced. The one bright spot for John DeLorean was having his car prominently featured in the *Back to the Future* movies.

113. A caveat: the Model T was selling at a time when there were far less than thirty million total households in the United States, and those households usually had just one car. Today, there are in excess of 120 million US households, with an average of two cars each. The Model T was incredibly dominant. At the same time, the two automobiles were very much alike. They were both robust rugged cars, easy to maintain, affordable, high mileage, high quality, with a huge supporting aftermarket. They were both produced with "Fordism" techniques. And, they both achieved very high standing and visibility in their times and culture.

114. The boy was purportedly the son of Henry's assistant, Evangeline Dahlinger. She and her husband Ray became managers of Ford's Greenfield Village. Henry built a lavish mansion for the Dahlingers near his Fairlane estate. It included a secret passage by which Ford was able to visit Evangeline. The boy was quite possibly Henry's second though illegitimate son.

115. C. Harold Wills joined in 1899 and left in 1919 amid disagreements (he walked out with $1.5 million, though). James Couzens joined with the formation of the Ford Motor Company in 1902 and left in 1915. Charles Sorensen left during World War II amid disagreement with both Henry Ford and Henry Ford II. Norval Hawkins, super salesman sales manager, joined in 1907 and left in 1919 to join General Motors. Bill Knudsen came on board with Keim in 1911 and left in 1921, frustrated with Henry countermanding his decisions. He went to work for GM in 1919.

Bibliography

Essential Periodicals

For life in the small farm towns, there is no greater resource than the local newspapers. This is especially true of their reporting in the late nineteenth and early twentieth centuries. The papers were the heartbeat of the community. No minutiae of daily life were too small. Reading through the issues week after week, I felt like I was reliving the times. For this book in particular, the timing was fortuitous. As I mentioned, in the early years of the automobile, just about anything relating to these amazing new machines was duly reported. The shine did not wear off until the late 1920s.

The *Brimfield News* ran from 1876 to 1977. Most amazingly, most of the issues in that time span have been digitized and indexed, and the entire record is available online. This electronic library includes the *Brimfield Gazette* and *Princeville Telephone*. The indexing supercharges the resource. You can enter all search criteria and it will instantly bring up all the references. If you want to know who bought the first Cadillac in the area, you are just a few keystrokes away from the answer. Many thanks to the Brimfield Public Library for both this resource and its assistance.

The *Williamsfield Times* debuted in 1889, a year after the railroad arrived. The paper ran until 1992. While the issues are not available online, several libraries have digitized the issues to microfilm. The archivist at Knox College pointed me to the Galesburg Public Library, which had nearly all of the issues in the paper's run. I traveled to Galesburg and spent many hours over the course of a week with the microfilm reader. I believe I got pretty good at tracking down key information. The trick was to understand the layout of the newspaper. Each was typically 8–10 pages in length, with certain content always on the same page number. Community news was on page seven, so I headed straight there.

Another invaluable resource was the Automotive Research Library of the Horseless Carriage Foundation. This group, founded in 1985, digitized many of the early automotive industry's essential periodicals. The foundation's core holdings include *Cycle and Automobile Trade Journal*, *The Horseless Age*, *Motor Age*, *Motor World*, *The Automobile*, and several others. Together, they represent a priceless compendium of early automobile history.

Books

Before I get to the list, I must call out one particular resource, *The Standard Catalog of American Cars, 1805–1942*. This heavyweight volume by Beverly Rae Kimes and Henry Austin Clark Jr. is the bible of automotive history. It is truly a wonder, a compendium of thousands of automobile companies replete with both automobile details and backstory. The sheer research work required to put it together is astounding. Led by Beverly Kimes ("the first lady of automotive history"), it is the definitive source with over five thousand entries, from Abbott-Akin (who incorporated but never produced a car) to Zip (a car built by B. T. Wagner in his Texas backyard) and everything in between.

Adler, Dennis, *Daimler and Benz*, Harper, 2006.

Albert, Dan, *Are We There Yet?*, W. W. Norton, 2019.

Apps, Jerry, *Horse Drawn Days*, Wisconsin Historical Society, 2010.

Banham, Russ, *The Ford Century*, Artisan, 2002.

Barnard, Harry, *Independent Man: The Life of Senator James Couzens*, Wayne State University Press, 2002.

Barnett, William, *NAS Melbourne*, Xlibris, 2001.

Bel Geddes, Norman, *Horizons*, Little, Brown, 1932.

Berkebile, Don H., *The 1893 Duryea Automobile in the Museum of History and Technology*, FQ Books, 2009.

Bonsall, Thomas, *More than Promised*, Stanford University Press, 2000.

Brinkley, Douglas, *Wheels of the World*, Viking, 2003.

Bryan, Ford R., *The Birth of the Ford Motor Company*. Henry Ford Heritage Association, 2003.

Casey, Robert H., *The Model T*, Johns Hopkins University Press, 2016.

Chapman, Giles, *Car: The Definitive Visual History*, DK Publishing, 2011.

Clymer, Floyd, *Treasury of Early Automobiles*, Bonanza, 1950.

Collier, David and David Horowitz, *The Fords: An American Epic*, Encounter Books, 2002.

Collins, Tom, *The Legendary Model T*, Krause Publications, 2007.

Crabb, Richard, *Birth of a Giant*, Chilton, 1969.

Crawshaw, Fred, *Ultimate Guide to Farm Mechanics*, Skyhorse, 2015.

Curcio, Vincent, *Chrysler: Life and Times*, Oxford University Press, 2000.

Currierv, Vic, *Goodbye, Lord, I'm Going to New York*, Xlibris, 2015.

Cutler, Richard, and Joseph Persico, *Memoirs of a Counterintelligence Officer*, Potomac Books, 2004.

Davis, Michael, *Detroit War Time*, Arcadia, 2007.

Duncan, John, *Designing the Model T*, Exisle, 2015.

Dunford, Chauney, ed. *Bicycle: The Definitive Visual History*, DK Publishing, 2016.

Earley, Helen, and James Wackinshaw, *Olds: Setting the Pace*, Publications International, 1997.

Flink, James J., *The Automobile Age*, MIT Press, 1990.

Federal Writers Project, *The WPA Guide to Illinois*, Pantheon, 1983.

Ford, Henry, and Samuel Crowther, *My Life and Work*, Garden City, 1922.

Foster, Patrick, *Jeep*, Motorbooks, 2014.

Foster, Patrick, *Studebaker*, Crestline, 2015.

Freyssenet, Michael, *The Second Automobile Revolution*, Palgrave MacMillan, 2009.

Gardner, Bruce, *American Agriculture in the Twentieth Century*, Harvard University Press, 2002.

Gelderman, Carol, *The Wayward Capitalist*, Dial Press, 1981.

Georgano, Nick, *The American Automobile*, Smithmark, 1993.

Goldstone, Lawrence, *Drive*, Ballantine, 2016.

Greene, Ann Norton, *Horses at Work*, Harvard University Press, 2008.

Gunnell, John, *The Standard Catalog of American Cars, 1946–1975*, Krause Publications, 2002.

Gustin, Lawrence, *Billy Durant: Creator of General Motors,* University of Michigan Press, 2012.

Halberstam, David, *The Reckoning*, William Morrow, 1986.

Haskew, Michael, *M4 Sherman Tanks*, Voyageur Press, 2016.

Heitmann, John, *The Automobile and American Life*, revised. McFarland, 2018.

Henderson, Jason, and Nathan Kauffman, *Farm Investment and Leverage Cycles*, Economic Review, 2017.

Hyde, Charles K., *Riding the Roller Coaster: A History of the Chrysler Corporation.* Wayne State University Press, 2003.

Hyde, Charles K., *The Dodge Brothers: The Men, The Motor Cars, and the Legacy*, Wayne State University Press, 2005.

Ingram, Tammy, *Dixie Highway*, University of North Carolina Press, 2014.

Jackson, Clay, *Down the Asphalt Path*, Columbia University Press, 1994.

Jamison, Dorothy, *Family History*, 1991.

Kaszynski, William, *The American Highway*, McFarland, 2000.

Kay, Jane Holtz, *Asphalt Nation*, Crown, 1997.

Keller, Edward, *Mr. Ford*, Keaton Keller, 1997.

Kimes, Beverly Rae, *The Standard Catalog of American Cars, 1805–1942*, Krause Publications, 1996.

Knoedelseder, William, *Fins: Harley Earl, The Rise of General Motors and the Glory Days of Detroit.* Harper-Collins, 2018.

Lacey, Robert, *The Man and the Machine*, Little, Brown, 1986.

Langworth, Richard, *The Complete History of Chrysler*, Beekman House Crown, 1985.

Larson, Olaf, *When Horses Pulled the Plow*, University of Wisconsin Press, 2011.

Leavitt, Judith, *Birthing and Anesthesia: The Debate over Twilight Sleep.* University of Chicago Press, 1980.

Levin, Jonathan, *Where Have All the Horses Gone*, McFarland, 2017.

Lin, James, *A Brief History of the Lincoln Highway.* Lincoln Highway Association, 1999.

Lindert, Peter, *Long Run Trends in American Farmland Values*, Agriculture History Center, 1988.

Local Automobile Registrations, 1911, Illinois Secretary of State, 1911.

Lynd, Robert, and Helen Lynd, *Middletown*, Harcourt, Brace, 1929.

Maffai, Nicolas, *Norman Bel Geddes: American Design Visionary*, Bloomsbury, 2018.

Martini, Dinah, *Technological Change in U.S. Agriculture*, University of Washington Press, 2003.

McCulloch, David, ed., "Elmwood Town History," in *Historical Encyclopedia of Illinois*, Munsell Publishing, 1902.

McKenzie, Hamish, *Insane Mode: How Elon Musk's Tesla Sparked an Electric Revolution*, Dutton, 2018.

McKibben, Eugene, and John Hopkin, *Changes in Farm Power and Equipment*, WPA Report, 1938.

Memler, Henrietta, *History of Elmwood 1831–2004*.

Memler, Henrietta, *A History of Brimfield, Illinois, 1836–1986*, self-published manuscript, 1937.

Meyer, Carrie, *Days on the Farm*, University of Minnesota Press, 2007.

Meyer, Carrie, *The Farm Debut of the Gasoline Engine*, George Mason University Press, 2011.

Miller, G. Wayne, *Car Crazy*. Hachette, 2015.

Moritz, Michael, and Barrett Seaman, *Going for Broke*, Doubleday, 1981.

Naldrett, Alan, *Lost Car Companies of Detroit*, History Press, 2016.

Naldrett, Alan and Lynn Naldrett, *Michigan's C. Harold Wills: The Genius Behind the Model T and the Wills Sainte Claire Automobiles*, Arcadia Publishing, 2017.

Nelsen, Walter Henry, *Small Wonder Volkswagen*, Little, Brown, 1965.

Nevins, Allan, and Frank Hill, *Ford: The Times, The Man, The Company*, Scribner, 1954.

Nixon, John, *The Invention of the Automobile*, Edizioni Savine, 2016.

Nolan, William, *Barney Oldfield: The Life and Times of America's Legendary Speed King*, Brown Fox Books, 2002.

Northey, Tom, *The World of Automobiles*, Columbia House, 1974.

Olson, Sidney, and David Lewis, *Young Henry Ford*, Wayne State University Press, 2015.

Page, Victor, *The Model T Ford Car*, Henley Publications, 1917.

Palmer, Cyrus, *The Farmer's Guide Book*, Palala Press, 2016.

Parisienne, Steven, *The Life of the Automobile*, Thomas Dunne Books, 2014.

Phillips, Stanley, *The Farm Tractor*, Power Wagon Reference, 1920.

Pooley, William, *The Settlement of Illinois from 1830 to 1850*, University of Wisconsin, 1908.

Prairie Farmers Directory—1917, Prairie Farmer Publishing, 1917.

Pripps, Robert, *Vintage Ford Tractors*, Voyageur Press, 1997.

Rae, John Bell, *American Automobile Manufacturers*, Chilton, 1959.

Reid, Carlton, *Roads Not Built for Cars*, Island Press, 2015.

Reiger, Bernhard, *The People's Car*, Harvard University Press, 2013.

Rhodes, Richard, *Energy*, Simon and Shuster, 2019.

Rocheleau, Paul, and Verlyn Klinkenborg, *The One-Room Schoolhouse*, Universe Publishing, 2003.

Rubenstein, James, *Making and Selling Cars*, Johns Hopkins University Press, 2001.

Sears, Stephen, *The Automobile in America*, Scribner, 1977.

Sedgwick, Michael, *Cars of the Thirties*, Beekman House, 1980.

Shurtleff, William, and Akiko Aoyagi, *Henry Ford and His Researchers*, Chemurgy, 2011.

Sinsibaugh, Chris, *Who Me? Forty Years of Automotive History*, Arnold-Powers, 1940.

Smitka, Mike, and Peter Warrian, *A Profile of the Global Automobile Industry*, Business Expert Press, 2016.

Snow, Richard, *I Invented the Modern Age*, Scribner, 2014.

Sorensen, Charles, and David Lewis, *My Forty Years at Ford*, Norton, 1956.

Sumner, Gregory, *Detroit in World War II*, History Press, 2015.

Swift, Earl, *The Big Roads*, Mariner Books, 2012.

Taylor, Karl, *Saturday Night in a Small Country Town*, published on storiesfromsmalltownillinois.com, 2016.

Throm, Edward, and James Crenshaw, *Popular Mechanics Automobile Album*, Popular Mechanics Press, 1952.

Tillman, Barrett, *Hellcat: The F6F in World War II*, Naval Institute Press, 1979.

United States Bureau of the Census, *The Farm Horse*, Government Printing Office, 1933.

Vance, Ashlee, *Musk*, Ecco, 2017.

Warren, Paul, *To War in a Hellcat*, Sea Classics, 2013.

Watts, Steven, *The People's Tycoon*, Random House, 1980.

Weiss, H. Eugene, *Chrysler, Ford, Durant, and Sloan*, McFarland, 2003.

White, Williams, *Economic History of Tractors in the U.S.*, EH.Net, 2008.

Wik, Reynold, *Henry Ford and Grassroots America*, University of Michigan Press, 1972.

Williams, Michael, *Farm Tractors*, Silverdale Books, 1977.

Williams, Robert, *Fordson, Farmall, and Poppin Johnny*, University of Illinois Press, 1987.

Yerkes, Arnold, and L. M. Church, *Tractor Experience in Illinois*, USDA, 1918.

Zaroga, Steve, *Armored Thunderbolt*, Stackpole Books, 2008.

Articles

"1915 Automobile Registrations," December 23, 1915, *The Automobile*.

"Alexander Winton," October 1898, *The Horseless Age*, pp. 11–12.

"Automobile Deaths, April 19, 1923, *Automotive Industries*.

"Buick Cuts Prices Ranging $300–$660," June 2, 1921, *Automotive Industries*, p. 1185.

"Buick: Nineteen Twenty One," August 1, 1920, *Automobile Trade Journal*, p. 187.

"Charles Duryea Dies at 76," October 1, 1938, *Automobile Topics*.

"Chicago to Have 276 Exhibitors," January 22, 1914, *The Automobile*.

"Chryslers Are Announced," October 23, 1937, *Automotive Industry*, p. 538.

"Curtains Raised on Chicago's Row," April 20, 1911, *The Automobile*, Vol. XXIV, No. 16.

"Ford Model N," November 28, 1906, *The Horseless Age*.

"Ford Pinto," April 16, 2020, Wikipedia.

"Ford Restores Rural School," September 23, 1931, *Herald-Press*, St. Joseph, Michigan.

"Green Light on Training," *The Navy's Air War*, Aviation History Unit, 1946.

"Henry Ford, Simply Life," *Simply Knowledge*, Aatman Innovations.

"Henry Ford II is Dead at 70", September 30, 1987, *New York Times*.

"Low Point of Tractor Production Far Behind," December 28, 1935, *Automotive Industries*, p. 855.

"Many New Features in 1914 Detroit Electrics," *Automobile Trade Journal*, November 1913, p. 220.

"Motor Row District," April 5, 2000, *Landmark Designation Report*, Commission on Chicago Landmarks.

"Nearly the Whole Industry Place for New York Show," December 5, 1903), *The Automobile*, p. 584.

"Pioneers of the Industry at NACC Banquet," January 8, 1925, *Automotive Industries*.

"Thanksgiving Day Route," December 1895, *The Horseless Age*.

"The Ford Rebate," July 22, 1915, *The Automobile*.

"The Otto Gasoline Engine," November 14, 1891, *Scientific American*.

"The Real Fordson Story," July 1985, *Gas Engine Magazine*.

Armstrong, James, "Thinking Small: The Volkswagen Beetle in History," January 2011, State University of New York.

Barger, Melvin, "The Tucker Car," January 1, 1989, Foundation for Economic Education.

Brent, Thomas G., "The Real Fordson Story," July/August 1985, *Gas Engine Magazine*.

Burton, J. R., "I Christen Thee," May 22, 1913, *Motor Age*.

Ceppos, Rich, "Learning to Drive the Model T," June 16, 2003, *Autoweek*.

Donnelly, Jim, "David Dunbar Buick: Founder of the Buick Company," June 2016, *Hemming Classic Car*.

Duryea, J. Frank, "Who Designed and Built Those Early Duryea Automobiles," privately published, 1944.

Garrett, Jerry, "Where Credit Is Due: A Fresh Look on the Exner Designs," October 21, 2007, *New York Times*.

Gourlie, John C., and P. M. Heldt, "Interest Created by Ford Should Benefit Whole Industry," December 10, 1927, *Automotive Industries*.

Grubb, Farley, "Morbidity and Mortality on the North Atlantic Passage: Eighteenth-Century Germain Immigration," Volume 17, No. 3 (Winter, 1987), *The MIT Press - The Journal of Interdisciplinary History*.

Heldt, P. M., "Willys' Colorful Career in Automotive Industry Ends with Death," August 31, 1935, *Automotive Industries*.

Hilton, Gregory, "The 20th Anniversary of Roger and Me," May 7, 2009, DC World Affairs blog.

Howell, Mark, "The Chrysler Six: America's First Modern Automobile," March-April 1972), *Antique Automobile*.

Jackson, David D., "The American Automobile Industry in World War Two," 2020, author's website.

Johnson, D. E., "The Rise and Fall of Detroit's Early Electrics," August 19, 2014, *Michigan History Magazine*.

Johnson, Grace, "Williamsfield Born at Time of Santa Fe," March 13, 1952, *Daily Register Mail*.

Kane, Sharyn, and Richard Keeton, "A Soldier's Place in History: Fort Polk, Louisiana," Southeast Archeological Center, 2004.

Kelly, Fred, "The Great Bicycle Craze," December 1956, *American Heritage*.

Kiley, David, "The New Heat on Ford," May 29, 2007, *Bloomberg Business Week*.

Kraus, James, "Who Killed the Corvair," January 6, 2018, *Auto Universum*.

Larson, Sara, "Soybeans in Midwest Farming," 1950, Transactions of the Kansas Academy of Science.

Loewy, Raymond, "Jukebox on Wheels," April 1955, *The Atlantic*.

Mateja, Jim, "Wanted: Ford Punch Bowl, Slightly Used in 100 Years," February 25, 2001, *Chicago Tribune*.

McNessor, Mike, "The Accident that Started It All," February 27, 2012), *Automobilia*.

Meyer, Corkly, "Grumman Hellcat: Just in the Nick of Time," April 2002, *Flight Journal*.

Morgan, Thomas, "The Industrial Mobilization of World War II," 1994, *Army History*.

Neil, Don, "General Motors: The Road from Icon to Bankrupt," June 6, 2009, *Los Angeles Times*.

Nikel, David, "Electric Cars: Why Little Norway Leads the World in EV Usage," June 18, 2019, *Forbes*.

Olmstead, Alan, and Paul Rhodes, "The Impact and Diffusion of the Tractor in American Agriculture 1910–1960," 2001, *Journal of Economic History*.

Quinn, James, "As General Motors Goes, So Goes the Nation," February 26, 2009, Market Oracle.

Rae, John B., "The Fabulous Billy Durant," Autumn 1958, *Business History Review*.

Raftery, Tom, "Seven Reasons Why the Internal Combustion Engine Is a Dead Man Walking," September 6, 2018, *Forbes*.

Roberts, Bruce D. "Ford Fiasco: Tracking the Rise and Fall of the Edsel." (September 2013, Volume 8 Issue 3, *Readex Report*).

Roy, Rex, "Detroit's Original Three: A Patriotic Trip in an Automotive Time Machine," July 3, 2010), Verizon Media.

Schreiber, Ronnie, "How the Nazis Made Daimler and Benz the Inventors of the Automobile," March 9, 2014, The Truth About Cars.

Schreiber, Ronnie, "Swedish Airflow, Anyone? Volvos Weren't Always Boxy." April 9, 2019, Hagerty Media.

Severson, Aaron, "Falling Empires: The Road Back," November 30, 2008, Ate Up with Motor.

Severson, Aaron, "Lark and Super Lark: The Last Days of Studebaker," October 17, 2009, Ate Up with Motor.

Severson, Aaron, "Fork-Tailed Devil: The P-38 Lightning and the Birth of Cadillac's Famous Fins," March 8, 2009, Ate Up with Motor.

Severson, Aaron, "Hydra-Matic History: GM's First Automatic Transmission," May 29, 2010, Ate Up with Motor.

Severson, Aaron, "The Unlikely Studebaker: The Birth (and Rebirth) of the Avanti," June 10, 2009, Ate Up with Motor.

Seward, Keith, "Henry Ford Buys Out Ford Motor Company, 1919," 2014, Salt of America.

Szerlip, Alexandra, "Too Good to Succeed," *Paris Review*, 2013.

Tedlow, Richard, "The Struggle for Dominance in the Automobile Market: The Early Years of Ford and General Motors," 1988, Business History Conference.

Thibodeau, Ian, "Hot Seat Has Scorched Many Top Ford Execs," May 29, 2017, *Detroit News*.

Trescott, Martha, "The Bicycle, a Technical Precursor of the Automobile," SMU Department of History, 1976.

Vlasic, Bill, "Prized Logo Is Returned to Ford," May 22, 2012, *New York Times*.

Weber, Austin, "Assembly Then and Now: The Man Behind the Moving Assembly Line," February 1, 2003, *Assembly*.

Weber, Austin, "The Rouge an Industrial Icon," May 20, 2003, *Assembly*.

Wells, Brian, "Revolution in Farm Tractor Design," May/June 2006, *Belt Pulley Magazine*.

Wells, Christopher, "The Road to the Model T," July 2007, Johns Hopkins University Press and the Society for the History of Technology.

White, Joseph, "How Detroit's Automakers Went from Kings of the Road to Roadkill," February 2009, *Wall Street Journal*.

Williams, Casey, "Driving the Ford Model T," July 3, 2018, *Chicago Tribune*.

Williams, Gurney, "When Cars Were Easier to Drive," February 1934, *Life*.

Williams, Stephen, "Station Wagons on Endangered List as SUVs Crush All in Their Path," November 26, 2019, *New York Times*.

Wollering, Max F. "The Reminiscences of Mr. Max F. Wollering," April 1955, Benson Ford Research Center.

Photo Credits for Chapter Headings

Chapter 2: Sailing ship *Gibraltar* painted by Heinrich Andreas Petersen (public domain).

Chapter 3: 1893 Safety bike (*Wheel and Cycling Trade Review*, Smithsonian Libraries, public domain).

Chapter 4: 1903 Curved Dash Oldsmobile (US National Museum, public domain).

Chapter 5: Henry Ford with 1896 Quadricycle (public domain).

Chapter 6: Santa Fe at depot (Caldwell House Museum, Williamsfield).

Chapter 7: 1906 Ford Model N (Hennepin County Library).

Chapter 8: 1911 Ford Model T (1911 Ford catalog).

Chapter 9: Ford Model TT truck (Pixabay, Emslicher).

Chapter 10: 1927 Ford Model A (Pixabay).

Chapter 11: 1921 Buick Touring (New York Public Library).

Chapter 12: 1924 Chrysler (Old Cars Canada).

Chapter 13: 1938 Chrysler Royal (Wikimedia Commons).

Chapter 14: M4 Sherman tank (Imperial War Museum).

Chapter 15: F6F-3 Hellcat from the VF-27 USS *Princeton*, October 1944 (Wikimedia Commons, Stephane Hernault).

Chapter 16: Tucker 48 (Tucker Corporation Christmas Car, public domain).

Chapter 17: 1942 Studebaker Commander (author's collection).

Chapter 18: Volkswagen (Pixabay).

Chapter 19: Ford Mustang (standard clipart).

Index

About the Author

William "Bill" Shaffer has had a half-century love affair with the automobile, including the Ford Mustang above. Over the course of forty plus years with IBM, he has written numerous feature articles but they were all about computers not cars. The discovery of the Model T photograph that is reproduced on the cover, with his grandfather and namesake at the wheel, set him off on a five-year journey to trace the family's history with the automobile as well as the stories of the cars and the car pioneers. It has been quite a ride, literally, taking Bill to automobile museums, university libraries, and even small town newspapers in order to weave a multi-generational story.

Bill lives in Boulder, Colorado, with his wife. Their two sons live in New York City and Seattle, respectively, and much to the chagrin of their father, neither owns an automobile.

CPSIA information can be obtained
at www.ICGtesting.com
Printed in the USA
BVHW042321161221
624207BV00013B/349

9 781735 807805